MznLnx

Missing Links Exam Preps

Exam Prep for

American Economic History

Hughes & Cain, 7th Edition

The MznLnx Exam Prep is your link from the texbook and lecture to your exams.
The MznLnx Exam Preps are unauthorized and comprehensive reviews of your textbooks.

All material provided by MznLnx and Rico Publications (c) 2010
Textbook publishers and textbook authors do not particpate in or contribute to these reviews.

MznLnx

Rico Publications

Exam Prep for American Economic History
7th Edition
Hughes & Cain

Publisher: Raymond Houge	*Product Manager:* Dave Mason
Assistant Editor: Michael Rouger	*Editorial Assitant:* Rachel Guzmanji
Text and Cover Designer: Lisa Buckner	*Pedagogy:* Debra Long
Marketing Manager: Sara Swagger	*Cover Image:* Jim Reed/Getty Images
Project Manager, Editorial Production: Jerry Emerson	*Text and Cover Printer:* City Printing, Inc.
Art Director: Vernon Lowerui	*Compositor:* Media Mix, Inc.

(c) 2010 Rico Publications
ALL RIGHTS RESERVED. No part of this work covered by the copyright may be reproduced or used in any form or by an means--graphic, electronic, or mechanical, including photocopying, recording, taping, Web distribution, information storage, and retrieval systems, or in any other manner--without the written permission of the publisher.

Printed in the United States
ISBN:

For more information about our products, contact us at:
Dave.Mason@RicoPublications.com

For permission to use material from this text or product, submit a request online to:
Dave.Mason@RicoPublications.com

Contents

CHAPTER 1
Overseas Empire — 1

CHAPTER 2
Colonial Development — 7

CHAPTER 3
America on the Eve of Revolution — 13

CHAPTER 4
Gaining Independence — 18

CHAPTER 5
Westward Expansion — 23

CHAPTER 6
Population and Labor Force — 27

CHAPTER 7
Law and the Rise of Classical American Capitalism — 33

CHAPTER 8
Transportation, Internal Improvements, and Urbanization — 39

CHAPTER 9
Agricultural Expansion: The Conflict of Two Systems on the Land — 41

CHAPTER 10
The Debate over Slavery — 45

CHAPTER 11
The Early Industrial Sector — 47

CHAPTER 12
The Financial System and the International Economy — 51

CHAPTER 13
Economic Effects of the Civil War — 61

CHAPTER 14
Railroads and Economic Development — 67

CHAPTER 15
Post—Civil War Agriculture — 71

CHAPTER 16
Population Growth and the Atlantic Migration — 74

CHAPTER 17
Industrialization and Urban Growth — 77

CHAPTER 18
Big Business and Government Intervention — 85

CHAPTER 19
Financial Developments (1863-1914) — 90

CHAPTER 20
The Giant Economy and Its International Relations — 98

Contents (Cont.)

CHAPTER 21
Labor and the Law — 105

CHAPTER 22
The Command Economy Emerges: World War I — 109

CHAPTER 23
Normalcy (1919-1929) — 114

CHAPTER 24
The Great Depression — 119

CHAPTER 25
The New Deal — 125

CHAPTER 26
The Prosperity of Wartime — 131

CHAPTER 27
Before the New Frontier: The Postwar Economy — 135

CHAPTER 28
Population, Labor, and the Tertiary Sector — 142

CHAPTER 29
Postwar Industry and Agriculture — 149

CHAPTER 30
To the New Millennium and Beyond — 155

CHAPTER 31
Does Our Past Have a Future? — 168

ANSWER KEY — 171

TO THE STUDENT

COMPREHENSIVE

The *MznLnx* Exam Prep series is designed to help you pass your exams. Editors at MznLnx review your textbooks and then prepare these practice exams to help you master the textbook material. Unlike study guides, workbooks, and practice tests provided by the texbook publisher and textbook authors, *MznLnx* gives you **all** of the material in each chapter in exam form, not just samples, so you can be sure to nail your exam.

MECHANICAL

The MznLnx Exam Prep series creates exams that will help you learn the subject matter as well as test you on your understanding. Each question is designed to help you master the concept. Just working through the exams, you gain an understanding of the subject--its a simple mechanical process that produces success.

INTEGRATED STUDY GUIDE AND REVIEW

MznLnx is not just a set of exams designed to test you, its also a comprehensive review of the subject content. Each exam question is also a review of the concept, making sure that you will get the answer correct without having to go to other sources of material. You learn as you go! Its the easiest way to pass an exam.

HUMOR

Studying can be tedious and dry. MznLnx's instructional design includes moderate humor within the exam questions on occassion, to break the tedium and revitalize the brain

Chapter 1. Overseas Empire

1. The _____ was a period in the late 18th and early 19th centuries when major changes in agriculture, manufacturing, mining, and transportation had a profound effect on the socioeconomic and cultural conditions in Britain. The changes subsequently spread throughout Europe, North America, and eventually the world. The onset of the _____ marked a major turning point in human society; almost every aspect of daily life was eventually influenced in some way.

    a. Adam Smith
    b. Industrial Revolution
    c. Adolph Fischer
    d. Adolf Hitler

2. _____ is an economic theory that holds that the prosperity of a nation is dependent upon its supply of capital, and that the global volume of international trade is 'unchangeable.' Economic assets or capital, are represented by bullion (gold, silver, and trade value) held by the state, which is best increased through a positive balance of trade with other nations (exports minus imports.) _____ suggests that the ruling government should advance these goals by playing a protectionist role in the economy; by encouraging exports and discouraging imports, notably through the use of tariffs and subsidies.

    _____ was the dominant school of thought throughout the early modern period (from the 16th to the 18th century.)

    a. Consumer theory
    b. General equilibrium theory
    c. Mercantilism
    d. Nominal value

Chapter 1. Overseas Empire

3. A _____ is:

   - Rewrite _____, in generative grammar and computer science
   - Standardization, a formal and widely-accepted statement, fact, definition, or qualification
   - Operation, a determinate _____ for performing a mathematical operation and obtaining a certain result (Mathematics, Logic)
     - Unary operation
     - Binary operation
   - _____ of inference, a function from sets of formulae to formulae (Mathematics, Logic)
   - _____ of thumb, principle with broad application that is not intended to be strictly accurate or reliable for every situation. Also often simply referred to as a _____
   - Moral, an atomic element of a moral code for guiding choices in human behavior
   - Heuristic, a quantized '_____' which shows a tendency or probability for successful function
   - A regulation, as in sports
   - A Production _____, as in computer science
   - Procedural law, a _____ set governing the application of laws to cases
     - A law, which may informally be called a '_____'
     - A court ruling, a decision by a court
   - In the U.S. Government, a regulation mandated by Congress, but written or expanded upon by the Executive Branch.
   - Norm (sociology), an informal but widely accepted _____, concept, truth, definition, or qualification (social norms, legal norms, coding norms)
   - Norm (philosophy), a kind of sentence or a reason to act, feel or believe
   - 'Rulership' is the concept of governance by a government:
     - Military _____, governance by a military body
     - Monastic _____, a collection of precepts that guides the life of monks or nuns in a religious order where the superior holds the place of Christ
   - Slide _____

   - '_____,' a song by Ayumi Hamasaki
   - '_____,' a song by rapper Nas
   - '_____s,' an album by the band The Whitest Boy Alive
   - _____s: Pyaar Ka Superhit Formula, a 2003 Bollywood film
   - ruler, an instrument for measuring lengths
   - _____, a component of an astrolabe, circumferator or similar instrument
   - The _____s, a bestselling self-help book
   - _____ Project (Run Up-to-date Linux Everywhere), a project that aims to use up-to-date Linux software on old PCs
   - _____ engine, a software system that helps managing business _____s
   - Ja _____, a hip hop artist
     - R.U.L.E., a 2005 greatest hits album by rapper Ja _____
   - '_____s,' a KMFDM song

a. Procter ' Gamble
b. Technocracy
c. Demand
d. Rule

Chapter 1. Overseas Empire

4. _____ is the change in population over time, and can be quantified as the change in the number of individuals in a population using 'per unit time' for measurement. The term _____ can technically refer to any species, but almost always refers to humans, and it is often used informally for the more specific demographic term _____ rate , and is often used to refer specifically to the growth of the population of the world.

Simple models of _____ include the Malthusian Growth Model and the logistic model.

   a. 100-year flood
   b. 130-30 fund
   c. Population dynamics
   d. Population growth

5. The term _____ used by politicians and economists to measure broader social effects of policies, such as the effect that reducing graffiti or vandalism might have on the wellbeing of local residents.

Two widely known measures of a country's liveability are the Economist Intelligence Unit's _____ index and the Mercer Quality of Living Survey. Both measures calculate the liveability of countries around the world through a combination of subjective life-satisfaction surveys and objective determinants of _____ such as divorce rates, safety, and infrastructure.

   a. Compliance cost
   b. Genuine progress indicator
   c. Quality of life
   d. Culture of capitalism

6. In microeconomics, _____ is quite simply the conversion of inputs into outputs. It is an economic process that uses resources to create a good or service that is suitable for exchange. This can include manufacturing, storing, shipping, and packaging.
   a. Red Guards
   b. Solved
   c. MET
   d. Production

7. Competition law, known in the United States as _____ law, has three main elements:

   - prohibiting agreements or practices that restrict free trading and competition between business entities. This includes in particular the repression of cartels.
   - banning abusive behaviour by a firm dominating a market, or anti-competitive practices that tend to lead to such a dominant position. Practices controlled in this way may include predatory pricing, tying, price gouging, refusal to deal, and many others.
   - supervising the mergers and acquisitions of large corporations, including some joint ventures. Transactions that are considered to threaten the competitive process can be prohibited altogether, or approved subject to 'remedies' such as an obligation to divest part of the merged business or to offer licences or access to facilities to enable other businesses to continue competing.

The substance and practice of competition law varies from jurisdiction to jurisdiction. Protecting the interests of consumers (consumer welfare) and ensuring that entrepreneurs have an opportunity to compete in the market economy are often treated as important objectives. Competition law is closely connected with law on deregulation of access to markets, state aids and subsidies, the privatisation of state owned assets and the establishment of independent sector regulators. In recent decades, competition law has been viewed as a way to provide better public services.

4   *Chapter 1. Overseas Empire*

    a. Antitrust   b. Anti-Inflation Act
    c. Intellectual property law   d. United Kingdom competition law

8. An _____ is a form of debt bondage worker. The laborer is under contract of an employer for usually three to seven years, in exchange for their transportation, food, drink, clothing, lodging and other necessities. Unlike a slave, an _____ is required to work only for a limited term specified in a signed contract.

    a. AD-IA Model   b. Indentured servant
    c. ACEA agreement   d. ACCRA Cost of Living Index

9. The _____ was one of the peace treaties at the end of World War I. It ended the state of war between Germany and the Allied Powers. It was signed on 28 June 1919, exactly five years after the assassination of Archduke Franz Ferdinand. The other Central Powers on the German side of World War I were dealt with in separate treaties.

    a. 100-year flood   b. 130-30 fund
    c. 1921 recession   d. Treaty of Versailles

10. Economics:

- _____, the desire to own something and the ability to pay for it
- _____ curve, a graphic representation of a _____ schedule
- _____ deposit, the money in checking accounts
- _____ pull theory, the theory that inflation occurs when _____ for goods and services exceeds existing supplies
- _____ schedule, a table that lists the quantity of a good a person will buy it each different price
- _____ side economics, the school of economics at believes government spending and tax cuts open economy by raising _____

    a. Demand   b. Variability
    c. Production   d. McKesson ' Robbins scandal

11. A _____ is the exclusive authority to determine how a resource is used, whether that resource is owned by government or by individuals. All economic goods have a _____s attribute. This attribute has three broad components

1. The right to use the good
2. The right to earn income from the good
3. The right to transfer the good to others

The concept of _____s as used by economists and legal scholars are related but distinct. The distinction is largely seen in the economists' focus on the ability of an individual or collective to control the use of the good.

    a. Post-sale restraint   b. Holder in due course
    c. High-reeve   d. Property right

12. Under the system of feudalism, a _____, fief, feud, feoff often consisted of inheritable lands or revenue-producing property granted by a liege lord, generally to a vassal, in return for a form of allegiance, originally to give him the means to fulfill his military duties when called upon. However anything of value could be held in fief, such as an office, a right of exploitation (e.g., hunting, fishing) or any other type of revenue, rather than the land it comes from.

Originally, the feudal institution of vassalage did not imply the giving or receiving of landholdings (which were granted only as a reward for loyalty), but by the eighth century the giving of a landholding was becoming standard.

a. 130-30 fund
b. 100-year flood
c. 1921 recession
d. Fiefdom

13. A _____ is an estate in land. It is the most common way real estate is owned in common law countries, and is ordinarily the most complete ownership interest that can be had in real property short of allodial title, which is often reserved for governments. _____ ownership represents absolute ownership of real property but it is limited by the four basic government powers of taxation, eminent domain, police power, and escheat and could also be limited by certain encumbrances or a condition in the deed.

a. Deficiency judgment
b. Leave of absence
c. Fraudulent trading
d. Fee simple

14. Economic _____ is defined as an excess distribution to any factor in a production process above that which is required to induce the factor into the process or any excess above that which is necessary to keep the factor in its current use..

Classical Factor _____ is primarily concerned with the fee paid for the use of fixed (e.g. natural) resources. The classical definition is expressed as any excess payment above that required to induce or provide for production.

a. 1921 recession
b. Rent
c. 100-year flood
d. 130-30 fund

15. _____ is the practice within the banking industry of authorizing electronic transactions done with a debit card or credit card and holding this balance as unavailable either until the merchant clears the transaction _____s can fall off the account anywhere from 1-5 days after the transaction date depending on the bank's policy; in the case of credit cards, holds may last as long as 30 days, depending on the issuing bank.

Signature-based credit and debit card transactions are a two-step process, consisting of an authorization and a settlement.

When a merchant swipes a customer's credit card, the credit card terminal connects to the merchant's acquirer which verifies that the customer's account is valid and that sufficient funds are available to cover the transaction's cost.

a. Interbank network
b. Authorization hold
c. Issuing bank
d. Electronic funds transfer

16. _____ to the arrival of new individuals into a habitat or population. It is a biological concept and is important in population ecology, differentiated from emigration and migration.

_____ is a modern phenomenon.

a. AD-IA Model
b. Immigration
c. ACCRA Cost of Living Index
d. ACEA agreement

17. In economics, the _____ measures the payments that flow between any individual country and all other countries. It is used to summarize all international economic transactions for that country during a specific time period, usually a year. The _____ is determined by the country's exports and imports of goods, services, and financial capital, as well as financial transfers.

a. Balance of payments
b. Gross domestic product per barrel
c. Skyscraper Index
d. Gross world product

18. A _____ is the transfer of wealth from one party (such as a person or company) to another. A _____ is usually made in exchange for the provision of goods, services or both, or to fulfill a legal obligation.

The simplest and oldest form of _____ is barter, the exchange of one good or service for another.

a. Soft count
b. Social gravity
c. Going concern
d. Payment

19. _____s is the social science that studies the production, distribution, and consumption of goods and services. The term _____s comes from the Ancient Greek oἰκονομῖα from oἶκος (oikos, 'house') + νΐŒμος (nomos, 'custom' or 'law'), hence 'rules of the house(hold)'. Current _____ models developed out of the broader field of political economy in the late 19th century, owing to a desire to use an empirical approach more akin to the physical sciences.

a. Inflation
b. Opportunity cost
c. Energy economics
d. Economic

Chapter 2. Colonial Development

1. _____ is the physical growth of rural or natural land into urban areas as a result of population immigration to an existing urban area. Effects include change in density and administration services. While the exact definition and population size of urbanized areas varies among different countries, _____ is attributed to growth of cities.

   a. Urban prairie
   b. Urban renewal
   c. ACCRA Cost of Living Index
   d. Urbanization

2. In algebra, a _____ is a function depending on n that associates a scalar, det(A), to an n×n square matrix A. The fundamental geometric meaning of a _____ is a scale factor for measure when A is regarded as a linear transformation. _____s are important both in calculus, where they enter the substitution rule for several variables, and in multilinear algebra.

   For a fixed nonnegative integer n, there is a unique _____ function for the n×n matrices over any commutative ring R. In particular, this function exists when R is the field of real or complex numbers.

   a. Determinant
   b. 130-30 fund
   c. 1921 recession
   d. 100-year flood

3. A _____ is the exclusive authority to determine how a resource is used, whether that resource is owned by government or by individuals. All economic goods have a _____s attribute. This attribute has three broad components

   1. The right to use the good
   2. The right to earn income from the good
   3. The right to transfer the good to others

   The concept of _____s as used by economists and legal scholars are related but distinct. The distinction is largely seen in the economists' focus on the ability of an individual or collective to control the use of the good.

   a. Holder in due course
   b. Post-sale restraint
   c. High-reeve
   d. Property right

4. The _____ is institutions that comprise the World Bank Group. The IBRD is an international organization whose original mission was to finance the reconstruction of nations devastated by World War II. Now, its mission has expanded to fight poverty by means of financing states.

   a. ACCRA Cost of Living Index
   b. International Bank for Reconstruction and Development
   c. International Development Association
   d. United Nations Monetary and Financial Conference

5. _____ is the change in population over time, and can be quantified as the change in the number of individuals in a population using 'per unit time' for measurement. The term _____ can technically refer to any species, but almost always refers to humans, and it is often used informally for the more specific demographic term _____ rate , and is often used to refer specifically to the growth of the population of the world.

   Simple models of _____ include the Malthusian Growth Model and the logistic model.

   a. Population dynamics
   b. Population growth
   c. 100-year flood
   d. 130-30 fund

Chapter 2. Colonial Development

6. In economics, _____ refers to the ability of a person or a country to produce a particular good at a lower marginal cost and opportunity cost than another person or country. It is the ability to produce a product most efficiently given all the other products that could be produced. It can be contrasted with absolute advantage which refers to the ability of a person or a country to produce a particular good at a lower absolute cost than another.
   a. Gravity model of trade
   b. Comparative advantage
   c. Hot money
   d. Triffin dilemma

7. _____ or economic opportunity loss is the value of the next best alternative foregone as the result of making a decision. _____ analysis is an important part of a company's decision-making processes but is not treated as an actual cost in any financial statement. The next best thing that a person can engage in is referred to as the _____ of doing the best thing and ignoring the next best thing to be done.
   a. Industrial organization
   b. Economic
   c. Economic ideology
   d. Opportunity cost

8. In economics, the _____ measures the payments that flow between any individual country and all other countries. It is used to summarize all international economic transactions for that country during a specific time period, usually a year. The _____ is determined by the country's exports and imports of goods, services, and financial capital, as well as financial transfers.
   a. Gross domestic product per barrel
   b. Balance of payments
   c. Gross world product
   d. Skyscraper Index

9. A _____ is the transfer of wealth from one party (such as a person or company) to another. A _____ is usually made in exchange for the provision of goods, services or both, or to fulfill a legal obligation.

The simplest and oldest form of _____ is barter, the exchange of one good or service for another.

   a. Going concern
   b. Social gravity
   c. Payment
   d. Soft count

10. In microeconomics, _____ is quite simply the conversion of inputs into outputs. It is an economic process that uses resources to create a good or service that is suitable for exchange. This can include manufacturing, storing, shipping, and packaging.
    a. Red Guards
    b. MET
    c. Solved
    d. Production

11. _____, in microeconomics, are the cost advantages that a business obtains due to expansion. They are factors that cause a producere;s average cost per unit to fall as scale is increased. _____ is a long run concept and refers to reductions in unit cost as the size of a facility, or scale, increases.
    a. Underinvestment employment relationship
    b. Economic production quantity
    c. Isoquant
    d. Economies of scale

12. _____ to the arrival of new individuals into a habitat or population. It is a biological concept and is important in population ecology, differentiated from emigration and migration.

_____ is a modern phenomenon.

Chapter 2. Colonial Development   9

a. ACEA agreement
b. AD-IA Model
c. ACCRA Cost of Living Index
d. Immigration

13. Network externalities resemble economies of scale, but they are not considered such because they are a function of the number of users of a good or service in an industry, not of the production efficiency within a business. _____ are only considered examples of network externalities if they are driven by demand side economies.

Formally, a production function $F(K, L)$ is defined to have:

- constant returns to scale if (for any constant a greater than or equal to 0) $F(aK, aL) = aF(K, L)$
- increasing returns to scale if (for any constant a greater than 1) $F(aK, aL) > aF(K, L)$,
- decreasing returns to scale if (for any constant a greater than 1) $F(aK, aL) < aF(K, L)$

where K and L are factors of production, capital and labour, respectively.

As an example, the Cobb-Douglas functional form has constant returns to scale when the sum of the exponents adds up to one.

a. AD-IA Model
b. ACEA agreement
c. Economies of scale external to the firm
d. ACCRA Cost of Living Index

14. Economics:

- _____, the desire to own something and the ability to pay for it
- _____ curve, a graphic representation of a _____ schedule
- _____ deposit, the money in checking accounts
- _____ pull theory, the theory that inflation occurs when _____ for goods and services exceeds existing supplies
- _____ schedule, a table that lists the quantity of a good a person will buy it each different price
- _____ side economics, the school of economics at believes government spending and tax cuts open economy by raising _____

a. McKesson ' Robbins scandal
b. Production
c. Variability
d. Demand

15. The term '_____' refers to the concept of collecting information and attempting to spot a pattern in the information. In some fields of study, the term '_____' has more formally-defined meanings.

In project management _____ is a mathematical technique that uses historical results to predict future outcome.

a. Coefficient of determination
b. Probit model
c. Trend analysis
d. Quantile regression

16. The _____ was a period in the late 18th and early 19th centuries when major changes in agriculture, manufacturing, mining, and transportation had a profound effect on the socioeconomic and cultural conditions in Britain. The changes subsequently spread throughout Europe, North America, and eventually the world. The onset of the _____ marked a major turning point in human society; almost every aspect of daily life was eventually influenced in some way.
    a. Adam Smith
    b. Industrial Revolution
    c. Adolph Fischer
    d. Adolf Hitler

17. Competition law, known in the United States as _____ law, has three main elements:

    - prohibiting agreements or practices that restrict free trading and competition between business entities. This includes in particular the repression of cartels.
    - banning abusive behaviour by a firm dominating a market, or anti-competitive practices that tend to lead to such a dominant position. Practices controlled in this way may include predatory pricing, tying, price gouging, refusal to deal, and many others.
    - supervising the mergers and acquisitions of large corporations, including some joint ventures. Transactions that are considered to threaten the competitive process can be prohibited altogether, or approved subject to 'remedies' such as an obligation to divest part of the merged business or to offer licences or access to facilities to enable other businesses to continue competing.

    The substance and practice of competition law varies from jurisdiction to jurisdiction. Protecting the interests of consumers (consumer welfare) and ensuring that entrepreneurs have an opportunity to compete in the market economy are often treated as important objectives. Competition law is closely connected with law on deregulation of access to markets, state aids and subsidies, the privatisation of state owned assets and the establishment of independent sector regulators. In recent decades, competition law has been viewed as a way to provide better public services.

    a. Anti-Inflation Act
    b. Intellectual property law
    c. Antitrust
    d. United Kingdom competition law

18. _____ is a term used to describe a policy of allowing events to take their own course. The term is a French phrase literally meaning 'let do'. It is a doctrine that states that government generally should not intervene in the marketplace.
    a. Communization
    b. Heroic capitalism
    c. Theory of Productive Forces
    d. Laissez-faire

19. _____ is Latin for 'Let the buyer beware'. Generally _____ is the property law doctrine that controls the sale of real property after the date of closing.

    Under the doctrine of _____, the buyer could not recover from the seller for defects on the property that rendered the property unfit for ordinary purposes.

    a. 100-year flood
    b. 1921 recession
    c. Caveat emptor
    d. 130-30 fund

20. A _____ is an object whose consumption increases the utility of the consumer, for which the quantity demanded exceeds the quantity supplied at zero price. _____s are usually modeled as having diminishing marginal utility. The first individual purchase has high utility; the second has less.
   a. Composite good
   b. Good
   c. Merit good
   d. Pie method

21. In economics, a _____ exists when a specific individual or enterprise has sufficient control over a particular product or service to determine significantly the terms on which other individuals shall have access to it. Monopolies are thus characterized by a lack of economic competition for the good or service that they provide and a lack of viable substitute goods. The verb 'monopolize' refers to the process by which a firm gains persistently greater market share than what is expected under perfect competition.
   a. 100-year flood
   b. 1921 recession
   c. 130-30 fund
   d. Monopoly

22. _____ is a system of training a new generation of practitioners of a skill. Apprentices (or in early modern usage 'prentices') or protégés build their careers from _____s. Most of their training is done on the job while working for an employer who helps the apprentices learn their trade, in exchange for their continuing labour for an agreed period after they become skilled.
   a. AD-IA Model
   b. ACEA agreement
   c. ACCRA Cost of Living Index
   d. Apprenticeship

23. In economics, the people in the _____ are the suppliers of labor. The _____ is all the nonmilitary people who are employed or unemployed. In 2005, the worldwide _____ was over 3 billion people.
   a. Distributed workforce
   b. Grenelle agreements
   c. Departmentalization
   d. Labor force

24.

The _____ was the first United States Federal statute to limit cartels and monopolies. It falls under antitrust law.

The Act provides: 'Every contract, combination in the form of trust or otherwise, or conspiracy, in restraint of trade or commerce among the several States, or with foreign nations, is declared to be illegal'. The Act also provides: 'Every person who shall monopolize, or attempt to monopolize, or combine or conspire with any other person or persons, to monopolize any part of the trade or commerce among the several States, or with foreign nations, shall be deemed guilty of a felony [. . .]' The Act put responsibility upon government attorneys and district courts to pursue and investigate trusts, companies and organizations suspected of violating the Act. The Clayton Act extended the right to sue under the antitrust laws to 'any person who shall be injured in his business or property by reason of anything forbidden in the antitrust laws.' Under the Clayton Act, private parties may sue in U.S. district court and should they prevail, they may be awarded treble damages and the cost of suit, including reasonable attorney's fees.

   a. 1921 recession
   b. Sherman Antitrust Act
   c. 100-year flood
   d. 130-30 fund

25. _____ is the shortage of common things such as food, clothing, shelter and safe drinking water, all of which determine the quality of life. It may also include the lack of access to opportunities such as education and employment which aid the escape from _____ and/or allow one to enjoy the respect of fellow citizens. According to Mollie Orshansky who developed the _____ measurements used by the U.S. government, 'to be poor is to be deprived of those goods and services and pleasures which others around us take for granted.' Ongoing debates over causes, effects and best ways to measure _____, directly influence the design and implementation of _____-reduction programs and are therefore relevant to the fields of public administration and international development.
   a. Poverty
   b. Liberal welfare reforms
   c. Growth Elasticity of Poverty
   d. Poverty map

Chapter 3. America on the Eve of Revolution

1. _____ to the arrival of new individuals into a habitat or population. It is a biological concept and is important in population ecology, differentiated from emigration and migration.

   _____ is a modern phenomenon.

   a. ACCRA Cost of Living Index
   b. AD-IA Model
   c. Immigration
   d. ACEA agreement

2. _____ is a measure of the number of deaths (in general scaled to the size of that population, per unit time. _____ is typically expressed in units of deaths per 1000 individuals per year; thus, a _____ of 9.5 in a population of 100,000 would mean 950 deaths per year in that entire population. It is distinct from morbidity rate, which refers to the number of individuals in poor health during a given time period (the prevalence rate) or the number who currently have that disease (the incidence rate), scaled to the size of the population.

   a. Mortality rate
   b. 130-30 fund
   c. 100-year flood
   d. 1921 recession

3. _____ is the change in population over time, and can be quantified as the change in the number of individuals in a population using 'per unit time' for measurement. The term _____ can technically refer to any species, but almost always refers to humans, and it is often used informally for the more specific demographic term _____ rate, and is often used to refer specifically to the growth of the population of the world.

   Simple models of _____ include the Malthusian Growth Model and the logistic model.

   a. 100-year flood
   b. 130-30 fund
   c. Population dynamics
   d. Population growth

4. Crude _____ is the nativity or childbirths per 1,000 people per year.

   It can be represented by number of childbirths in that year, and p is the current population. This figure is combined with the crude death rate to produce the rate of natural population growth (natural in that it does not take into account net migration.)

   a. Neo-Malthusianism
   b. Malthusian equilibrium
   c. Depensation
   d. Birth rate

5. _____s is the social science that studies the production, distribution, and consumption of goods and services. The term _____s comes from the Ancient Greek oá¼°κονομῖα from oá¼¶κος (oikos, 'house') + νÏŒμος (nomos, 'custom' or 'law'), hence 'rules of the house(hold)'. Current _____ models developed out of the broader field of political economy in the late 19th century, owing to a desire to use an empirical approach more akin to the physical sciences.

   a. Energy economics
   b. Opportunity cost
   c. Inflation
   d. Economic

6. _____ is the increase in the amount of the goods and services produced by an economy over time. It is conventionally measured as the percent rate of increase in real gross domestic product, or real GDP. Growth is usually calculated in real terms, i.e. inflation-adjusted terms, in order to net out the effect of inflation on the price of the goods and services produced.

Chapter 3. America on the Eve of Revolution

a. ACEA agreement
b. ACCRA Cost of Living Index
c. AD-IA Model
d. Economic growth

7. In economics, _____ are the resources employed to produce goods and services. They facilitate production but do not become part of the product (as with raw materials) or significantly transformed by the production process (as with fuel used to power machinery.) To 19th century economists, the _____ were land (natural resources, gifts from nature), labor (the ability to work), and capital goods (human-made tools and equipment.)

a. Hicks-neutral technical change
b. Factors of production
c. Long-run
d. Product Pipeline

8. In microeconomics, _____ is quite simply the conversion of inputs into outputs. It is an economic process that uses resources to create a good or service that is suitable for exchange. This can include manufacturing, storing, shipping, and packaging.

a. Production
b. Solved
c. MET
d. Red Guards

9. _____ in economics refers to metrics and measures of output from production processes, per unit of input. Labor _____, for example, is typically measured as a ratio of output per labor-hour, an input. _____ may be conceived of as a metrics of the technical or engineering efficiency of production.

a. Production-possibility frontier
b. Fordism
c. Piece work
d. Productivity

10. _____ is generally measured by standards such as real (i.e. inflation adjusted) income per person and poverty rate. Other measures such as access and quality of health care, income growth inequality and educational standards are also used. Examples are access to certain goods (such as number of refrigerators per 1000 people), or measures of health such as life expectancy.

a. 130-30 fund
b. 100-year flood
c. Remuneration
d. Standard of living

11. _____ is a comparison of the wealth of various members or groups in a society. It differs from the distribution of income in a manner analogous to the difference between position and speed.

Wealth is a person's net worth, expressed as:

   wealth = assets - liabilities

The word 'wealth' is often confused with 'income'.

a. Distribution of wealth
b. 130-30 fund
c. Wealth condensation
d. 100-year flood

12. In economics, the _____ of money is a theory emphasizing the positive relationship of overall prices or the nominal value of expenditures to the quantity of money.

It is the mainstream economic theory of the price level. Alternative theories include the real bills doctrine and the more recent fiscal theory of the price level.

Chapter 3. America on the Eve of Revolution

a. Real business cycle
b. Quantity theory
c. Romer Model
d. Dishoarding

13. In economics, _____ is a monetary standard in which the value of the monetary unit is defined as equivalent either to a certain quantity of gold or to a certain quantity of silver. Such a system effectively establishes a fixed rate of exchange for the two metals. The merits of the system were the subject of debate in the late 19th century.
   a. 100-year flood
   b. 130-30 fund
   c. 1921 recession
   d. Bimetallism

14. _____ or forced tender is payment that, by law, cannot be refused in settlement of a debt.

_____ is variously defined in different jurisdictions. Formally, it is anything which when offered in payment extinguishes the debt.

   a. Legal tender
   b. Landsbanki Freezing Order 2008
   c. Patent portfolio
   d. Leave of absence

15. In economics, the _____ measures the payments that flow between any individual country and all other countries. It is used to summarize all international economic transactions for that country during a specific time period, usually a year. The _____ is determined by the country's exports and imports of goods, services, and financial capital, as well as financial transfers.
   a. Balance of payments
   b. Skyscraper Index
   c. Gross world product
   d. Gross domestic product per barrel

16. A _____ is the transfer of wealth from one party (such as a person or company) to another. A _____ is usually made in exchange for the provision of goods, services or both, or to fulfill a legal obligation.

The simplest and oldest form of _____ is barter, the exchange of one good or service for another.

   a. Social gravity
   b. Soft count
   c. Going concern
   d. Payment

17. The _____ is the central bank of the United Kingdom and is the model on which most modern, large central banks have been based. Since 1946 it has been a state-owned institution. It was established in 1694 to act as the English Government's banker, and to this day it still acts as the banker for the UK Government.
   a. 130-30 fund
   b. 100-year flood
   c. 1921 recession
   d. Bank of England

18. _____ is a reduction in the value of a currency with respect to other monetary units. In common modern usage, it specifically implies an official lowering of the value of a country's currency within a fixed exchange rate system, by which the monetary authority formally sets a new fixed rate with respect to a foreign reference currency. In contrast, (currency) depreciation is used for the unofficial decrease in the exchange rate in a floating exchange rate system.
   a. Texas redbacks
   b. Reserve currency
   c. Devaluation
   d. Petrodollar recycling

Chapter 3. America on the Eve of Revolution

19. In economics, _____ is a rise in the general level of prices of goods and services in an economy over a period of time. When the general price level rises, each unit of currency buys fewer goods and services; consequently, _____ is also a decline in the real value of money--a loss of purchasing power in the medium of exchange which is also the monetary unit of account in the economy. A chief measure of general price-level _____ is the general _____ rate, which is the percentage change in a general price index (normally the Consumer Price Index) over time.
   - a. Opportunity cost
   - b. Economic
   - c. Energy economics
   - d. Inflation

20. The _____ was enacted in July 14, 1890 as a United States federal law. While not authorizing the free and unlimited coinage of silver that the Free Silver supporters wanted, it increased the amount of silver the government was required to purchase every month. The _____ had been passed in response to the growing complaints of farmers and mining interests.
   - a. Pure Food and Drug Act
   - b. Security and Freedom Through Encryption Act
   - c. 100-year flood
   - d. Sherman Silver Purchase Act

21. A _____ is a kind of negotiable instrument, a promissory note made by a bank payable to the bearer on demand, used as money, and in many jurisdictions is legal tender. Along with coins, _____s make up the cash or bearer forms of all modern money. With the exception of non-circulating high-value or precious metal commemorative issues, coins are generally used for lower valued monetary units, while _____s are used for higher values.
   - a. Local currency
   - b. Security thread
   - c. Microprinting
   - d. Banknote

22. _____ is a term used in accounting, economics and finance to spread the cost of an asset over the span of several years.

   In simple words we can say that _____ is the reduction in the value of an asset due to usage, passage of time, wear and tear, technological outdating or obsolescence, depletion, inadequacy, rot, rust, decay or other such factors.

   In accounting, _____ is a term used to describe any method of attributing the historical or purchase cost of an asset across its useful life, roughly corresponding to normal wear and tear.
   - a. Historical cost
   - b. Salvage value
   - c. Net income per employee
   - d. Depreciation

23. _____ is money declared by a government to be legal tender. The term derives from the Latin fiat, meaning 'let it be done'. _____ achieves value because a government accepts it in payment of taxes and says it can be used within the country as a 'tender' to pay all debts.
   - a. Currency board
   - b. World currency
   - c. Devaluation
   - d. Fiat money

24. _____ is a term used to describe large corporations, in either an individual or collective sense. The term first came into use in a symbolic sense subsequent to the American Civil War, particularly after 1880, in connection with the combination movement that began in American business at that time. Organizations that fall into the category of '_____' include ExxonMobil, Wal-Mart, Google, Microsoft, General Motors, Citigroup and Arcelor Mittal.

a. First-mover advantage
b. Brainsworking
c. Sole proprietorship
d. Big business

Chapter 4. Gaining Independence

1. Competition law, known in the United States as _____ law, has three main elements:

   - prohibiting agreements or practices that restrict free trading and competition between business entities. This includes in particular the repression of cartels.
   - banning abusive behaviour by a firm dominating a market, or anti-competitive practices that tend to lead to such a dominant position. Practices controlled in this way may include predatory pricing, tying, price gouging, refusal to deal, and many others.
   - supervising the mergers and acquisitions of large corporations, including some joint ventures. Transactions that are considered to threaten the competitive process can be prohibited altogether, or approved subject to 'remedies' such as an obligation to divest part of the merged business or to offer licences or access to facilities to enable other businesses to continue competing.

   The substance and practice of competition law varies from jurisdiction to jurisdiction. Protecting the interests of consumers (consumer welfare) and ensuring that entrepreneurs have an opportunity to compete in the market economy are often treated as important objectives. Competition law is closely connected with law on deregulation of access to markets, state aids and subsidies, the privatisation of state owned assets and the establishment of independent sector regulators. In recent decades, competition law has been viewed as a way to provide better public services.

   a. Antitrust
   b. United Kingdom competition law
   c. Intellectual property law
   d. Anti-Inflation Act

2. _____s is the social science that studies the production, distribution, and consumption of goods and services. The term _____s comes from the Ancient Greek οἰκονομία from οἶκος (oikos, 'house') + νόμος (nomos, 'custom' or 'law'), hence 'rules of the house(hold)'. Current _____ models developed out of the broader field of political economy in the late 19th century, owing to a desire to use an empirical approach more akin to the physical sciences.

   a. Economic
   b. Energy economics
   c. Inflation
   d. Opportunity cost

3. In economics, the _____ measures the payments that flow between any individual country and all other countries. It is used to summarize all international economic transactions for that country during a specific time period, usually a year. The _____ is determined by the country's exports and imports of goods, services, and financial capital, as well as financial transfers.

   a. Skyscraper Index
   b. Gross domestic product per barrel
   c. Gross world product
   d. Balance of payments

4. A _____ is the transfer of wealth from one party (such as a person or company) to another. A _____ is usually made in exchange for the provision of goods, services or both, or to fulfill a legal obligation.

   The simplest and oldest form of _____ is barter, the exchange of one good or service for another.

   a. Going concern
   b. Soft count
   c. Social gravity
   d. Payment

Chapter 4. Gaining Independence

5. _____ is an economic theory that holds that the prosperity of a nation is dependent upon its supply of capital, and that the global volume of international trade is 'unchangeable.' Economic assets or capital, are represented by bullion (gold, silver, and trade value) held by the state, which is best increased through a positive balance of trade with other nations (exports minus imports.) _____ suggests that the ruling government should advance these goals by playing a protectionist role in the economy; by encouraging exports and discouraging imports, notably through the use of tariffs and subsidies.

_____ was the dominant school of thought throughout the early modern period (from the 16th to the 18th century.)

   a. Consumer theory
   c. Nominal value
   b. General equilibrium theory
   d. Mercantilism

6. In economics, an _____ is any good or commodity, transported from one country to another country in a legitimate fashion, typically for use in trade. _____ goods or services are provided to foreign consumers by domestic producers. _____ is an important part of international trade.
   a. ACEA agreement
   c. ACCRA Cost of Living Index
   b. AD-IA Model
   d. Export

7. _____ is the increase in the amount of the goods and services produced by an economy over time. It is conventionally measured as the percent rate of increase in real gross domestic product, or real GDP. Growth is usually calculated in real terms, i.e. inflation-adjusted terms, in order to net out the effect of inflation on the price of the goods and services produced.
   a. ACCRA Cost of Living Index
   c. AD-IA Model
   b. ACEA agreement
   d. Economic growth

8. In macroeconomics, _____ is a condition of the national economy, where all or nearly all persons willing and able to work at the prevailing wages and working conditions are able to do so. It is defined either as 0% unemployment, literally, no unemployment (the rate of unemployment is the fraction of the work force unable to find work), as by James Tobin, or as the level of employment rates when there is no cyclical unemployment. It is defined by the majority of mainstream economists as being an acceptable level of natural unemployment above 0%, the discrepancy from 0% being due to non-cyclical types of unemployment.
   a. Demand shock
   c. Harrod-Johnson diagram
   b. Marginal propensity to consume
   d. Full employment

9. In economics, the people in the _____ are the suppliers of labor. The _____ is all the nonmilitary people who are employed or unemployed. In 2005, the worldwide _____ was over 3 billion people.
   a. Grenelle agreements
   c. Labor force
   b. Distributed workforce
   d. Departmentalization

10. The _____ was a period in the late 18th and early 19th centuries when major changes in agriculture, manufacturing, mining, and transportation had a profound effect on the socioeconomic and cultural conditions in Britain. The changes subsequently spread throughout Europe, North America, and eventually the world. The onset of the _____ marked a major turning point in human society; almost every aspect of daily life was eventually influenced in some way.

a. Industrial Revolution
b. Adolph Fischer
c. Adam Smith
d. Adolf Hitler

11. The _____ is a term used for industries primarily concerned with the design or manufacture of clothing as well as the distribution and use of textiles.

Prior to the manufacturing processes were mechanized, textiles were produced in the home, and excess sold for extra money. Most cloth was made from either wool, cotton, or flax, depending on the era and location.

a. Textile manufacture during the Industrial Revolution
b. 100-year flood
c. 130-30 fund
d. Textile industry

12. _____ ndustrialization in North America, is the process of social and economic change whereby a human group is transformed from a pre-industrial society into an industrial one. _____ t is a part of a wider modernisation process, where social change and economic development are closely related with technological innovation, particularly with the development of large-scale energy and metallurgy production. _____ t is the extensive organisation of an economy for the purpose of manufacturing.

a. AD-IA Model
b. Industrialization
c. ACCRA Cost of Living Index
d. ACEA agreement

13. In microeconomics, _____ is quite simply the conversion of inputs into outputs. It is an economic process that uses resources to create a good or service that is suitable for exchange. This can include manufacturing, storing, shipping, and packaging.

a. Production
b. Solved
c. MET
d. Red Guards

14. _____ is money accepted for exchange of goods in an economy. The prevalence of one money over another arises, usually, when a government designates through decrees that the government shall accept only particular notes and coins in payment for taxes. Typically, money of _____ consists of stamped coins and minted paper bills.

a. Local currency
b. Currency
c. Security thread
d. Totnes pound

15. The _____ was an early English joint-stock company that was formed initially for pursuing trade with the East Indies, but that ended up trading with the Indian subcontinent and China. The oldest among several similarly formed European East India Companies, the Company was granted an English Royal Charter, under the name Governor and Company of Merchants of London Trading into the East Indies, by Elizabeth I on 31 December 1600. After a rival English company challenged its monopoly in the late 17th century, the two companies were merged in 1708 to form the United Company of Merchants of England Trading to the East Indies, commonly styled the Honourable _____, and abbreviated, HEast India Company; the Company was colloquially referred to as John Company, and in India as Company Bahadur .

a. ACCRA Cost of Living Index
b. East India Company
c. AD-IA Model
d. ACEA agreement

16. A _____ is a kind of negotiable instrument, a promissory note made by a bank payable to the bearer on demand, used as money, and in many jurisdictions is legal tender. Along with coins, _____s make up the cash or bearer forms of all modern money. With the exception of non-circulating high-value or precious metal commemorative issues, coins are generally used for lower valued monetary units, while _____s are used for higher values.

Chapter 4. Gaining Independence

a. Microprinting
b. Banknote
c. Security thread
d. Local currency

17. A _____ is a law enacted by a government that requires a tax to be paid on the transfer of certain documents. Those that pay the tax receive an official stamp on their documents. The tax raised, called stamp duty, was first devised in the Netherlands in 1624 after a public competition to find a new form of tax.
a. Tax law
b. Tax and spend
c. Honorarium
d. Stamp Act

18. _____ is a term used in accounting, economics and finance to spread the cost of an asset over the span of several years.

In simple words we can say that _____ is the reduction in the value of an asset due to usage, passage of time, wear and tear, technological outdating or obsolescence, depletion, inadequacy, rot, rust, decay or other such factors.

In accounting, _____ is a term used to describe any method of attributing the historical or purchase cost of an asset across its useful life, roughly corresponding to normal wear and tear.

a. Historical cost
b. Net income per employee
c. Salvage value
d. Depreciation

19. In economics, _____ is a rise in the general level of prices of goods and services in an economy over a period of time. When the general price level rises, each unit of currency buys fewer goods and services; consequently, _____ is also a decline in the real value of money--a loss of purchasing power in the medium of exchange which is also the monetary unit of account in the economy. A chief measure of general price-level _____ is the general _____ rate, which is the percentage change in a general price index (normally the Consumer Price Index) over time.
a. Energy economics
b. Opportunity cost
c. Inflation
d. Economic

20. _____ is an economic situation in which inflation and economic stagnation occur simultaneously and remain unchecked for a period of time. The portmanteau _____ is generally attributed to British politician Iain Macleod, who coined the term in a speech to Parliament in 1965. The concept is notable partly because, in postwar macroeconomic theory, inflation and recession were regarded as mutually exclusive, and also because _____ has generally proven to be difficult and costly to eradicate once it gets started.
a. Chronic inflation
b. Stagflation
c. Real interest rate
d. Price/wage spiral

21. In economics, _____ refers to the ability of a person or a country to produce a particular good at a lower marginal cost and opportunity cost than another person or country. It is the ability to produce a product most efficiently given all the other products that could be produced. It can be contrasted with absolute advantage which refers to the ability of a person or a country to produce a particular good at a lower absolute cost than another.
a. Comparative advantage
b. Hot money
c. Triffin dilemma
d. Gravity model of trade

Chapter 4. Gaining Independence

22. The _____ or gross domestic income (GDI), a basic measure of an economy's economic performance, is the market value of all final goods and services produced within the borders of a nation in a year. _____ can be defined in three ways, all of which are conceptually identical. First, it is equal to the total expenditures for all final goods and services produced within the country in a stipulated period of time (usually a 365-day year.)

a. Countercyclical
b. Monopolistic competition
c. Market structure
d. Gross domestic product

1. _____ is the practice within the banking industry of authorizing electronic transactions done with a debit card or credit card and holding this balance as unavailable either until the merchant clears the transaction _____s can fall off the account anywhere from 1-5 days after the transaction date depending on the bank's policy; in the case of credit cards, holds may last as long as 30 days, depending on the issuing bank.

Signature-based credit and debit card transactions are a two-step process, consisting of an authorization and a settlement.

When a merchant swipes a customer's credit card, the credit card terminal connects to the merchant's acquirer which verifies that the customer's account is valid and that sufficient funds are available to cover the transaction's cost.

   a. Electronic funds transfer
   b. Interbank network
   c. Issuing bank
   d. Authorization hold

2. Competition law, known in the United States as _____ law, has three main elements:

   - prohibiting agreements or practices that restrict free trading and competition between business entities. This includes in particular the repression of cartels.
   - banning abusive behaviour by a firm dominating a market, or anti-competitive practices that tend to lead to such a dominant position. Practices controlled in this way may include predatory pricing, tying, price gouging, refusal to deal, and many others.
   - supervising the mergers and acquisitions of large corporations, including some joint ventures. Transactions that are considered to threaten the competitive process can be prohibited altogether, or approved subject to 'remedies' such as an obligation to divest part of the merged business or to offer licences or access to facilities to enable other businesses to continue competing.

The substance and practice of competition law varies from jurisdiction to jurisdiction. Protecting the interests of consumers (consumer welfare) and ensuring that entrepreneurs have an opportunity to compete in the market economy are often treated as important objectives. Competition law is closely connected with law on deregulation of access to markets, state aids and subsidies, the privatisation of state owned assets and the establishment of independent sector regulators. In recent decades, competition law has been viewed as a way to provide better public services.

   a. United Kingdom competition law
   b. Anti-Inflation Act
   c. Intellectual property law
   d. Antitrust

3. A _____ refers to any type debt instrument, such as a loan, bond, mortgage that does not have a fixed rate of interest over the life of the instrument. Such debt typically uses an index or other base rate for establishing the interest rate for each relevant period. One of the most common rates to use as the basis for applying interest rates is the London Inter-bank Offered Rate, or LIBOR
   a. Moneylender
   b. Money market
   c. Disposal tax effect
   d. Floating interest rate

4. _____s is the social science that studies the production, distribution, and consumption of goods and services. The term _____s comes from the Ancient Greek oá¼°κονομῖα from oá¼¶κος (oikos, 'house') + vÏŒμος (nomos, 'custom' or 'law'), hence 'rules of the house(hold)'. Current _____ models developed out of the broader field of political economy in the late 19th century, owing to a desire to use an empirical approach more akin to the physical sciences.
   a. Energy economics
   b. Economic
   c. Inflation
   d. Opportunity cost

5. _____ is the increase in the amount of the goods and services produced by an economy over time. It is conventionally measured as the percent rate of increase in real gross domestic product, or real GDP. Growth is usually calculated in real terms, i.e. inflation-adjusted terms, in order to net out the effect of inflation on the price of the goods and services produced.
   a. Economic growth
   b. AD-IA Model
   c. ACCRA Cost of Living Index
   d. ACEA agreement

6. A _____ is the exclusive authority to determine how a resource is used, whether that resource is owned by government or by individuals. All economic goods have a _____s attribute. This attribute has three broad components

   1. The right to use the good
   2. The right to earn income from the good
   3. The right to transfer the good to others

The concept of _____s as used by economists and legal scholars are related but distinct. The distinction is largely seen in the economists' focus on the ability of an individual or collective to control the use of the good.

   a. Property right
   b. High-reeve
   c. Post-sale restraint
   d. Holder in due course

7. The _____ is institutions that comprise the World Bank Group. The IBRD is an international organization whose original mission was to finance the reconstruction of nations devastated by World War II. Now, its mission has expanded to fight poverty by means of financing states.
   a. United Nations Monetary and Financial Conference
   b. ACCRA Cost of Living Index
   c. International Bank for Reconstruction and Development
   d. International Development Association

8. _____ is an economic system in which wealth, and the means of producing wealth, are privately owned. Through _____, the land, labor, and capital are owned, operated, and traded for the purpose of generating profits, without force or fraud, by private individuals either singly or jointly, and investments, distribution, income, production, pricing and supply of goods, commodities and services are determined by voluntary private decision in a market economy. A distinguishing feature of _____ is that each person owns his or her own labor and therefore is allowed to sell the use of it to employers.
   a. Late capitalism
   b. Creative capitalism
   c. Socialism for the rich and capitalism for the poor
   d. Capitalism

9. In microeconomics, the reservation (or reserve) price is the maximum price a buyer is willing to pay for a good or service; or, conversely, the minimum price at which a seller is willing to sell a good or service. _____s are commonly used in auctions.

_____s vary for the buyer according to their disposable income, their desire for the good, and the prices of, and their information about substitute goods.

- a. Producer surplus
- b. Mohring effect
- c. Returns to scale
- d. Reservation price

10. _____ in economics and business is the result of an exchange and from that trade we assign a numerical monetary value to a good, service or asset. If Alice trades Bob 4 apples for an orange, the _____ of an orange is 4 apples. Inversely, the _____ of an apple is 1/4 oranges.

- a. Price war
- b. Price
- c. Price book
- d. Premium pricing

11. In finance, _____ is a financial action that does not promise safety of the initial investment along with the return on the principal sum. _____ typically involves the lending of money or the purchase of assets, equity or debt but in a manner that has not been given thorough analysis or is deemed to have low margin of safety or a significant risk of the loss of the principal investment. The term, '_____,' which is formally defined as above in Graham and Dodd's 1934 text, Security Analysis, contrasts with the term 'investment,' which is a financial operation that, upon thorough analysis, promises safety of principal and a satisfactory return.

- a. Global Financial Centres Index
- b. Municipal Bond Arbitrage
- c. Speculation
- d. Hybrid market

12. The term _____ refers to economy-wide fluctuations in production or economic activity over several months or years. These fluctuations occur around a long-term growth trend, and typically involve shifts over time between periods of relatively rapid economic growth (expansion or boom), and periods of relative stagnation or decline (contraction or recession.)

These fluctuations are often measured using the growth rate of real gross domestic product.

- a. Tobit model
- b. Nominal value
- c. Business cycle
- d. Consumer theory

13. _____ to the arrival of new individuals into a habitat or population. It is a biological concept and is important in population ecology, differentiated from emigration and migration.

_____ is a modern phenomenon.

- a. Immigration
- b. AD-IA Model
- c. ACCRA Cost of Living Index
- d. ACEA agreement

14. In economics, the _____ measures the payments that flow between any individual country and all other countries. It is used to summarize all international economic transactions for that country during a specific time period, usually a year. The _____ is determined by the country's exports and imports of goods, services, and financial capital, as well as financial transfers.

a. Gross world product
b. Gross domestic product per barrel
c. Skyscraper Index
d. Balance of payments

15. A _____ is the transfer of wealth from one party (such as a person or company) to another. A _____ is usually made in exchange for the provision of goods, services or both, or to fulfill a legal obligation.

The simplest and oldest form of _____ is barter, the exchange of one good or service for another.

a. Payment
b. Soft count
c. Going concern
d. Social gravity

Chapter 6. Population and Labor Force

1. _____ is the change in population over time, and can be quantified as the change in the number of individuals in a population using 'per unit time' for measurement. The term _____ can technically refer to any species, but almost always refers to humans, and it is often used informally for the more specific demographic term _____ rate, and is often used to refer specifically to the growth of the population of the world.

Simple models of _____ include the Malthusian Growth Model and the logistic model.

   a. 130-30 fund
   b. Population dynamics
   c. Population growth
   d. 100-year flood

2. Crude _____ is the nativity or childbirths per 1,000 people per year.

It can be represented by number of childbirths in that year, and p is the current population. This figure is combined with the crude death rate to produce the rate of natural population growth (natural in that it does not take into account net migration.)

   a. Birth rate
   b. Malthusian equilibrium
   c. Depensation
   d. Neo-Malthusianism

3. In economics, a _____ or a hard good is a good which does not quickly wear out it yields services or utility over time rather than being completely used up when used once. Most goods are therefore _____s to a certain degree. These are goods that can last for a relatively long time, such as refrigerators, cars, and DVD players.
   a. Luxury good
   b. Superior goods
   c. Search good
   d. Durable good

4. The _____ was a worldwide economic downturn starting in most places in 1929 and ending at different times in the 1930s or early 1940s for different countries. It was the largest and most important economic depression in the 20th century, and is used in the 21st century as an example of how far the world's economy can fall. The _____ originated in the United States; historians most often use as a starting date the stock market crash on October 29, 1929, known as Black Tuesday.
   a. Wall Street Crash of 1929
   b. British Empire Economic Conference
   c. Great Depression
   d. Jarrow March

5. In economics, _____ are the plant, machinery, and equipment that enable production, and are the main input into new installed capital.
   a. Occupational licensing
   b. Investment goods
   c. Indexation of contracts
   d. Equipment trust certificate

6. A _____ is an object whose consumption increases the utility of the consumer, for which the quantity demanded exceeds the quantity supplied at zero price. _____s are usually modeled as having diminishing marginal utility. The first individual purchase has high utility; the second has less.
   a. Merit good
   b. Pie method
   c. Composite good
   d. Good

7. _____ is the a method of technical and economic research of the systems for purpose to optimize a parity between system's consumer functions or properties and expenses to achieve those functions or properties.

Chapter 6. Population and Labor Force

This methodology for continuous perfection of production, industrial technologies, organizational structures was developed by Juryj Sobolev in 1948 at the 'Perm telephone factory'

- 1948 Juryj Sobolev - the first success in application of a method analysis at the 'Perm telephone factory'.
- 1949 - the first application for the invention as result of use of the new method.

Today in economically developed countries practically each enterprise or the company use methodology of the kind of functional-cost analysis as a practice of the quality management, most full satisfying to principles of standards of series ISO 9000.

- Interest of consumer not in products itself, but the advantage which it will receive from its usage.
- The consumer aspires to reduce his expenses
- Functions needed by consumer can be executed in the various ways, and, hence, with various efficiency and expenses. Among possible alternatives of realization of functions exist such in which the parity of quality and the price is the optimal for the consumer.

The goal of _____ is achievement of the highest consumer satisfaction of production at simultaneous decrease in all kinds of industrial expenses Classical _____ has three English synonyms - Value Engineering, Value Management, Value Analysis.

   a. Staple financing
   c. Willingness to pay
   b. Monopoly wage
   d. Function cost analysis

8. _____ to the arrival of new individuals into a habitat or population. It is a biological concept and is important in population ecology, differentiated from emigration and migration.

_____ is a modern phenomenon.

   a. ACEA agreement
   c. AD-IA Model
   b. ACCRA Cost of Living Index
   d. Immigration

9. The _____ was a period in the late 18th and early 19th centuries when major changes in agriculture, manufacturing, mining, and transportation had a profound effect on the socioeconomic and cultural conditions in Britain. The changes subsequently spread throughout Europe, North America, and eventually the world. The onset of the _____ marked a major turning point in human society; almost every aspect of daily life was eventually influenced in some way.
   a. Adam Smith
   c. Adolph Fischer
   b. Adolf Hitler
   d. Industrial Revolution

10. _____s is the social science that studies the production, distribution, and consumption of goods and services. The term _____s comes from the Ancient Greek oá¼°κονομῖα from oá¼¶κος (oikos, 'house') + vÏŒμος (nomos, 'custom' or 'law'), hence 'rules of the house(hold)'. Current _____ models developed out of the broader field of political economy in the late 19th century, owing to a desire to use an empirical approach more akin to the physical sciences.

a. Inflation
b. Economic
c. Energy economics
d. Opportunity cost

11. _____ the Great War, and the War to End All Wars, was a global military conflict which involved the majority of the world's great powers, organized into two opposing military alliances: the Entente Powers and the Central Powers. Over 70 million military personnel were mobilized in one of the largest wars in history. In a state of total war, the major combatants fully placed their scientific and industrial capabilities at the service of the war effort.
   a. 1921 recession
   b. World War I
   c. 100-year flood
   d. 130-30 fund

12. _____ is the increase in the amount of the goods and services produced by an economy over time. It is conventionally measured as the percent rate of increase in real gross domestic product, or real GDP. Growth is usually calculated in real terms, i.e. inflation-adjusted terms, in order to net out the effect of inflation on the price of the goods and services produced.
   a. ACEA agreement
   b. ACCRA Cost of Living Index
   c. AD-IA Model
   d. Economic growth

13. An _____ is a form of debt bondage worker. The laborer is under contract of an employer for usually three to seven years, in exchange for their transportation, food, drink, clothing, lodging and other necessities. Unlike a slave, an _____ is required to work only for a limited term specified in a signed contract.
   a. ACEA agreement
   b. AD-IA Model
   c. ACCRA Cost of Living Index
   d. Indentured servant

14. Economics:

    - _____,the desire to own something and the ability to pay for it
    - _____ curve,a graphic representation of a _____ schedule
    - _____ deposit, the money in checking accounts
    - _____ pull theory,the theory that inflation occurs when _____ for goods and services exceeds existing supplies
    - _____ schedule,a table that lists the quantity of a good a person will buy it each different price
    - _____ side economics,the school of economics at believes government spending and tax cuts open economy by raising _____

a. Production
b. Variability
c. Demand
d. McKesson ' Robbins scandal

Chapter 6. Population and Labor Force

15. Competition law, known in the United States as _____ law, has three main elements:

- prohibiting agreements or practices that restrict free trading and competition between business entities. This includes in particular the repression of cartels.
- banning abusive behaviour by a firm dominating a market, or anti-competitive practices that tend to lead to such a dominant position. Practices controlled in this way may include predatory pricing, tying, price gouging, refusal to deal, and many others.
- supervising the mergers and acquisitions of large corporations, including some joint ventures. Transactions that are considered to threaten the competitive process can be prohibited altogether, or approved subject to 'remedies' such as an obligation to divest part of the merged business or to offer licences or access to facilities to enable other businesses to continue competing.

The substance and practice of competition law varies from jurisdiction to jurisdiction. Protecting the interests of consumers (consumer welfare) and ensuring that entrepreneurs have an opportunity to compete in the market economy are often treated as important objectives. Competition law is closely connected with law on deregulation of access to markets, state aids and subsidies, the privatisation of state owned assets and the establishment of independent sector regulators. In recent decades, competition law has been viewed as a way to provide better public services.

a. United Kingdom competition law
b. Intellectual property law
c. Anti-Inflation Act
d. Antitrust

16. In economics, the _____ measures the payments that flow between any individual country and all other countries. It is used to summarize all international economic transactions for that country during a specific time period, usually a year. The _____ is determined by the country's exports and imports of goods, services, and financial capital, as well as financial transfers.

a. Gross domestic product per barrel
b. Gross world product
c. Skyscraper Index
d. Balance of payments

17. A _____ is the transfer of wealth from one party (such as a person or company) to another. A _____ is usually made in exchange for the provision of goods, services or both, or to fulfill a legal obligation.

The simplest and oldest form of _____ is barter, the exchange of one good or service for another.

a. Social gravity
b. Going concern
c. Soft count
d. Payment

18. In economics, the people in the _____ are the suppliers of labor. The _____ is all the nonmilitary people who are employed or unemployed. In 2005, the worldwide _____ was over 3 billion people.

a. Departmentalization
b. Labor force
c. Grenelle agreements
d. Distributed workforce

19. The _____ is a term used for industries primarily concerned with the design or manufacture of clothing as well as the distribution and use of textiles.

Prior to the manufacturing processes were mechanized, textiles were produced in the home, and excess sold for extra money. Most cloth was made from either wool, cotton, or flax, depending on the era and location.

   a. Textile manufacture during the Industrial Revolution
   b. Textile industry
   c. 130-30 fund
   d. 100-year flood

20. _____ is the physical growth of rural or natural land into urban areas as a result of population immigration to an existing urban area. Effects include change in density and administration services. While the exact definition and population size of urbanized areas varies among different countries, _____ is attributed to growth of cities.
   a. Urban renewal
   b. Urbanization
   c. ACCRA Cost of Living Index
   d. Urban prairie

21. The _____ was one of the first federations of labor unions in the United States. It was founded in Columbus, Ohio in 1886 by Samuel Gompers as a reorganization of its predecessor, the Federation of Organized Trades and Labor Unions. Gompers became president of the AFL in 1886 and was reelected every year except one until his death on December 13, 1924.
   a. American Federation of Labor
   b. ACEA agreement
   c. ACCRA Cost of Living Index
   d. AD-IA Model

22. A trade union or _____ is an organization of workers who have banded together to achieve common goals in key areas and working conditions. The trade union, through its leadership, bargains with the employer on behalf of union members (rank and file members) and negotiates labor contracts (Collective bargaining) with employers. This may include the negotiation of wages, work rules, complaint procedures, rules governing hiring, firing and promotion of workers, benefits, workplace safety and policies.
   a. Business valuation standards
   b. Demand-side technologies
   c. Basis of futures
   d. Labor union

23. _____, known in the United States as antitrust law, has three main elements:

   - prohibiting agreements or practices that restrict free trading and competition between business entities. This includes in particular the repression of cartels.
   - banning abusive behaviour by a firm dominating a market, or anti-competitive practices that tend to lead to such a dominant position. Practices controlled in this way may include predatory pricing, tying, price gouging, refusal to deal, and many others.
   - supervising the mergers and acquisitions of large corporations, including some joint ventures. Transactions that are considered to threaten the competitive process can be prohibited altogether, or approved subject to 'remedies' such as an obligation to divest part of the merged business or to offer licences or access to facilities to enable other businesses to continue competing.

The substance and practice of _____ varies from jurisdiction to jurisdiction. Protecting the interests of consumers (consumer welfare) and ensuring that entrepreneurs have an opportunity to compete in the market economy are often treated as important objectives. _____ is closely connected with law on deregulation of access to markets, state aids and subsidies, the privatisation of state owned assets and the establishment of independent sector regulators. In recent decades, _____ has been viewed as a way to provide better public services.

Chapter 6. Population and Labor Force

a. Hostile work environment
b. Due diligence
c. Fee simple
d. Competition law

24. In mathematics, an _____ is a statement about the relative size or order of two objects, or about whether they are the same or not

- The notation a < b means that a is less than b.
- The notation a > b means that a is greater than b.
- The notation a ≠ b means that a is not equal to b, but does not say that one is greater than the other or even that they can be compared in size.

In each statement above, a is not equal to b. These relations are known as strict inequalities. The notation a < b may also be read as 'a is strictly less than b'.

a. ACCRA Cost of Living Index
b. AD-IA Model
c. ACEA agreement
d. Inequality

25. A _____ or labor union is an organization of workers who have banded together to achieve common goals in key areas and working conditions. The _____, through its leadership, bargains with the employer on behalf of union members (rank and file members) and negotiates labor contracts (Collective bargaining) with employers. This may include the negotiation of wages, work rules, complaint procedures, rules governing hiring, firing and promotion of workers, benefits, workplace safety and policies.

a. Trade union
b. Consumer goods
c. Guaranteed investment contracts
d. Case-Shiller Home Price Indices

26. In economics, _____ is how a natione;s total economy is distributed among its population. ._____ has always been a central concern of economic theory and economic policy. Classical economists such as Adam Smith, Thomas Malthus and David Ricardo were mainly concerned with factor _____, that is, the distribution of income between the main factors of production, land, labour and capital.

a. Authorised capital
b. Eco commerce
c. Equipment trust certificate
d. Income distribution

Chapter 7. Law and the Rise of Classical American Capitalism

1. _____ is an economic system in which wealth, and the means of producing wealth, are privately owned. Through _____, the land, labor, and capital are owned, operated, and traded for the purpose of generating profits, without force or fraud, by private individuals either singly or jointly, and investments, distribution, income, production, pricing and supply of goods, commodities and services are determined by voluntary private decision in a market economy. A distinguishing feature of _____ is that each person owns his or her own labor and therefore is allowed to sell the use of it to employers.
   - a. Late capitalism
   - b. Capitalism
   - c. Socialism for the rich and capitalism for the poor
   - d. Creative capitalism

2. A _____ is the exclusive authority to determine how a resource is used, whether that resource is owned by government or by individuals. All economic goods have a _____s attribute. This attribute has three broad components

   1. The right to use the good
   2. The right to earn income from the good
   3. The right to transfer the good to others

   The concept of _____s as used by economists and legal scholars are related but distinct. The distinction is largely seen in the economists' focus on the ability of an individual or collective to control the use of the good.
   - a. High-reeve
   - b. Post-sale restraint
   - c. Property right
   - d. Holder in due course

3. _____s is the social science that studies the production, distribution, and consumption of goods and services. The term _____s comes from the Ancient Greek οἰκονομία from οἶκος (oikos, 'house') + νόμος (nomos, 'custom' or 'law'), hence 'rules of the house(hold)'. Current _____ models developed out of the broader field of political economy in the late 19th century, owing to a desire to use an empirical approach more akin to the physical sciences.
   - a. Economic
   - b. Opportunity cost
   - c. Energy economics
   - d. Inflation

4. _____ is the increase in the amount of the goods and services produced by an economy over time. It is conventionally measured as the percent rate of increase in real gross domestic product, or real GDP. Growth is usually calculated in real terms, i.e. inflation-adjusted terms, in order to net out the effect of inflation on the price of the goods and services produced.
   - a. ACEA agreement
   - b. ACCRA Cost of Living Index
   - c. AD-IA Model
   - d. Economic growth

34   *Chapter 7. Law and the Rise of Classical American Capitalism*

5. _____ has several particular meanings:

   - in mathematics
     - _____ function
     - Euler _____
     - _____
     - _____ subgroup
     - method of _____s (partial differential equations)
   - in physics and engineering
     - any _____ curve that shows the relationship between certain input- and output parameters, e.g.
     - an I-V or current-voltage _____ is the current in a circuit as a function of the applied voltage
     - Receiver-Operator _____
   - in fiction
     - in Dungeons ' Dragons, _____ is another name for ability score

   a. Demand
   b. Technocracy
   c. Characteristic
   d. Russian financial crisis

6. _____ is the development of economic wealth of countries or regions for the well-being of their inhabitants. It is the process by which a nation improves the economic, political, and social well being of its people. From a policy perspective, _____ can be defined as efforts that seek to improve the economic well-being and quality of life for a community by creating and/or retaining jobs and supporting or growing incomes and the tax base.

   a. Economic development
   b. Inflation
   c. Experimental economics
   d. Economic methodology

7. _____ is the change in population over time, and can be quantified as the change in the number of individuals in a population using 'per unit time' for measurement. The term _____ can technically refer to any species, but almost always refers to humans, and it is often used informally for the more specific demographic term _____ rate , and is often used to refer specifically to the growth of the population of the world.

   Simple models of _____ include the Malthusian Growth Model and the logistic model.

   a. 100-year flood
   b. Population dynamics
   c. Population growth
   d. 130-30 fund

Chapter 7. Law and the Rise of Classical American Capitalism

8. Competition law, known in the United States as _____ law, has three main elements:

   - prohibiting agreements or practices that restrict free trading and competition between business entities. This includes in particular the repression of cartels.
   - banning abusive behaviour by a firm dominating a market, or anti-competitive practices that tend to lead to such a dominant position. Practices controlled in this way may include predatory pricing, tying, price gouging, refusal to deal, and many others.
   - supervising the mergers and acquisitions of large corporations, including some joint ventures. Transactions that are considered to threaten the competitive process can be prohibited altogether, or approved subject to 'remedies' such as an obligation to divest part of the merged business or to offer licences or access to facilities to enable other businesses to continue competing.

The substance and practice of competition law varies from jurisdiction to jurisdiction. Protecting the interests of consumers (consumer welfare) and ensuring that entrepreneurs have an opportunity to compete in the market economy are often treated as important objectives. Competition law is closely connected with law on deregulation of access to markets, state aids and subsidies, the privatisation of state owned assets and the establishment of independent sector regulators. In recent decades, competition law has been viewed as a way to provide better public services.

   a. Antitrust
   b. Intellectual property law
   c. Anti-Inflation Act
   d. United Kingdom competition law

9. _____ is a term used to describe a policy of allowing events to take their own course. The term is a French phrase literally meaning 'let do'. It is a doctrine that states that government generally should not intervene in the marketplace.
   a. Heroic capitalism
   b. Communization
   c. Theory of Productive Forces
   d. Laissez-faire

10. _____ is Latin for 'Let the buyer beware'. Generally _____ is the property law doctrine that controls the sale of real property after the date of closing.

Under the doctrine of _____, the buyer could not recover from the seller for defects on the property that rendered the property unfit for ordinary purposes.

   a. Caveat emptor
   b. 1921 recession
   c. 100-year flood
   d. 130-30 fund

11. In economics, a _____ exists when a specific individual or enterprise has sufficient control over a particular product or service to determine significantly the terms on which other individuals shall have access to it. Monopolies are thus characterized by a lack of economic competition for the good or service that they provide and a lack of viable substitute goods. The verb 'monopolize' refers to the process by which a firm gains persistently greater market share than what is expected under perfect competition.
   a. 100-year flood
   b. Monopoly
   c. 1921 recession
   d. 130-30 fund

Chapter 7. Law and the Rise of Classical American Capitalism

12. A _____ is a group of people who share or are motivated by at least one common issue or interest, or work together on a specific project(s) to achieve a common objective. _____s are also characterised by attempts to share and exercise political and social power and to make decisions on a consensus-driven and egalitarian basis. _____s differ from cooperatives in that they are not necessarily focused upon an economic benefit or saving (but can be that as well.)
   a. 100-year flood
   b. Collective
   c. 1921 recession
   d. 130-30 fund

13. _____ are defined as public goods that could be delivered as private goods, but are usually delivered by the government for various reasons, including social policy, and finances from public funds like taxes.

Common examples of public goods include: defense and law enforcement (including the system of property rights), public fireworks, lighthouses, clean air and other environmental goods, and information goods, such as software development, authorship, and invention.

   a. Government monopoly
   b. Common property
   c. Privatizing profits and socializing losses
   d. Collective goods

14. Economic _____ is defined as an excess distribution to any factor in a production process above that which is required to induce the factor into the process or any excess above that which is necessary to keep the factor in its current use..

Classical Factor _____ is primarily concerned with the fee paid for the use of fixed (e.g. natural) resources. The classical definition is expressed as any excess payment above that required to induce or provide for production.

   a. 1921 recession
   b. 100-year flood
   c. 130-30 fund
   d. Rent

15. A _____ is an object whose consumption increases the utility of the consumer, for which the quantity demanded exceeds the quantity supplied at zero price. _____s are usually modeled as having diminishing marginal utility. The first individual purchase has high utility; the second has less.
   a. Composite good
   b. Good
   c. Merit good
   d. Pie method

16. Many _____ are related to the environmental consequences of production and use

   - Systemic risk describes the risks to the overall economy arising from the risks which the banking system takes. That the private costs of banking failure may be smaller than the social costs justifies banking regulations, although regulations could create a moral hazard.

   - Anthropogenic climate change is attributed to greenhouse gas emissions from burning oil, gas, and coal. Global warming has been ranked as the #1 externality of all economic activity, in the magnitude of potential harms and yet remains unmitigated.

Chapter 7. Law and the Rise of Classical American Capitalism

    a. White certificates
    c. Green certificate
    b. Total Economic Value
    d. Negative externalities

17. In economics, _____ is the transfer of income, wealth or property from some individuals to others.

One premise of _____ is that money should be distributed to benefit the poorer members of society, and that the rich have an obligation to assist the poor, thus creating a more financially egalitarian society. Another argument is that the rich exploit the poor or otherwise gain unfair benefits.

    a. 100-year flood
    c. 130-30 fund
    b. 1921 recession
    d. Redistribution

18. _____ is a concept whereby a person's financial liability is limited to a fixed sum, most commonly the value of a person's investment in a company or partnership with _____. A shareholder in a limited company is not personally liable for any of the debts of the company, other than for the value of his investment in that company. The same is true for the members of a _____ partnership and the limited partners in a limited partnership.

    a. Personal Responsibility and Work Opportunity Reconciliation Act of 1996
    c. Nexus of contracts
    b. Deficiency judgment
    d. Limited liability

19. The _____ consists of a number of economic theories which describe the nature of the firm, company including its existence, its behaviour, and its relationship with the market.

In simplified terms, the _____ aims to answer these questions:

1. Existence - why do firms emerge, why are not all transactions in the economy mediated over the market?
2. Boundaries - why the boundary between firms and the market is located exactly there? Which transactions are performed internally and which are negotiated on the market?
3. Organization - why are firms structured in such specific way? What is the interplay of formal and informal relationships?

Despite looking simple, these questions are not answered by the established economic theory, which usually views firms as given, and treats them as black boxes without any internal structure.

The First World War period saw a change of emphasis in economic theory away from industry-level analysis which mainly included analysing markets to analysis at the level of the firm, as it became increasingly clear that perfect competition was no longer an adequate model of how firms behaved. Economic theory till then had focussed on trying to understand markets alone and there had been little study on understanding why firms or organisations exist.

    a. Policy Ineffectiveness Proposition
    c. Theory of the firm
    b. Khazzoom-Brookes postulate
    d. Technology gap

20. _____, compulsory purchase (United Kingdom, New Zealand, Ireland), resumption/compulsory acquisition (Australia) or expropriation (South Africa and Canada) or land acqusition (India) in common law legal systems is the inherent power of the state to seize a citizen's private property, expropriate property but without the owner's consent. The property is taken either for government use or by delegation to third parties who will devote it to public or civic use or, in some cases, economic development. The most common uses of property taken by _____ are for public utilities, highways, and railroads.

a. AD-IA Model
b. ACEA agreement
c. Eminent domain
d. ACCRA Cost of Living Index

21. The _____ is the central bank of the United Kingdom and is the model on which most modern, large central banks have been based. Since 1946 it has been a state-owned institution. It was established in 1694 to act as the English Government's banker, and to this day it still acts as the banker for the UK Government.

a. 100-year flood
b. 130-30 fund
c. 1921 recession
d. Bank of England

22. A _____ refers to any type debt instrument, such as a loan, bond, mortgage that does not have a fixed rate of interest over the life of the instrument. Such debt typically uses an index or other base rate for establishing the interest rate for each relevant period. One of the most common rates to use as the basis for applying interest rates is the London Inter-bank Offered Rate, or LIBOR

a. Money market
b. Disposal tax effect
c. Moneylender
d. Floating interest rate

23. The _____ was an alliance of trading cities and their guilds that established and maintained a trade monopoly along the coast of Northern Europe, from the Baltic to the North Sea and inland, during the Late Middle Ages and Early modern period The Hanseatic cities had their own law system and furnished their own protection and mutual aid.

Historians generally trace the origins of the League to the rebuilding of the North German town of Lübeck in 1159 by Duke Henry the Lion of Saxony, after Henry had captured the area from Count Adolf II of Holstein.

a. Smithsonian Agreement
b. Hanseatic League
c. Land reform
d. Putting-out system

Chapter 8. Transportation, Internal Improvements, and Urbanization

1. The _____ was a period in the late 18th and early 19th centuries when major changes in agriculture, manufacturing, mining, and transportation had a profound effect on the socioeconomic and cultural conditions in Britain. The changes subsequently spread throughout Europe, North America, and eventually the world. The onset of the _____ marked a major turning point in human society; almost every aspect of daily life was eventually influenced in some way.
   a. Industrial Revolution
   b. Adolf Hitler
   c. Adam Smith
   d. Adolph Fischer

2. _____ in economics refers to metrics and measures of output from production processes, per unit of input. Labor _____, for example, is typically measured as a ratio of output per labor-hour, an input. _____ may be conceived of as a metrics of the technical or engineering efficiency of production.
   a. Productivity
   b. Fordism
   c. Piece work
   d. Production-possibility frontier

3. The _____ was a panic in the United States built on a speculative fever. The bubble burst on May 10, 1837 in New York City, when every bank stopped payment in specie (gold and silver coinage.) The Panic was followed by a five-year depression, with the failure of banks and record high unemployment levels.
   a. 130-30 fund
   b. 1921 recession
   c. 100-year flood
   d. Panic of 1837

4. _____ is a term used to describe large corporations, in either an individual or collective sense. The term first came into use in a symbolic sense subsequent to the American Civil War, particularly after 1880, in connection with the combination movement that began in American business at that time. Organizations that fall into the category of '_____' include ExxonMobil, Wal-Mart, Google, Microsoft, General Motors, Citigroup and Arcelor Mittal.
   a. Brainsworking
   b. First-mover advantage
   c. Sole proprietorship
   d. Big business

5. A variety of measures of national income and output are used in economics to estimate total economic activity in a country or region, including gross domestic product (GDP), _____ , and net national income (NNI.)

   There are three main ways of calculating these numbers; the output approach, the income approach and the expenditure approach. In theory, the three must yield the same, because total expenditures on goods and services must equal the total income paid to the producers (GNI), and that must also equal the total value of the output of goods and services (_____.)

   a. Gross world product
   b. Purchasing power parity
   c. Gross national product
   d. Household final consumption expenditure

6. _____ is the process of sharing of skills, knowledge, technologies, methods of manufacturing, samples of manufacturing and facilities among governments and other institutions to ensure that scientific and technological developments are accessible to a wider range of users who can then further develop and exploit the technology into new products, processes, applications, materials or services. It is closely related to (and may arguably be considered a subset of) Knowledge transfer. Related terms, used almost synonymously, include 'technology valorisation' and 'technology commercialisation'.
   a. Law of increasing relative cost
   b. Judgment summons
   c. Patent
   d. Technology transfer

7. The term _____ refers to economy-wide fluctuations in production or economic activity over several months or years. These fluctuations occur around a long-term growth trend, and typically involve shifts over time between periods of relatively rapid economic growth (expansion or boom), and periods of relative stagnation or decline (contraction or recession.)

These fluctuations are often measured using the growth rate of real gross domestic product.

   a. Nominal value
   b. Tobit model
   c. Consumer theory
   d. Business cycle

8. _____ is the physical growth of rural or natural land into urban areas as a result of population immigration to an existing urban area. Effects include change in density and administration services. While the exact definition and population size of urbanized areas varies among different countries, _____ is attributed to growth of cities.
   a. ACCRA Cost of Living Index
   b. Urban renewal
   c. Urban prairie
   d. Urbanization

9. In economics, the _____ measures the payments that flow between any individual country and all other countries. It is used to summarize all international economic transactions for that country during a specific time period, usually a year. The _____ is determined by the country's exports and imports of goods, services, and financial capital, as well as financial transfers.
   a. Skyscraper Index
   b. Balance of payments
   c. Gross world product
   d. Gross domestic product per barrel

10. A _____ is the transfer of wealth from one party (such as a person or company) to another. A _____ is usually made in exchange for the provision of goods, services or both, or to fulfill a legal obligation.

The simplest and oldest form of _____ is barter, the exchange of one good or service for another.

   a. Social gravity
   b. Payment
   c. Going concern
   d. Soft count

11. _____s is the social science that studies the production, distribution, and consumption of goods and services. The term _____s comes from the Ancient Greek οἰκονομία from οἶκος (oikos, 'house') + νόμος (nomos, 'custom' or 'law'), hence 'rules of the house(hold)'. Current _____ models developed out of the broader field of political economy in the late 19th century, owing to a desire to use an empirical approach more akin to the physical sciences.
   a. Energy economics
   b. Inflation
   c. Opportunity cost
   d. Economic

Chapter 9. Agricultural Expansion: The Conflict of Two Systems on the Land

1. An _____ is a form of debt bondage worker. The laborer is under contract of an employer for usually three to seven years, in exchange for their transportation, food, drink, clothing, lodging and other necessities. Unlike a slave, an _____ is required to work only for a limited term specified in a signed contract.
   a. Indentured servant
   b. ACCRA Cost of Living Index
   c. AD-IA Model
   d. ACEA agreement

2. The _____ is institutions that comprise the World Bank Group. The IBRD is an international organization whose original mission was to finance the reconstruction of nations devastated by World War II. Now, its mission has expanded to fight poverty by means of financing states.
   a. United Nations Monetary and Financial Conference
   b. International Development Association
   c. ACCRA Cost of Living Index
   d. International Bank for Reconstruction and Development

3. _____ is the change in population over time, and can be quantified as the change in the number of individuals in a population using 'per unit time' for measurement. The term _____ can technically refer to any species, but almost always refers to humans, and it is often used informally for the more specific demographic term _____ rate , and is often used to refer specifically to the growth of the population of the world.

   Simple models of _____ include the Malthusian Growth Model and the logistic model.

   a. Population dynamics
   b. Population growth
   c. 100-year flood
   d. 130-30 fund

4. _____ in economics refers to metrics and measures of output from production processes, per unit of input. Labor _____, for example, is typically measured as a ratio of output per labor-hour, an input. _____ may be conceived of as a metrics of the technical or engineering efficiency of production.
   a. Piece work
   b. Fordism
   c. Production-possibility frontier
   d. Productivity

5. _____, in microeconomics, are the cost advantages that a business obtains due to expansion. They are factors that cause a producere;s average cost per unit to fall as scale is increased. _____ is a long run concept and refers to reductions in unit cost as the size of a facility, or scale, increases.
   a. Economies of scale
   b. Isoquant
   c. Economic production quantity
   d. Underinvestment employment relationship

6. Network externalities resemble economies of scale, but they are not considered such because they are a function of the number of users of a good or service in an industry, not of the production efficiency within a business. _____ are only considered examples of network externalities if they are driven by demand side economies.

Formally, a production function $F(K, L)$ is defined to have:

- constant returns to scale if (for any constant a greater than or equal to 0) $F(aK, aL) = aF(K, L)$
- increasing returns to scale if (for any constant a greater than 1) $F(aK, aL) > aF(K, L)$,
- decreasing returns to scale if (for any constant a greater than 1) $F(aK, aL) < aF(K, L)$

where K and L are factors of production, capital and labour, respectively.

As an example, the Cobb-Douglas functional form has constant returns to scale when the sum of the exponents adds up to one.

- a. AD-IA Model
- b. ACCRA Cost of Living Index
- c. Economies of scale external to the firm
- d. ACEA agreement

7. In economics, the _____ measures the payments that flow between any individual country and all other countries. It is used to summarize all international economic transactions for that country during a specific time period, usually a year. The _____ is determined by the country's exports and imports of goods, services, and financial capital, as well as financial transfers.
- a. Balance of payments
- b. Gross world product
- c. Gross domestic product per barrel
- d. Skyscraper Index

8. _____ is a specific term used in companies' financial reporting from the company-whole point of view. Because that use excludes the effects of changing ownership interest, an economic measure of _____ is necessary for financial analysis from the shareholders' point of view

_____ is defined by the Financial Accounting Standards Board, or FASB, as e;the change in equity [net assets] of a business enterprise during a period from transactions and other events and circumstances from nonowner sources. It includes all changes in equity during a period except those resulting from investments by owners and distributions to owners.e;

_____ is the sum of net income and other items that must bypass the income statement because they have not been realized, including items like an unrealized holding gain or loss from available for sale securities and foreign currency translation gains or losses.

- a. Net national income
- b. Real income
- c. Windfall gain
- d. Comprehensive income

9. In economics, an _____ is any good or commodity, transported from one country to another country in a legitimate fashion, typically for use in trade. _____ goods or services are provided to foreign consumers by domestic producers. _____ is an important part of international trade.
- a. Export
- b. ACEA agreement
- c. AD-IA Model
- d. ACCRA Cost of Living Index

10. A _____ is the transfer of wealth from one party (such as a person or company) to another. A _____ is usually made in exchange for the provision of goods, services or both, or to fulfill a legal obligation.

The simplest and oldest form of _____ is barter, the exchange of one good or service for another.

- a. Going concern
- b. Payment
- c. Soft count
- d. Social gravity

Chapter 9. Agricultural Expansion: The Conflict of Two Systems on the Land

11. The _____ was a period in the late 18th and early 19th centuries when major changes in agriculture, manufacturing, mining, and transportation had a profound effect on the socioeconomic and cultural conditions in Britain. The changes subsequently spread throughout Europe, North America, and eventually the world. The onset of the _____ marked a major turning point in human society; almost every aspect of daily life was eventually influenced in some way.
    a. Industrial Revolution
    b. Adolf Hitler
    c. Adam Smith
    d. Adolph Fischer

12. In economics, the people in the _____ are the suppliers of labor. The _____ is all the nonmilitary people who are employed or unemployed. In 2005, the worldwide _____ was over 3 billion people.
    a. Departmentalization
    b. Distributed workforce
    c. Grenelle agreements
    d. Labor force

13. The _____ is a term used for industries primarily concerned with the design or manufacture of clothing as well as the distribution and use of textiles.

Prior to the manufacturing processes were mechanized, textiles were produced in the home, and excess sold for extra money. Most cloth was made from either wool, cotton, or flax, depending on the era and location.

    a. 100-year flood
    b. 130-30 fund
    c. Textile manufacture during the Industrial Revolution
    d. Textile industry

14. In microeconomics, _____ is quite simply the conversion of inputs into outputs. It is an economic process that uses resources to create a good or service that is suitable for exchange. This can include manufacturing, storing, shipping, and packaging.
    a. Solved
    b. Production
    c. MET
    d. Red Guards

15. _____ refers to the state of not requiring any outside aid, support for survival; it is therefore a type of personal or collective autonomy. On a large scale, a totally self-sufficient economy that does not trade with the outside world is called an autarky.

The term _____ is usually applied to varieties of sustainable living in which nothing is consumed outside of what is produced by the self-sufficient individuals.

    a. Sustainability science
    b. Sustainable forest management
    c. Global Reporting Initiative
    d. Self-sufficiency

16. _____ is a misspelled phrase from Latin 'pro capite' phrase meaning per head with pro meaning 'per' or 'for each' and capite meaning 'head.' Both words together equate to the phrase 'for each head.'

It is usually used in the field of statistics to indicate the average per person for any given concern, such as income, crime rate, etc.

It is also used in wills to indicate that each of the named beneficiaries should receive, by devise or bequest, equal shares of the estate. This is in contrast to a per stirpes division, in which each branch of the inheriting family inherits an equal share of the estate.

a. Sargan test
b. Population statistics
c. False positive rate
d. Per capita

17. The thrashing machine, or, in modern spelling, _____, was a machine first invented by Scottish mechanical engineer Andrew Meikle for use in agriculture. It was invented (c.1784) for the separation of grain from stalks and husks. For thousands of years, grain was separated by hand with flails, and was very laborious and time consuming.
a. Threshing machine
b. 130-30 fund
c. 100-year flood
d. 1921 recession

Chapter 10. The Debate over Slavery 45

1. The _____ was a worldwide economic downturn starting in most places in 1929 and ending at different times in the 1930s or early 1940s for different countries. It was the largest and most important economic depression in the 20th century, and is used in the 21st century as an example of how far the world's economy can fall. The _____ originated in the United States; historians most often use as a starting date the stock market crash on October 29, 1929, known as Black Tuesday.
    a. Jarrow March
    b. British Empire Economic Conference
    c. Great Depression
    d. Wall Street Crash of 1929

2. _____ is the change in population over time, and can be quantified as the change in the number of individuals in a population using 'per unit time' for measurement. The term _____ can technically refer to any species, but almost always refers to humans, and it is often used informally for the more specific demographic term _____ rate , and is often used to refer specifically to the growth of the population of the world.

Simple models of _____ include the Malthusian Growth Model and the logistic model.

    a. Population dynamics
    b. Population growth
    c. 130-30 fund
    d. 100-year flood

3. In statistics, the _____ problem occurs when one considers a set of statistical inferences simultaneously. Errors in inference, including confidence intervals that fail to include their corresponding population parameters are more likely to occur when one considers the family as a whole. Several statistical techniques have been developed to prevent this from happening, allowing significance levels for single and _____ to be directly compared.
    a. False discovery rate
    b. Familywise error rate
    c. Multiple comparisons
    d. Hypotheses suggested by the data

4. _____ to the arrival of new individuals into a habitat or population. It is a biological concept and is important in population ecology, differentiated from emigration and migration.

_____ is a modern phenomenon.

    a. ACEA agreement
    b. ACCRA Cost of Living Index
    c. Immigration
    d. AD-IA Model

5. _____ is generally measured by standards such as real (i.e. inflation adjusted) income per person and poverty rate. Other measures such as access and quality of health care, income growth inequality and educational standards are also used. Examples are access to certain goods (such as number of refrigerators per 1000 people), or measures of health such as life expectancy.
    a. 130-30 fund
    b. Remuneration
    c. 100-year flood
    d. Standard of living

6. _____ is a measure of the number of deaths (in general scaled to the size of that population, per unit time. _____ is typically expressed in units of deaths per 1000 individuals per year; thus, a _____ of 9.5 in a population of 100,000 would mean 950 deaths per year in that entire population. It is distinct from morbidity rate, which refers to the number of individuals in poor health during a given time period (the prevalence rate) or the number who currently have that disease (the incidence rate), scaled to the size of the population.

a. 1921 recession
b. Mortality rate
c. 130-30 fund
d. 100-year flood

7. In economics, _____ is how a natione;s total economy is distributed among its population. ._____ has always been a central concern of economic theory and economic policy. Classical economists such as Adam Smith, Thomas Malthus and David Ricardo were mainly concerned with factor _____, that is, the distribution of income between the main factors of production, land, labour and capital.

a. Authorised capital
b. Equipment trust certificate
c. Eco commerce
d. Income distribution

Chapter 11. The Early Industrial Sector

1. _____ is an economic system in which wealth, and the means of producing wealth, are privately owned. Through _____, the land, labor, and capital are owned, operated, and traded for the purpose of generating profits, without force or fraud, by private individuals either singly or jointly, and investments, distribution, income, production, pricing and supply of goods, commodities and services are determined by voluntary private decision in a market economy. A distinguishing feature of _____ is that each person owns his or her own labor and therefore is allowed to sell the use of it to employers.
   a. Creative capitalism
   b. Late capitalism
   c. Socialism for the rich and capitalism for the poor
   d. Capitalism

2. The _____ was a period in the late 18th and early 19th centuries when major changes in agriculture, manufacturing, mining, and transportation had a profound effect on the socioeconomic and cultural conditions in Britain. The changes subsequently spread throughout Europe, North America, and eventually the world. The onset of the _____ marked a major turning point in human society; almost every aspect of daily life was eventually influenced in some way.
   a. Adolf Hitler
   b. Industrial Revolution
   c. Adam Smith
   d. Adolph Fischer

3. In economics, an _____ is any good or commodity, transported from one country to another country in a legitimate fashion, typically for use in trade. _____ goods or services are provided to foreign consumers by domestic producers. _____ is an important part of international trade.
   a. AD-IA Model
   b. ACEA agreement
   c. ACCRA Cost of Living Index
   d. Export

4. The _____ is a term used for industries primarily concerned with the design or manufacture of clothing as well as the distribution and use of textiles.

Prior to the manufacturing processes were mechanized, textiles were produced in the home, and excess sold for extra money. Most cloth was made from either wool, cotton, or flax, depending on the era and location.

   a. Textile industry
   b. 130-30 fund
   c. 100-year flood
   d. Textile manufacture during the Industrial Revolution

5. _____ has several particular meanings:

   - in mathematics
     - _____ function
     - Euler _____
     - _____
     - _____ subgroup
     - method of _____s (partial differential equations)
   - in physics and engineering
     - any _____ curve that shows the relationship between certain input- and output parameters, e.g.
     - an I-V or current-voltage _____ is the current in a circuit as a function of the applied voltage
     - Receiver-Operator _____
   - in fiction
     - in Dungeons ' Dragons, _____ is another name for ability score

a. Russian financial crisis
b. Technocracy
c. Demand
d. Characteristic

6. _____ in economics refers to metrics and measures of output from production processes, per unit of input. Labor _____, for example, is typically measured as a ratio of output per labor-hour, an input. _____ may be conceived of as a metrics of the technical or engineering efficiency of production.
   a. Fordism
   b. Productivity
   c. Piece work
   d. Production-possibility frontier

7. The _____ involves semi-skilled labor using machine tools and templates (or jigs) to make standardized, identical, interchangeable parts, manufactured to a tolerance. The system is also known as the armory practice because of the history of its development by the United States Department of War in the Springfield and Harpers Ferry armories.

Since parts are interchangeable, it is also possible to separate manufacture from assembly, and assembly may be carried out by semi-skilled labor on an assembly line - an example of the division of labor.
   a. American System of Manufacturing
   b. AD-IA Model
   c. ACCRA Cost of Living Index
   d. ACEA agreement

8. In economics, the people in the _____ are the suppliers of labor. The _____ is all the nonmilitary people who are employed or unemployed. In 2005, the worldwide _____ was over 3 billion people.
   a. Labor force
   b. Grenelle agreements
   c. Departmentalization
   d. Distributed workforce

9. _____s is the social science that studies the production, distribution, and consumption of goods and services. The term _____s comes from the Ancient Greek oá¼°κονομῖα from oá¼¶κος (oikos, 'house') + vÏŒμος (nomos, 'custom' or 'law'), hence 'rules of the house(hold)'. Current _____ models developed out of the broader field of political economy in the late 19th century, owing to a desire to use an empirical approach more akin to the physical sciences.
   a. Energy economics
   b. Inflation
   c. Economic
   d. Opportunity cost

10. _____, in microeconomics, are the cost advantages that a business obtains due to expansion. They are factors that cause a producere;s average cost per unit to fall as scale is increased. _____ is a long run concept and refers to reductions in unit cost as the size of a facility, or scale, increases.
    a. Economic production quantity
    b. Isoquant
    c. Economies of scale
    d. Underinvestment employment relationship

11. A _____ is a set of exclusive rights granted by a state to an inventor or his assignee for a limited period of time in exchange for a disclosure of an invention.

The procedure for granting _____s, the requirements placed on the _____ee and the extent of the exclusive rights vary widely between countries according to national laws and international agreements. Typically, however, a _____ application must include one or more claims defining the invention which must be new, inventive, and useful or industrially applicable.

Chapter 11. The Early Industrial Sector

    a. Patent
    b. Bank regulation
    c. Long service leave
    d. Bona fide occupational qualification

12. _____ is a common concept in economics, and gives rise to derived concepts such as consumer debt. Generally _____ is defined by opposition to production. But the precise definition can vary because different schools of economists define production quite differently.
    a. Federal Reserve Bank Notes
    b. Cash or share options
    c. Foreclosure data providers
    d. Consumption

13. _____s (economically referred to as land or raw materials) occur naturally within environments that exist relatively undisturbed by mankind, in a natural form. A _____'s is often characterized by amounts of biodiversity existent in various ecosystems.

Mining, petroleum extraction, fishing, hunting, and forestry are generally considered natural-resource industries.

    a. 1921 recession
    b. 100-year flood
    c. 130-30 fund
    d. Natural resource

14. The _____ was a sudden downturn in the economy of the United States that occurred in 1857. A general recession first emerged late in 1856, but the successive failure of banks and businesses that characterized the panic began in mid-1857. While the overall economic downturn was brief, the recovery was unequal, and the lasting impact was more political than economic.
    a. Panic of 1857
    b. 130-30 fund
    c. 100-year flood
    d. 1921 recession

15. In algebra, a _____ is a function depending on n that associates a scalar, det(A), to an n×n square matrix A. The fundamental geometric meaning of a _____ is a scale factor for measure when A is regarded as a linear transformation. _____s are important both in calculus, where they enter the substitution rule for several variables, and in multilinear algebra.

For a fixed nonnegative integer n, there is a unique _____ function for the n×n matrices over any commutative ring R. In particular, this function exists when R is the field of real or complex numbers.

    a. 1921 recession
    b. Determinant
    c. 100-year flood
    d. 130-30 fund

16. _____ is the physical growth of rural or natural land into urban areas as a result of population immigration to an existing urban area. Effects include change in density and administration services. While the exact definition and population size of urbanized areas varies among different countries, _____ is attributed to growth of cities.
    a. ACCRA Cost of Living Index
    b. Urban prairie
    c. Urban renewal
    d. Urbanization

17. In economics, _____ refers to the ability of a person or a country to produce a particular good at a lower marginal cost and opportunity cost than another person or country. It is the ability to produce a product most efficiently given all the other products that could be produced. It can be contrasted with absolute advantage which refers to the ability of a person or a country to produce a particular good at a lower absolute cost than another.

Chapter 11. The Early Industrial Sector

a. Hot money
c. Triffin dilemma
b. Comparative advantage
d. Gravity model of trade

18. In economics, the _____ measures the payments that flow between any individual country and all other countries. It is used to summarize all international economic transactions for that country during a specific time period, usually a year. The _____ is determined by the country's exports and imports of goods, services, and financial capital, as well as financial transfers.
   a. Gross world product
   c. Gross domestic product per barrel
   b. Balance of payments
   d. Skyscraper Index

19. A _____ is the transfer of wealth from one party (such as a person or company) to another. A _____ is usually made in exchange for the provision of goods, services or both, or to fulfill a legal obligation.

The simplest and oldest form of _____ is barter, the exchange of one good or service for another.

   a. Going concern
   c. Social gravity
   b. Soft count
   d. Payment

20. _____ refers to the stock of skills and knowledge embodied in the ability to perform labor so as to produce economic value. It is the skills and knowledge gained by a worker through education and experience. Many early economic theories refer to it simply as labor, one of three factors of production, and consider it to be a fungible resource -- homogeneous and easily interchangeable. Other conceptions of labor dispense with these assumptions.
   a. Price theory
   c. General equilibrium
   b. Law of increasing costs
   d. Human capital

21. _____ ndustrialization in North America, is the process of social and economic change whereby a human group is transformed from a pre-industrial society into an industrial one. _____ t is a part of a wider modernisation process, where social change and economic development are closely related with technological innovation, particularly with the development of large-scale energy and metallurgy production. _____ t is the extensive organisation of an economy for the purpose of manufacturing.
   a. AD-IA Model
   c. ACEA agreement
   b. ACCRA Cost of Living Index
   d. Industrialization

22. A _____ is a duty imposed on goods when they are moved across a political boundary. They are usually associated with protectionism, the economic policy of restraining trade between nations. For political reasons, _____ s are usually imposed on imported goods, although they may also be imposed on exported goods.
   a. 100-year flood
   c. 1921 recession
   b. Tariff
   d. 130-30 fund

Chapter 12. The Financial System and the International Economy   51

1. The _____ was chartered on December 31, 1781 by the Congress of the Confederation and opened on January 7, 1782, at the prodding of Superintendent of Finance Robert Morris. This was thus the first modern United States bank. In 1785, the Banke;s charter was not renewed.
   a. 130-30 fund
   b. 100-year flood
   c. 1921 recession
   d. Bank of North America

2. A _____, reserve bank, or monetary authority is the entity responsible for the monetary policy of a country or of a group of member states. It is a bank that can lend money to other banks in times of need. Its primary responsibility is to maintain the stability of the national currency and money supply, but more active duties include controlling subsidized-loan interest rates, and acting as a lender of last resort to the banking sector during times of financial crisis (private banks often being integral to the national financial system.)
   a. Central bank
   b. 130-30 fund
   c. 1921 recession
   d. 100-year flood

3. _____ is a term used in accounting, economics and finance to spread the cost of an asset over the span of several years.

In simple words we can say that _____ is the reduction in the value of an asset due to usage, passage of time, wear and tear, technological outdating or obsolescence, depletion, inadequacy, rot, rust, decay or other such factors.

In accounting, _____ is a term used to describe any method of attributing the historical or purchase cost of an asset across its useful life, roughly corresponding to normal wear and tear.

   a. Historical cost
   b. Net income per employee
   c. Salvage value
   d. Depreciation

4. The _____ is the central banking system of the United States. Created in 1913 by the enactment of the Federal Reserve Act (signed by Woodrow Wilson), it is a quasi-public and quasi-private (government entity with private components) banking system that comprises (1) the presidentially appointed Board of Governors of the _____ in Washington, D.C.; (2) the Federal Open Market Committee; (3) twelve regional Federal Reserve Banks located in major cities throughout the nation acting as fiscal agents for the U.S. Treasury, each with its own nine-member board of directors; (4) numerous other private U.S. member banks, which subscribe to required amounts of non-transferable stock in their regional Federal Reserve Banks; and (5) various advisory councils. Since February 2006, Ben Bernanke has served as the Chairman of the Board of Governors of the _____.
   a. Federal Reserve System
   b. Term auction facility
   c. Federal Reserve System Open Market Account
   d. Monetary Policy Report to the Congress

5. _____ is a concept whereby a person's financial liability is limited to a fixed sum, most commonly the value of a person's investment in a company or partnership with _____. A shareholder in a limited company is not personally liable for any of the debts of the company, other than for the value of his investment in that company. The same is true for the members of a _____ partnership and the limited partners in a limited partnership.
   a. Limited liability
   b. Deficiency judgment
   c. Personal Responsibility and Work Opportunity Reconciliation Act of 1996
   d. Nexus of contracts

Chapter 12. The Financial System and the International Economy

6. _____ involves the 'matching' of lenders with savings to borrowers who need money by an agent or third party, such as a bank.

If this matching is successful, the lender obtains a positive rate of return, the borrower receives a return for risk taking and entrepeneurship and the banker receives a marginal return for making the successful match. If the borrower's speculative play with the depositor's funds does not pay off, the depositor can lose the savings borrowed by the borrower and the bank can face significant losses on its loan portfolio.

- a. Origination fee
- b. Arranger
- c. Annual percentage rate
- d. Intermediation

7. A _____ is a fund established by a government agency or business for the purpose of reducing debt.

The _____ was first used in Great Britain in the 18th century to reduce national debt. While used by Robert Walpole in 1716 and effectively in the 1720s and early 1730s, it originated in the commercial tax syndicates of the Italian peninsula of the 14th century to retire redeemable public debt of those cities.

- a. Secured loan
- b. Bankruptcy remote
- c. Cost of living
- d. Sinking fund

8. A _____ is a duty imposed on goods when they are moved across a political boundary. They are usually associated with protectionism, the economic policy of restraining trade between nations. For political reasons, _____s are usually imposed on imported goods, although they may also be imposed on exported goods.

- a. 130-30 fund
- b. 1921 recession
- c. Tariff
- d. 100-year flood

9. _____ is that which is owed; usually referencing assets owed, but the term can also cover moral obligations and other interactions not requiring money. In the case of assets, _____ is a means of using future purchasing power in the present before a summation has been earned. Some companies and corporations use _____ as a part of their overall corporate finance strategy.

- a. Collateral Management
- b. Debenture
- c. Hard money loan
- d. Debt

10. In economics, _____ is a monetary standard in which the value of the monetary unit is defined as equivalent either to a certain quantity of gold or to a certain quantity of silver. Such a system effectively establishes a fixed rate of exchange for the two metals. The merits of the system were the subject of debate in the late 19th century.

- a. 130-30 fund
- b. 100-year flood
- c. 1921 recession
- d. Bimetallism

11. The _____ was a panic in the United States built on a speculative fever. The bubble burst on May 10, 1837 in New York City, when every bank stopped payment in specie (gold and silver coinage.) The Panic was followed by a five-year depression, with the failure of banks and record high unemployment levels.

- a. 1921 recession
- b. Panic of 1837
- c. 100-year flood
- d. 130-30 fund

Chapter 12. The Financial System and the International Economy

12. A _____ is a kind of negotiable instrument, a promissory note made by a bank payable to the bearer on demand, used as money, and in many jurisdictions is legal tender. Along with coins, _____s make up the cash or bearer forms of all modern money. With the exception of non-circulating high-value or precious metal commemorative issues, coins are generally used for lower valued monetary units, while _____s are used for higher values.

a. Local currency
b. Microprinting
c. Security thread
d. Banknote

13. Economics:

- _____,the desire to own something and the ability to pay for it
- _____ curve,a graphic representation of a _____ schedule
- _____ deposit, the money in checking accounts
- _____ pull theory,the theory that inflation occurs when _____ for goods and services exceeds existing supplies
- _____ schedule,a table that lists the quantity of a good a person will buy it each different price
- _____ side economics,the school of economics at believes government spending and tax cuts open economy by raising _____

a. McKesson ' Robbins scandal
b. Production
c. Variability
d. Demand

14. _____ is a type of bank account where the money in the account is legally able to be withdrawn immediately upon demand (or 'at call'.) This type of bank account can also be referred to as a 'cheque' or 'checking' or transactional account.

This type of bank account, allowing immediate conversion of the account balance into cash or withdrawal to another account, can be contrasted with a time deposit (also known as a certificate of deposit or term deposit), where the funds are not legally available for immediate withdrawal by the depositor.

a. Tangible Common Equity
b. Debt rescheduling
c. Clawbacks in economic development
d. Demand deposit

15.

A _____ is a type of financial intermediary and a type of bank. Commercial banking is also known as business banking. It is a bank that provides checking accounts, savings accounts, and money market accounts and that accepts time deposits.

a. Lombard banking
b. Bought deal
c. Daylight overdraft
d. Commercial bank

16. A _____ or labor union is an organization of workers who have banded together to achieve common goals in key areas and working conditions. The _____, through its leadership, bargains with the employer on behalf of union members (rank and file members) and negotiates labor contracts (Collective bargaining) with employers. This may include the negotiation of wages, work rules, complaint procedures, rules governing hiring, firing and promotion of workers, benefits, workplace safety and policies.

54   Chapter 12. The Financial System and the International Economy

    a. Consumer goods
    b. Trade union
    c. Guaranteed investment contracts
    d. Case-Shiller Home Price Indices

17. A _____ refers to any type debt instrument, such as a loan, bond, mortgage that does not have a fixed rate of interest over the life of the instrument. Such debt typically uses an index or other base rate for establishing the interest rate for each relevant period. One of the most common rates to use as the basis for applying interest rates is the London Inter-bank Offered Rate, or LIBOR
    a. Money market
    b. Moneylender
    c. Disposal tax effect
    d. Floating interest rate

18. The _____ is the market for securities, where companies and governments can raise longterm funds. It is a market in which money is lent for periods longer than a year. The _____ includes the stock market and the bond market.
    a. Capital market
    b. Performance attribution
    c. Financial instrument
    d. Multi-family office

19. _____, in microeconomics, are the cost advantages that a business obtains due to expansion. They are factors that cause a producere;s average cost per unit to fall as scale is increased. _____ is a long run concept and refers to reductions in unit cost as the size of a facility, or scale, increases.
    a. Economies of scale
    b. Isoquant
    c. Economic production quantity
    d. Underinvestment employment relationship

20. Fractional-reserve banking is the banking practice in which banks keep only a fraction of their deposits in reserve (as cash and other highly liquid assets) and lend out the remainder, while maintaining the simultaneous obligation to redeem all these deposits upon demand. _____ necessarily occurs when banks lend out any fraction of the funds received from demand deposits. This practice is universal in modern banking.
    a. Private money
    b. Prime rate
    c. Narrow banking
    d. Fractional reserve banking

21. The _____ was the first major financial crisis in the United States, which occurred during the so-called 'Era of Good Feelings'. The new nation faced a depression in the late 1780s (which led directly to the establishment of the dollar and, perhaps indirectly, to the calls for a Constitutional Convention), and another severe economic downturn in the late 1790s following the Panic of 1797. In those earlier crises, however, the primary cause of economic turmoil originated in the broader Atlantic economy.
    a. Panic of 1819
    b. 100-year flood
    c. 130-30 fund
    d. 1921 recession

22. The _____ was a sudden downturn in the economy of the United States that occurred in 1857. A general recession first emerged late in 1856, but the successive failure of banks and businesses that characterized the panic began in mid-1857. While the overall economic downturn was brief, the recovery was unequal, and the lasting impact was more political than economic.
    a. Panic of 1857
    b. 1921 recession
    c. 100-year flood
    d. 130-30 fund

23. The reserve requirement (or required _____) is a bank regulation that sets the minimum reserves each bank must hold to customer deposits and notes. It would normally be in the form of fiat currency stored in a bank vault (vault cash), or with a central bank.

Chapter 12. The Financial System and the International Economy

The _____ is sometimes used as a tool in the monetary policy, influencing the country's economy, borrowing, and interest rates.

a. Bank-State-Branch
b. Dividend unit
c. First player wins
d. Reserve ratio

24. A _____ is an expression that compares quantities relative to each other. The most common examples involve two quantities, but any number of quantities can be compared. _____s are represented mathematically by separating each quantity with a colon, for example the _____ 2:3, which is read as the _____ 'two to three'.

a. Y-intercept
b. 100-year flood
c. 130-30 fund
d. Ratio

25. The _____ is a monetary system in which a region's common medium of exchange are paper notes that are normally freely convertible into pre-set, fixed quantities of gold. The _____ is not currently used by any government, having been replaced completely by fiat currency. Gold certificates were used as paper currency in the United States from 1882 to 1933, these certificates were freely convertable into gold coins.

In the 1790s Britain suffered a massive shortage of silver coinage and ceased to mint larger silver coins.

a. 100-year flood
b. 130-30 fund
c. 1921 recession
d. Gold Standard

26. The _____ of the United States was passed in 1900 (ratified on March 14) and established gold as the only standard for redeeming paper money, stopping bimetallism (which had allowed silver in exchange for gold.) It was signed by President William McKinley.

a. Flex dollars
b. Gold Standard Act
c. Fed Shreds
d. Remonetisation

27. The _____ consists of a number of economic theories which describe the nature of the firm, company including its existence, its behaviour, and its relationship with the market.

In simplified terms, the _____ aims to answer these questions:

1. Existence - why do firms emerge, why are not all transactions in the economy mediated over the market?
2. Boundaries - why the boundary between firms and the market is located exactly there? Which transactions are performed internally and which are negotiated on the market?
3. Organization - why are firms structured in such specific way? What is the interplay of formal and informal relationships?

Despite looking simple, these questions are not answered by the established economic theory, which usually views firms as given, and treats them as black boxes without any internal structure.

Chapter 12. The Financial System and the International Economy

The First World War period saw a change of emphasis in economic theory away from industry-level analysis which mainly included analysing markets to analysis at the level of the firm, as it became increasingly clear that perfect competition was no longer an adequate model of how firms behaved. Economic theory till then had focussed on trying to understand markets alone and there had been little study on understanding why firms or organisations exist.

a. Technology gap
b. Policy Ineffectiveness Proposition
c. Theory of the firm
d. Khazzoom-Brookes postulate

28. The _____ is a United States government corporation created by the Glass-Steagall Act of 1933. It provides deposit insurance, which guarantees the safety of deposits in member banks, currently up to $250,000 per depositor per bank. Funds in non-interest bearing transaction accounts are fully insured, with no limit, under the temporary Transaction Account Guarantee Program.

a. Great Leap Forward
b. Federal Deposit Insurance Corporation
c. Luxembourg Income Study
d. Foreign direct investment

29. _____, in law and economics, is a form of risk management primarily used to hedge against the risk of a contingent loss. _____ is defined as the equitable transfer of the risk of a loss, from one entity to another, in exchange for a premium, and can be thought of as a guaranteed small loss to prevent a large, possibly devastating loss. An insurer is a company selling the _____; an insured or policyholder is the person or entity buying the _____.

a. ACEA agreement
b. ACCRA Cost of Living Index
c. AD-IA Model
d. Insurance

30. In finance, a _____ is a debt security, in which the authorized issuer owes the holders a debt and, depending on the terms of the _____, is obliged to pay interest (the coupon) and/or to repay the principal at a later date, termed maturity. A _____ is a formal contract to repay borrowed money with interest at fixed intervals.

Thus a _____ is like a loan: the issuer is the borrower (debtor), the holder is the lender (creditor), and the coupon is the interest.

a. Prize Bond
b. Callable
c. Bond
d. Zero-coupon

31. A _____ is a customs union with common policies on product regulation, and freedom of movement of the factors of production (capital and labour) and of enterprise. The goal is that the movement of capital, labour, goods, and services between the members is as easy as within them. This is the fourth stage of economic integration.

a. Grey market
b. Common market
c. Competitiveness
d. Mutual recognition agreement

32. _____ is an equity (stock) exchange located at 11 Wall Street in lower Manhattan, New York, USA. It is the largest stock exchange in the world by dollar value of its listed companies' securities. As of October 2008, the combined capitalization of all domestic _____ listed companies was US$10.1 trillion.

a. 1921 recession
b. 130-30 fund
c. New York Stock Exchange
d. 100-year flood

Chapter 12. The Financial System and the International Economy

33. _____ is typically a 'higher ranking' stock than voting shares, and its terms are negotiated between the corporation and the investor.

_____ usually carries no voting rights, but may carry priority over common stock in the payment of dividends and upon liquidation. _____ may carry a dividend that is paid out prior to any dividends being paid to common stock holders.

a. Bookrunner
b. Financial accelerator
c. Book building
d. Preferred stock

34. A _____ is a corporation or mutual organization which provides trading facilities for stock brokers and traders, to trade stocks and other securities. It may be a physical trading room where the traders gather, or a formalised communications network. Creation of a _____ is a strategy of economic development.

a. 100-year flood
b. Stock Exchange
c. Primary shares
d. SEAQ

35. A _____ is a public market for the trading of company stock and derivatives at an agreed price; these are securities listed on a stock exchange as well as those only traded privately.

The size of the world _____ was estimated at about $36.6 trillion US at the beginning of October 2008 . The total world derivatives market has been estimated at about $791 trillion face or nominal value, 11 times the size of the entire world economy.

a. Stock market
b. Adolph Fischer
c. Adam Smith
d. Adolf Hitler

36. _____ are debt securities issued by a government for the purpose of financing military operations during times of war. _____ generate capital for the government and make civilians feel involved in their national militaries. Exhortations to buy _____ are often accompanied with appeals to patriotism and conscience.

a. 130-30 fund
b. 1921 recession
c. 100-year flood
d. War bonds

37. The _____ is the central bank of the United Kingdom and is the model on which most modern, large central banks have been based. Since 1946 it has been a state-owned institution. It was established in 1694 to act as the English Government's banker, and to this day it still acts as the banker for the UK Government.

a. 1921 recession
b. 100-year flood
c. 130-30 fund
d. Bank of England

38. _____s is the social science that studies the production, distribution, and consumption of goods and services. The term _____s comes from the Ancient Greek οἰκονομία from οἶκος (oikos, 'house') + νόμος (nomos, 'custom' or 'law'), hence 'rules of the house(hold)'. Current _____ models developed out of the broader field of political economy in the late 19th century, owing to a desire to use an empirical approach more akin to the physical sciences.

a. Energy economics
b. Opportunity cost
c. Inflation
d. Economic

Chapter 12. The Financial System and the International Economy

39. In finance, the _____s between two currencies specifies how much one currency is worth in terms of the other. It is the value of a foreign natione;s currency in terms of the home natione;s currency. For example an _____ of 102 Japanese yen to the United States dollar means that JPY 102 is worth the same as USD 1.
   a. ACCRA Cost of Living Index
   b. ACEA agreement
   c. Exchange rate
   d. Interbank market

40. The _____ was a period in the late 18th and early 19th centuries when major changes in agriculture, manufacturing, mining, and transportation had a profound effect on the socioeconomic and cultural conditions in Britain. The changes subsequently spread throughout Europe, North America, and eventually the world. The onset of the _____ marked a major turning point in human society; almost every aspect of daily life was eventually influenced in some way.
   a. Industrial Revolution
   b. Adam Smith
   c. Adolph Fischer
   d. Adolf Hitler

41. In economics, the _____ measures the payments that flow between any individual country and all other countries. It is used to summarize all international economic transactions for that country during a specific time period, usually a year. The _____ is determined by the country's exports and imports of goods, services, and financial capital, as well as financial transfers.
   a. Skyscraper Index
   b. Gross world product
   c. Balance of payments
   d. Gross domestic product per barrel

42. In economics, an _____ is any good or commodity, transported from one country to another country in a legitimate fashion, typically for use in trade. _____ goods or services are provided to foreign consumers by domestic producers. _____ is an important part of international trade.
   a. ACEA agreement
   b. ACCRA Cost of Living Index
   c. AD-IA Model
   d. Export

43. A _____ is the transfer of wealth from one party (such as a person or company) to another. A _____ is usually made in exchange for the provision of goods, services or both, or to fulfill a legal obligation.

   The simplest and oldest form of _____ is barter, the exchange of one good or service for another.

   a. Soft count
   b. Payment
   c. Going concern
   d. Social gravity

44. A _____ is a period of feverish migration of workers into the area of a dramatic discovery of commercial quantities of gold. _____es took place in the 19th century in Argentina, Australia, Brazil, Canada, Chile, New Zealand, South Africa, and the United States.

   _____es were typically marked by a general buoyant feeling of a 'free for all' in income mobility, in which any single individual might become abundantly wealthy almost instantly.

   a. Witwatersrand Gold Rush
   b. Carolina Gold Rush
   c. Fairbanks Gold Rush
   d. Gold rush

Chapter 12. The Financial System and the International Economy

45. The _____ was a worldwide economic downturn starting in most places in 1929 and ending at different times in the 1930s or early 1940s for different countries. It was the largest and most important economic depression in the 20th century, and is used in the 21st century as an example of how far the world's economy can fall. The _____ originated in the United States; historians most often use as a starting date the stock market crash on October 29, 1929, known as Black Tuesday.
   a. British Empire Economic Conference
   b. Wall Street Crash of 1929
   c. Jarrow March
   d. Great Depression

46. The term _____ refers to economy-wide fluctuations in production or economic activity over several months or years. These fluctuations occur around a long-term growth trend, and typically involve shifts over time between periods of relatively rapid economic growth (expansion or boom), and periods of relative stagnation or decline (contraction or recession.)

These fluctuations are often measured using the growth rate of real gross domestic product.

   a. Tobit model
   b. Consumer theory
   c. Nominal value
   d. Business cycle

47. In finance, the _____ is the system that allows the transfer of money between savers and borrowers.

Put another way: the _____ is a set of complex and closely interconnected financial institutions, markets, instruments, services, practices, and transactions.

   a. Foreign investment
   b. Lean consumption
   c. Financial system
   d. Hedonimetry

48. The _____ was started as a collapse of British financial markets associated with the end of the 1840s railroad boom. The Bank of China had to request a suspension of the Bank Charter Act to end the crisis. It was caused by excessive monetary inflation due to the Bank of China and fractional reserve banking.
   a. 100-year flood
   b. 1921 recession
   c. Panic of 1847
   d. 130-30 fund

49. In microeconomics, _____ is quite simply the conversion of inputs into outputs. It is an economic process that uses resources to create a good or service that is suitable for exchange. This can include manufacturing, storing, shipping, and packaging.
   a. Red Guards
   b. Solved
   c. MET
   d. Production

50. In international commerce and politics, an _____ is the prohibition of commerce (division of trade) and trade with a certain country, in order to isolate it and to put its government into a difficult internal situation, given that the effects of the _____ are often able to make its economy suffer from the initiative.

The _____ is usually used as a political punishment for some previous disagreed policies or acts, but its economic nature frequently raises doubts about the real interests that the prohibition serves.

One of the most comprehensive attempts at an _____ happened during the Napoleonic Wars.

a. Optimum currency area
b. International finance
c. Overshooting model
d. Embargo

51. The _____ includes the global processes of exploration, extraction, refining, transporting (often by oil tankers and pipelines), and marketing petroleum products. The largest volume products of the industry are fuel oil and gasoline (petrol.) Petroleum is also the raw material for many chemical products, including pharmaceuticals, solvents, fertilizers, pesticides, and plastics.
   a. 1921 recession
   b. Petroleum industry
   c. 100-year flood
   d. 130-30 fund

52. _____ is the change in population over time, and can be quantified as the change in the number of individuals in a population using 'per unit time' for measurement. The term _____ can technically refer to any species, but almost always refers to humans, and it is often used informally for the more specific demographic term _____ rate , and is often used to refer specifically to the growth of the population of the world.

Simple models of _____ include the Malthusian Growth Model and the logistic model.

   a. 100-year flood
   b. 130-30 fund
   c. Population growth
   d. Population dynamics

53. _____ is an economic system in which wealth, and the means of producing wealth, are privately owned. Through _____, the land, labor, and capital are owned, operated, and traded for the purpose of generating profits, without force or fraud, by private individuals either singly or jointly, and investments, distribution, income, production, pricing and supply of goods, commodities and services are determined by voluntary private decision in a market economy. A distinguishing feature of _____ is that each person owns his or her own labor and therefore is allowed to sell the use of it to employers.
   a. Late capitalism
   b. Capitalism
   c. Socialism for the rich and capitalism for the poor
   d. Creative capitalism

Chapter 13. Economic Effects of the Civil War

1. _____ refers to the stock of skills and knowledge embodied in the ability to perform labor so as to produce economic value. It is the skills and knowledge gained by a worker through education and experience.Many early economic theories refer to it simply as labor, one of three factors of production, and consider it to be a fungible resource -- homogeneous and easily interchangeable. Other conceptions of labor dispense with these assumptions.
   - a. Price theory
   - b. Human capital
   - c. Law of increasing costs
   - d. General equilibrium

2. The _____ was actually created in 1929, before the stock market crash on Black Tuesday, 1929, but its powers were later enlarged to meet the economic crisis farmers faced during the Great Depression. It was established by the Agricultural Marketing Act to stabilize prices and to promote the sale of agricultural products. The board would help farmers stabilize prices by holding surplus grain and cotton in storage.
   - a. Great Contraction
   - b. Great Depression
   - c. Great Depression in the United Kingdom
   - d. Federal Farm Board

3. The _____ is a monetary system in which a region's common medium of exchange are paper notes that are normally freely convertible into pre-set, fixed quantities of gold. The _____ is not currently used by any government, having been replaced completely by fiat currency. Gold certificates were used as paper currency in the United States from 1882 to 1933, these certificates were freely convertable into gold coins.

    In the 1790s Britain suffered a massive shortage of silver coinage and ceased to mint larger silver coins.

   - a. 130-30 fund
   - b. 100-year flood
   - c. 1921 recession
   - d. Gold Standard

4. The _____ of the United States was passed in 1900 (ratified on March 14) and established gold as the only standard for redeeming paper money, stopping bimetallism (which had allowed silver in exchange for gold.) It was signed by President William McKinley.
   - a. Flex dollars
   - b. Remonetisation
   - c. Fed Shreds
   - d. Gold Standard Act

5. In economics, _____ is inflation that is very high or 'out of control', a condition in which prices increase rapidly as a currency loses its value. Definitions used by the media vary from a cumulative inflation rate over three years approaching 100% to 'inflation exceeding 50% a month.' In informal usage the term is often applied to much lower rates. As a rule of thumb, normal inflation is reported per year, but _____ is often reported for much shorter intervals, often per month.
   - a. 1921 recession
   - b. Hyperinflation
   - c. 130-30 fund
   - d. 100-year flood

6. A _____ is a kind of negotiable instrument, a promissory note made by a bank payable to the bearer on demand, used as money, and in many jurisdictions is legal tender. Along with coins, _____s make up the cash or bearer forms of all modern money. With the exception of non-circulating high-value or precious metal commemorative issues, coins are generally used for lower valued monetary units, while _____s are used for higher values.
   - a. Security thread
   - b. Microprinting
   - c. Local currency
   - d. Banknote

Chapter 13. Economic Effects of the Civil War

7. _____ is that which is owed; usually referencing assets owed, but the term can also cover moral obligations and other interactions not requiring money. In the case of assets, _____ is a means of using future purchasing power in the present before a summation has been earned. Some companies and corporations use _____ as a part of their overall corporate finance strategy.
   - a. Collateral Management
   - b. Debt
   - c. Hard money loan
   - d. Debenture

8. In economics, the _____ measures the payments that flow between any individual country and all other countries. It is used to summarize all international economic transactions for that country during a specific time period, usually a year. The _____ is determined by the country's exports and imports of goods, services, and financial capital, as well as financial transfers.
   - a. Skyscraper Index
   - b. Gross world product
   - c. Balance of payments
   - d. Gross domestic product per barrel

9. A _____ is the transfer of wealth from one party (such as a person or company) to another. A _____ is usually made in exchange for the provision of goods, services or both, or to fulfill a legal obligation.

   The simplest and oldest form of _____ is barter, the exchange of one good or service for another.
   - a. Social gravity
   - b. Going concern
   - c. Soft count
   - d. Payment

10. In finance, a _____ is a debt security, in which the authorized issuer owes the holders a debt and, depending on the terms of the _____, is obliged to pay interest (the coupon) and/or to repay the principal at a later date, termed maturity. A _____ is a formal contract to repay borrowed money with interest at fixed intervals.

    Thus a _____ is like a loan: the issuer is the borrower (debtor), the holder is the lender (creditor), and the coupon is the interest.
    - a. Prize Bond
    - b. Callable
    - c. Zero-coupon
    - d. Bond

11. _____s is the social science that studies the production, distribution, and consumption of goods and services. The term _____s comes from the Ancient Greek οἰκονομία from οἶκος (oikos, 'house') + νόμος (nomos, 'custom' or 'law'), hence 'rules of the house(hold)'. Current _____ models developed out of the broader field of political economy in the late 19th century, owing to a desire to use an empirical approach more akin to the physical sciences.
    - a. Energy economics
    - b. Inflation
    - c. Opportunity cost
    - d. Economic

12. _____ is the increase in the amount of the goods and services produced by an economy over time. It is conventionally measured as the percent rate of increase in real gross domestic product, or real GDP. Growth is usually calculated in real terms, i.e. inflation-adjusted terms, in order to net out the effect of inflation on the price of the goods and services produced.
    - a. ACEA agreement
    - b. ACCRA Cost of Living Index
    - c. AD-IA Model
    - d. Economic growth

Chapter 13. Economic Effects of the Civil War

13. _____ ndustrialization in North America, is the process of social and economic change whereby a human group is transformed from a pre-industrial society into an industrial one. _____ t is a part of a wider modernisation process, where social change and economic development are closely related with technological innovation, particularly with the development of large-scale energy and metallurgy production. _____ t is the extensive organisation of an economy for the purpose of manufacturing.

   a. ACCRA Cost of Living Index
   b. ACEA agreement
   c. AD-IA Model
   d. Industrialization

14. _____ are debt securities issued by a government for the purpose of financing military operations during times of war. _____ generate capital for the government and make civilians feel involved in their national militaries. Exhortations to buy _____ are often accompanied with appeals to patriotism and conscience.

   a. 100-year flood
   b. 1921 recession
   c. War bonds
   d. 130-30 fund

15. _____ is an economic system in which wealth, and the means of producing wealth, are privately owned. Through _____, the land, labor, and capital are owned, operated, and traded for the purpose of generating profits, without force or fraud, by private individuals either singly or jointly, and investments, distribution, income, production, pricing and supply of goods, commodities and services are determined by voluntary private decision in a market economy. A distinguishing feature of _____ is that each person owns his or her own labor and therefore is allowed to sell the use of it to employers.

   a. Socialism for the rich and capitalism for the poor
   b. Creative capitalism
   c. Late capitalism
   d. Capitalism

16. Competition law, known in the United States as _____ law, has three main elements:

   - prohibiting agreements or practices that restrict free trading and competition between business entities. This includes in particular the repression of cartels.
   - banning abusive behaviour by a firm dominating a market, or anti-competitive practices that tend to lead to such a dominant position. Practices controlled in this way may include predatory pricing, tying, price gouging, refusal to deal, and many others.
   - supervising the mergers and acquisitions of large corporations, including some joint ventures. Transactions that are considered to threaten the competitive process can be prohibited altogether, or approved subject to 'remedies' such as an obligation to divest part of the merged business or to offer licences or access to facilities to enable other businesses to continue competing.

The substance and practice of competition law varies from jurisdiction to jurisdiction. Protecting the interests of consumers (consumer welfare) and ensuring that entrepreneurs have an opportunity to compete in the market economy are often treated as important objectives. Competition law is closely connected with law on deregulation of access to markets, state aids and subsidies, the privatisation of state owned assets and the establishment of independent sector regulators. In recent decades, competition law has been viewed as a way to provide better public services.

   a. Anti-Inflation Act
   b. United Kingdom competition law
   c. Intellectual property law
   d. Antitrust

17. In economics, the _____ is the agent who receives the net income (income after deducting all costs.)

Residual claimancy is generally required in order for there to be Moral Hazard, which is a problem typical of information asymmetry. This is specifically the case for the Principal-agent problem.

a. Horizontal merger
b. Free contract
c. Frontier markets
d. Residual claimant

18. A _____ is a duty imposed on goods when they are moved across a political boundary. They are usually associated with protectionism, the economic policy of restraining trade between nations. For political reasons, _____s are usually imposed on imported goods, although they may also be imposed on exported goods.

a. 1921 recession
b. 130-30 fund
c. 100-year flood
d. Tariff

19. In the legal system of the Soviet Union, _____ was the legal theory and system under which economic relations were a legal discipline independent of criminal law and civil law. In the Law of the United States and some other legal systems this approximately corresponds to the commercial law (business law.)

In the Soviet legal system, the purpose of the _____ is to regulate the relations arising from the economic activities.

a. Australian labour law
b. Economic Law
c. European Union Value Added Tax
d. Employment discrimination law in the United Kingdom

20. The _____ is 'the basic residential unit in which economic production, consumption, inheritance, child rearing, and shelter are organized and carried out'; [the _____] 'may or may not be synonomous with family'.

The _____ is the basic unit of analysis in many social, microeconomic and government models. The term refers to all individuals who live in the same dwelling.

a. 130-30 fund
b. 100-year flood
c. Household
d. Family economics

21. _____ is the a method of technical and economic research of the systems for purpose to optimize a parity between system's consumer functions or properties and expenses to achieve those functions or properties.

This methodology for continuous perfection of production, industrial technologies, organizational structures was developed by Juryj Sobolev in 1948 at the 'Perm telephone factory'

- 1948 Juryj Sobolev - the first success in application of a method analysis at the 'Perm telephone factory' .
- 1949 - the first application for the invention as result of use of the new method.

Chapter 13. Economic Effects of the Civil War

Today in economically developed countries practically each enterprise or the company use methodology of the kind of functional-cost analysis as a practice of the quality management, most full satisfying to principles of standards of series ISO 9000.

- Interest of consumer not in products itself, but the advantage which it will receive from its usage.
- The consumer aspires to reduce his expenses
- Functions needed by consumer can be executed in the various ways, and, hence, with various efficiency and expenses. Among possible alternatives of realization of functions exist such in which the parity of quality and the price is the optimal for the consumer.

The goal of _____ is achievement of the highest consumer satisfaction of production at simultaneous decrease in all kinds of industrial expenses Classical _____ has three English synonyms - Value Engineering, Value Management, Value Analysis.

   a. Willingness to pay
   b. Function cost analysis
   c. Staple financing
   d. Monopoly wage

22. _____ is the shortage of common things such as food, clothing, shelter and safe drinking water, all of which determine the quality of life. It may also include the lack of access to opportunities such as education and employment which aid the escape from _____ and/or allow one to enjoy the respect of fellow citizens. According to Mollie Orshansky who developed the _____ measurements used by the U.S. government, 'to be poor is to be deprived of those goods and services and pleasures which others around us take for granted.' Ongoing debates over causes, effects and best ways to measure _____, directly influence the design and implementation of _____-reduction programs and are therefore relevant to the fields of public administration and international development.
   a. Liberal welfare reforms
   b. Poverty map
   c. Poverty
   d. Growth Elasticity of Poverty

23. In economics, the people in the _____ are the suppliers of labor. The _____ is all the nonmilitary people who are employed or unemployed. In 2005, the worldwide _____ was over 3 billion people.
   a. Departmentalization
   b. Grenelle agreements
   c. Distributed workforce
   d. Labor force

24. The traditional definition of _____ is considered to be the ability to use language to read, write, listen, and speak. In modern contexts, the word refers to reading and writing at a level adequate for communication, or at a level that lets one understand and communicate ideas in a literate society, so as to take part in that society. The United Nations Educational, Scientific and Cultural Organization (UNESCO) has drafted the following definition: "_____' is the ability to identify, understand, interpret, create, communicate, compute and use printed and written materials associated with varying contexts.
   a. Literacy
   b. 100-year flood
   c. 1921 recession
   d. 130-30 fund

25. _____ is a system of agriculture or agricultural production in which a landowner allows a tenant to use the land in return for a share of the crop produced on the land (e.g., 50 percent of the crop.) This should not be confused with a crop fixed rent contract, in which a landowner allows a tenant to use the land in return for a fixed amount of crop per unit of land (e.g., 1 ton per hectare.) _____ has a long history and there are a wide range of different situations and types of agreements that have encompassed the system.

Chapter 13. Economic Effects of the Civil War

a. 100-year flood
b. 130-30 fund
c. Sharecropping
d. 1921 recession

26. A _____ is something for which there is demand, but which is supplied without qualitative differentiation across a market. It is a product that is the same no matter who produces it, such as petroleum, notebook paper, or milk. In other words, copper is copper.
   a. Hard commodity
   b. 100-year flood
   c. Commodity
   d. Soft commodity

27. _____ involves the 'matching' of lenders with savings to borrowers who need money by an agent or third party, such as a bank.

If this matching is successful, the lender obtains a positive rate of return, the borrower receives a return for risk taking and entrepeneurship and the banker receives a marginal return for making the successful match. If the borrower's speculative play with the depositor's funds does not pay off, the depositor can lose the savings borrowed by the borrower and the bank can face significant losses on its loan portfolio.

   a. Intermediation
   b. Annual percentage rate
   c. Arranger
   d. Origination fee

28. The _____ is the market for securities, where companies and governments can raise longterm funds. It is a market in which money is lent for periods longer than a year. The _____ includes the stock market and the bond market.
   a. Performance attribution
   b. Multi-family office
   c. Financial instrument
   d. Capital market

29. A _____ refers to any type debt instrument, such as a loan, bond, mortgage that does not have a fixed rate of interest over the life of the instrument. Such debt typically uses an index or other base rate for establishing the interest rate for each relevant period. One of the most common rates to use as the basis for applying interest rates is the London Inter-bank Offered Rate, or LIBOR
   a. Moneylender
   b. Floating interest rate
   c. Money market
   d. Disposal tax effect

Chapter 14. Railroads and Economic Development

1. _____s is the social science that studies the production, distribution, and consumption of goods and services. The term _____s comes from the Ancient Greek oá¼°κονομῖα from oá¼¶κος (oikos, 'house') + vĺŒμος (nomos, 'custom' or 'law'), hence 'rules of the house(hold)'. Current _____ models developed out of the broader field of political economy in the late 19th century, owing to a desire to use an empirical approach more akin to the physical sciences.
    a. Energy economics
    b. Opportunity cost
    c. Inflation
    d. Economic

2. _____ is the increase in the amount of the goods and services produced by an economy over time. It is conventionally measured as the percent rate of increase in real gross domestic product, or real GDP. Growth is usually calculated in real terms, i.e. inflation-adjusted terms, in order to net out the effect of inflation on the price of the goods and services produced.
    a. AD-IA Model
    b. ACEA agreement
    c. Economic growth
    d. ACCRA Cost of Living Index

3. _____ is a term used to describe large corporations, in either an individual or collective sense. The term first came into use in a symbolic sense subsequent to the American Civil War, particularly after 1880, in connection with the combination movement that began in American business at that time. Organizations that fall into the category of '_____' include ExxonMobil, Wal-Mart, Google, Microsoft, General Motors, Citigroup and Arcelor Mittal.
    a. Brainsworking
    b. Sole proprietorship
    c. First-mover advantage
    d. Big business

4. _____ is the change in population over time, and can be quantified as the change in the number of individuals in a population using 'per unit time' for measurement. The term _____ can technically refer to any species, but almost always refers to humans, and it is often used informally for the more specific demographic term _____ rate, and is often used to refer specifically to the growth of the population of the world.

Simple models of _____ include the Malthusian Growth Model and the logistic model.

    a. Population growth
    b. Population dynamics
    c. 130-30 fund
    d. 100-year flood

5. _____ is an economic system in which wealth, and the means of producing wealth, are privately owned. Through _____, the land, labor, and capital are owned, operated, and traded for the purpose of generating profits, without force or fraud, by private individuals either singly or jointly, and investments, distribution, income, production, pricing and supply of goods, commodities and services are determined by voluntary private decision in a market economy. A distinguishing feature of _____ is that each person owns his or her own labor and therefore is allowed to sell the use of it to employers.
    a. Socialism for the rich and capitalism for the poor
    b. Capitalism
    c. Late capitalism
    d. Creative capitalism

6. A variety of measures of national income and output are used in economics to estimate total economic activity in a country or region, including gross domestic product (GDP), _____ , and net national income (NNI.)

There are three main ways of calculating these numbers; the output approach, the income approach and the expenditure approach. In theory, the three must yield the same, because total expenditures on goods and services must equal the total income paid to the producers (GNI), and that must also equal the total value of the output of goods and services (_____.)

Chapter 14. Railroads and Economic Development

   a. Gross world product
   c. Purchasing power parity
   b. Household final consumption expenditure
   d. Gross national product

7. _____ is a common concept in economics, and gives rise to derived concepts such as consumer debt. Generally _____ is defined by opposition to production. But the precise definition can vary because different schools of economists define production quite differently.
   a. Federal Reserve Bank Notes
   c. Foreclosure data providers
   b. Cash or share options
   d. Consumption

8. _____ or economic opportunity loss is the value of the next best alternative foregone as the result of making a decision. _____ analysis is an important part of a company's decision-making processes but is not treated as an actual cost in any financial statement. The next best thing that a person can engage in is referred to as the _____ of doing the best thing and ignoring the next best thing to be done.
   a. Industrial organization
   c. Economic
   b. Economic ideology
   d. Opportunity cost

9. _____ is a growth accounting technique to evaluate the historic implications of new technology on economic growth. Developed in 1964 by American economic historian and scientist Robert Fogel, the methodology works to estimate the cost-savings of the new technology compared with the next best alternative. The amount of _____ may be calculated as _____ = $(P_{T0} - P_{T1})T_1$ where P_{T0} is the price of the alternative technology, P_{T1} is the price of the evaluated technology being evaluated, and T_1 is the quantity processed by the evaluated technology.
   a. Neoclassical synthesis
   c. Public good
   b. Reaganomics
   d. Social savings

10. In finance, a _____ is a debt security, in which the authorized issuer owes the holders a debt and, depending on the terms of the _____, is obliged to pay interest (the coupon) and/or to repay the principal at a later date, termed maturity. A _____ is a formal contract to repay borrowed money with interest at fixed intervals.

Thus a _____ is like a loan: the issuer is the borrower (debtor), the holder is the lender (creditor), and the coupon is the interest.

   a. Prize Bond
   c. Zero-coupon
   b. Callable
   d. Bond

11. In economics, a _____ exists when a specific individual or enterprise has sufficient control over a particular product or service to determine significantly the terms on which other individuals shall have access to it. Monopolies are thus characterized by a lack of economic competition for the good or service that they provide and a lack of viable substitute goods. The verb 'monopolize' refers to the process by which a firm gains persistently greater market share than what is expected under perfect competition.
   a. 100-year flood
   c. 1921 recession
   b. 130-30 fund
   d. Monopoly

12. _____ are debt securities issued by a government for the purpose of financing military operations during times of war. _____ generate capital for the government and make civilians feel involved in their national militaries. Exhortations to buy _____ are often accompanied with appeals to patriotism and conscience.

Chapter 14. Railroads and Economic Development

a. War bonds
b. 100-year flood
c. 130-30 fund
d. 1921 recession

13. _____ in economics and business is the result of an exchange and from that trade we assign a numerical monetary value to a good, service or asset. If Alice trades Bob 4 apples for an orange, the _____ of an orange is 4 apples. Inversely, the _____ of an apple is 1/4 oranges.
   a. Price book
   b. Price war
   c. Premium pricing
   d. Price

14. _____ exists when sales of identical goods or services are transacted at different prices from the same provider. In a theoretical market with perfect information, no transaction costs or prohibition on secondary exchange (or re-selling) to prevent arbitrage, _____ can only be a feature of monopoly and oligopoly markets, where market power can be exercised. Otherwise, the moment the seller tries to sell the same good at different prices, the buyer at the lower price can arbitrage by selling to the consumer buying at the higher price but with a tiny discount.
   a. Transfer pricing
   b. Loss leader
   c. Lerner Index
   d. Price discrimination

15. _____ is one of the four Ps of the marketing mix. The other three aspects are product, promotion, and place. It is also a key variable in microeconomic price allocation theory.
   a. Pricing
   b. Premium pricing
   c. Point of total assumption
   d. Guaranteed Maximum Price

16. Competition law, known in the United States as _____ law, has three main elements:

   - prohibiting agreements or practices that restrict free trading and competition between business entities. This includes in particular the repression of cartels.
   - banning abusive behaviour by a firm dominating a market, or anti-competitive practices that tend to lead to such a dominant position. Practices controlled in this way may include predatory pricing, tying, price gouging, refusal to deal, and many others.
   - supervising the mergers and acquisitions of large corporations, including some joint ventures. Transactions that are considered to threaten the competitive process can be prohibited altogether, or approved subject to 'remedies' such as an obligation to divest part of the merged business or to offer licences or access to facilities to enable other businesses to continue competing.

The substance and practice of competition law varies from jurisdiction to jurisdiction. Protecting the interests of consumers (consumer welfare) and ensuring that entrepreneurs have an opportunity to compete in the market economy are often treated as important objectives. Competition law is closely connected with law on deregulation of access to markets, state aids and subsidies, the privatisation of state owned assets and the establishment of independent sector regulators. In recent decades, competition law has been viewed as a way to provide better public services.

   a. Anti-Inflation Act
   b. Antitrust
   c. Intellectual property law
   d. United Kingdom competition law

17. In economics, _____ is a monetary standard in which the value of the monetary unit is defined as equivalent either to a certain quantity of gold or to a certain quantity of silver. Such a system effectively establishes a fixed rate of exchange for the two metals. The merits of the system were the subject of debate in the late 19th century.

   a. 1921 recession
   b. 100-year flood
   c. 130-30 fund
   d. Bimetallism

18. The _____ was a regulatory body in the United States created by the Interstate Commerce Act of 1887, which was signed into law by President Grover Cleveland. The agency was abolished in 1995, and the agency's remaining functions were transferred to the Surface Transportation Board.

The Commission's five members were appointed by the President with the consent of the United States Senate.

   a. Interstate Commerce Commission
   b. Office of Thrift Supervision
   c. ACEA agreement
   d. ACCRA Cost of Living Index

19. A security is a fungible, negotiable instrument representing financial value. _____ are broadly categorized into debt _____; equity _____, e.g., common stocks; and derivative (finance) contracts such as forwards, futures, options and swaps. The company or other entity issuing the security is called the issuer.

   a. Settlement risk
   b. Securities
   c. Pass-Through Certificates
   d. Red herring prospectus

20.

The _____ was the first United States Federal statute to limit cartels and monopolies. It falls under antitrust law.

The Act provides: 'Every contract, combination in the form of trust or otherwise, or conspiracy, in restraint of trade or commerce among the several States, or with foreign nations, is declared to be illegal'. The Act also provides: 'Every person who shall monopolize, or attempt to monopolize, or combine or conspire with any other person or persons, to monopolize any part of the trade or commerce among the several States, or with foreign nations, shall be deemed guilty of a felony [. . .]' The Act put responsibility upon government attorneys and district courts to pursue and investigate trusts, companies and organizations suspected of violating the Act. The Clayton Act extended the right to sue under the antitrust laws to 'any person who shall be injured in his business or property by reason of anything forbidden in the antitrust laws.' Under the Clayton Act, private parties may sue in U.S. district court and should they prevail, they may be awarded treble damages and the cost of suit, including reasonable attorney's fees.

   a. 1921 recession
   b. 100-year flood
   c. 130-30 fund
   d. Sherman Antitrust Act

Chapter 15. Post—Civil War Agriculture

1. _____ is a term used to describe large corporations, in either an individual or collective sense. The term first came into use in a symbolic sense subsequent to the American Civil War, particularly after 1880, in connection with the combination movement that began in American business at that time. Organizations that fall into the category of '_____' include ExxonMobil, Wal-Mart, Google, Microsoft, General Motors, Citigroup and Arcelor Mittal.
   a. First-mover advantage
   b. Sole proprietorship
   c. Brainsworking
   d. Big business

2. _____, in economics, is based on the expansion of the quantity of inputs in order to increase the quantity of outputs, opposite to that of intensive growth. Thus, _____ is likely to be subject to diminishing returns. It is therefore often viewed as having no effect on per-capita magnitudes in the long-run.
   a. Employee experience management
   b. Outside lag
   c. Implicit cost
   d. Extensive growth

3. In microeconomics, _____ is quite simply the conversion of inputs into outputs. It is an economic process that uses resources to create a good or service that is suitable for exchange. This can include manufacturing, storing, shipping, and packaging.
   a. MET
   b. Red Guards
   c. Solved
   d. Production

4. _____ in economics refers to metrics and measures of output from production processes, per unit of input. Labor _____, for example, is typically measured as a ratio of output per labor-hour, an input. _____ may be conceived of as a metrics of the technical or engineering efficiency of production.
   a. Piece work
   b. Fordism
   c. Production-possibility frontier
   d. Productivity

5. The _____ , established in 1848, is the world's oldest futures and options exchange. More than 50 different options and futures contracts are traded by over 3,600 _____ members through open outcry and eTrading. Volumes at the exchange in 2003 were a record breaking 454 million contracts.
   a. New York Mercantile Exchange
   b. 100-year flood
   c. 130-30 fund
   d. Chicago Board of Trade

6. _____ in economics and business is the result of an exchange and from that trade we assign a numerical monetary value to a good, service or asset. If Alice trades Bob 4 apples for an orange, the _____ of an orange is 4 apples. Inversely, the _____ of an apple is 1/4 oranges.
   a. Premium pricing
   b. Price book
   c. Price war
   d. Price

Chapter 15. Post—Civil War Agriculture

7. Economics:

    - _____, the desire to own something and the ability to pay for it
    - _____ curve, a graphic representation of a _____ schedule
    - _____ deposit, the money in checking accounts
    - _____ pull theory, the theory that inflation occurs when _____ for goods and services exceeds existing supplies
    - _____ schedule, a table that lists the quantity of a good a person will buy it each different price
    - _____ side economics, the school of economics at believes government spending and tax cuts open economy by raising _____

    a. Production
    b. Variability
    c. McKesson ' Robbins scandal
    d. Demand

8. The _____ was a regulatory body in the United States created by the Interstate Commerce Act of 1887, which was signed into law by President Grover Cleveland. The agency was abolished in 1995, and the agency's remaining functions were transferred to the Surface Transportation Board.

    The Commission's five members were appointed by the President with the consent of the United States Senate.

    a. ACCRA Cost of Living Index
    b. Office of Thrift Supervision
    c. ACEA agreement
    d. Interstate Commerce Commission

9. _____ is one of the four Ps of the marketing mix. The other three aspects are product, promotion, and place. It is also a key variable in microeconomic price allocation theory.

    a. Guaranteed Maximum Price
    b. Point of total assumption
    c. Premium pricing
    d. Pricing

10. _____ is a fee paid on borrowed assets. It is the price paid for the use of borrowed money, or, money earned by deposited funds. Assets that are sometimes lent with _____ include money, shares, consumer goods through hire purchase, major assets such as aircraft, and even entire factories in finance lease arrangements.

    a. Interest
    b. Internal debt
    c. Insolvency
    d. Asset protection

11. An _____ is the price a borrower pays for the use of money they do not own, for instance a small company might borrow from a bank to kick start their business, and the return a lender receives for deferring the use of funds, by lending it to the borrower. _____s are normally expressed as a percentage rate over the period of one year.

    _____s targets are also a vital tool of monetary policy and are used to control variables like investment, inflation, and unemployment.

    a. Arrow-Debreu model
    b. Enterprise value
    c. ACCRA Cost of Living Index
    d. Interest rate

Chapter 15. Post—Civil War Agriculture 73

12. _____ refers to the movement of cash into or out of a business or financial product. It is usually measured during a specified, finite period of time. Measurement of _____ can be used

- to determine a project's rate of return or value. The time of _____s into and out of projects are used as inputs in financial models such as internal rate of return, and net present value.
- to determine problems with a business's liquidity. Being profitable does not necessarily mean being liquid. A company can fail because of a shortage of cash, even while profitable.
- as an alternate measure of a business's profits when it is believed that accrual accounting concepts do not represent economic realities. For example, a company may be notionally profitable but generating little operational cash (as may be the case for a company that barters its products rather than selling for cash.) In such a case, the company may be deriving additional operating cash by issuing shares evaluating default risk, re-investment requirements, etc.

_____ is a generic term used differently depending on the context. It may be defined by users for their own purposes.

a. Restricted stock
c. Second lien loan
b. Cash flow
d. Strip financing

13. _____ is the act of taking possession of or assigning purpose to properties or ideas and is important in many topics, including:

- _____ in relation to the spread of knowledge
- _____ (art)
  - _____ (music) in reference to the re-use and proliferation of different types of music
- _____ (economics) origination of human ownership of previously unowned natural resources such as land
- _____ (law) as a component of government spending
- Cultural _____ is the borrowing, or theft, of an element of cultural expression of one group by another.
- The tort of _____ is one form of invasion of privacy.

a. Economic miracle
c. Appropriation
b. Augmentation
d. Oslo Agreements

14. The _____ is a federally owned corporation in the United States created by congressional charter in May 1933 to provide navigation, flood control, electricity generation, fertilizer manufacturing, and economic development in the Tennessee Valley, a region particularly impacted by the Great Depression. The _____ was envisioned not only as an electricity provider, but also as a regional economic development agency that would use federal experts and electricity to rapidly modernize the region's economy and society.

The _____'s jurisdiction covers most of Tennessee, parts of Alabama, Mississippi, and Kentucky, and small slices of Georgia, North Carolina, and Virginia.

a. 1921 recession
c. Tennessee Valley Authority
b. 100-year flood
d. 130-30 fund

Chapter 16. Population Growth and the Atlantic Migration

1. _____ is the change in population over time, and can be quantified as the change in the number of individuals in a population using 'per unit time' for measurement. The term _____ can technically refer to any species, but almost always refers to humans, and it is often used informally for the more specific demographic term _____ rate , and is often used to refer specifically to the growth of the population of the world.

Simple models of _____ include the Malthusian Growth Model and the logistic model.

   a. 100-year flood
   b. 130-30 fund
   c. Population dynamics
   d. Population growth

2. Crude _____ is the nativity or childbirths per 1,000 people per year.

It can be represented by number of childbirths in that year, and p is the current population. This figure is combined with the crude death rate to produce the rate of natural population growth (natural in that it does not take into account net migration.)

   a. Malthusian equilibrium
   b. Neo-Malthusianism
   c. Depensation
   d. Birth rate

3. _____s is the social science that studies the production, distribution, and consumption of goods and services. The term _____s comes from the Ancient Greek οἰκονομία from οἶκος (oikos, 'house') + νόμος (nomos, 'custom' or 'law'), hence 'rules of the house(hold)'. Current _____ models developed out of the broader field of political economy in the late 19th century, owing to a desire to use an empirical approach more akin to the physical sciences.
   a. Energy economics
   b. Opportunity cost
   c. Inflation
   d. Economic

4. _____ is the increase in the amount of the goods and services produced by an economy over time. It is conventionally measured as the percent rate of increase in real gross domestic product, or real GDP. Growth is usually calculated in real terms, i.e. inflation-adjusted terms, in order to net out the effect of inflation on the price of the goods and services produced.
   a. ACEA agreement
   b. Economic growth
   c. ACCRA Cost of Living Index
   d. AD-IA Model

5. _____ to the arrival of new individuals into a habitat or population. It is a biological concept and is important in population ecology, differentiated from emigration and migration.

_____ is a modern phenomenon.

   a. ACEA agreement
   b. ACCRA Cost of Living Index
   c. AD-IA Model
   d. Immigration

6. _____ndustrialization in North America, is the process of social and economic change whereby a human group is transformed from a pre-industrial society into an industrial one. _____t is a part of a wider modernisation process, where social change and economic development are closely related with technological innovation, particularly with the development of large-scale energy and metallurgy production. _____t is the extensive organisation of an economy for the purpose of manufacturing.

Chapter 16. Population Growth and the Atlantic Migration

a. ACEA agreement
b. AD-IA Model
c. ACCRA Cost of Living Index
d. Industrialization

7. _____ is an economic system in which wealth, and the means of producing wealth, are privately owned. Through _____, the land, labor, and capital are owned, operated, and traded for the purpose of generating profits, without force or fraud, by private individuals either singly or jointly, and investments, distribution, income, production, pricing and supply of goods, commodities and services are determined by voluntary private decision in a market economy. A distinguishing feature of _____ is that each person owns his or her own labor and therefore is allowed to sell the use of it to employers.
   a. Creative capitalism
   b. Capitalism
   c. Socialism for the rich and capitalism for the poor
   d. Late capitalism

8. The _____ or gross domestic income (GDI), a basic measure of an economy's economic performance, is the market value of all final goods and services produced within the borders of a nation in a year. _____ can be defined in three ways, all of which are conceptually identical. First, it is equal to the total expenditures for all final goods and services produced within the country in a stipulated period of time (usually a 365-day year.)
   a. Monopolistic competition
   b. Market structure
   c. Gross domestic product
   d. Countercyclical

9. The term '_____' refers to the concept of collecting information and attempting to spot a pattern in the information. In some fields of study, the term '_____' has more formally-defined meanings.

In project management _____ is a mathematical technique that uses historical results to predict future outcome.

   a. Probit model
   b. Coefficient of determination
   c. Quantile regression
   d. Trend analysis

10. _____ in economics refers to metrics and measures of output from production processes, per unit of input. Labor _____, for example, is typically measured as a ratio of output per labor-hour, an input. _____ may be conceived of as a metrics of the technical or engineering efficiency of production.
    a. Production-possibility frontier
    b. Fordism
    c. Productivity
    d. Piece work

11. The _____ is an international financial institution that provides financial and technical assistance to developing countries for development programs (e.g. bridges, roads, schools, etc.) with the stated goal of reducing poverty.

The _____ differs from the _____ Group, in that the _____ comprises only two institutions:

- International Bank for Reconstruction and Development (IBRD)
- International Development Association (IDA)

Whereas the latter incorporates these two in addition to three more:

- International Finance Corporation (IFC)
- Multilateral Investment Guarantee Agency (MIGA)
- International Centre for Settlement of Investment Disputes (ICSID)

John Maynard Keynes (right) represented the UK at the conference, and Harry Dexter White represented the US.

The _____ is one of two major financial institutions created as a result of the Bretton Woods Conference in 1944. The International Monetary Fund, a related but separate institution, is the second.

    a. Bank-State-Branch
    b. Financial costs of the 2003 Iraq War
    c. Flow to Equity-Approach
    d. World Bank

12. The _____ was a worldwide economic downturn starting in most places in 1929 and ending at different times in the 1930s or early 1940s for different countries. It was the largest and most important economic depression in the 20th century, and is used in the 21st century as an example of how far the world's economy can fall. The _____ originated in the United States; historians most often use as a starting date the stock market crash on October 29, 1929, known as Black Tuesday.

    a. Wall Street Crash of 1929
    b. Great Depression
    c. Jarrow March
    d. British Empire Economic Conference

13. _____ is that which is owed; usually referencing assets owed, but the term can also cover moral obligations and other interactions not requiring money. In the case of assets, _____ is a means of using future purchasing power in the present before a summation has been earned. Some companies and corporations use _____ as a part of their overall corporate finance strategy.

    a. Collateral Management
    b. Debenture
    c. Debt
    d. Hard money loan

14. The traditional definition of _____ is considered to be the ability to use language to read, write, listen, and speak. In modern contexts, the word refers to reading and writing at a level adequate for communication, or at a level that lets one understand and communicate ideas in a literate society, so as to take part in that society. The United Nations Educational, Scientific and Cultural Organization (UNESCO) has drafted the following definition: "_____' is the ability to identify, understand, interpret, create, communicate, compute and use printed and written materials associated with varying contexts.

    a. 100-year flood
    b. Literacy
    c. 130-30 fund
    d. 1921 recession

15. _____ the Great War, and the War to End All Wars, was a global military conflict which involved the majority of the world's great powers, organized into two opposing military alliances: the Entente Powers and the Central Powers. Over 70 million military personnel were mobilized in one of the largest wars in history. In a state of total war, the major combatants fully placed their scientific and industrial capabilities at the service of the war effort.

    a. 130-30 fund
    b. 100-year flood
    c. World War I
    d. 1921 recession

Chapter 17. Industrialization and Urban Growth

1. _____ ndustrialization in North America, is the process of social and economic change whereby a human group is transformed from a pre-industrial society into an industrial one. _____ t is a part of a wider modernisation process, where social change and economic development are closely related with technological innovation, particularly with the development of large-scale energy and metallurgy production. _____ t is the extensive organisation of an economy for the purpose of manufacturing.
   a. Industrialization
   b. AD-IA Model
   c. ACEA agreement
   d. ACCRA Cost of Living Index

2. _____ is an economic system in which wealth, and the means of producing wealth, are privately owned. Through _____, the land, labor, and capital are owned, operated, and traded for the purpose of generating profits, without force or fraud, by private individuals either singly or jointly, and investments, distribution, income, production, pricing and supply of goods, commodities and services are determined by voluntary private decision in a market economy. A distinguishing feature of _____ is that each person owns his or her own labor and therefore is allowed to sell the use of it to employers.
   a. Creative capitalism
   b. Late capitalism
   c. Socialism for the rich and capitalism for the poor
   d. Capitalism

3. _____ has several particular meanings:

   - in mathematics
     - _____ function
     - Euler _____
     - _____
     - _____ subgroup
     - method of _____ s (partial differential equations)
   - in physics and engineering
     - any _____ curve that shows the relationship between certain input- and output parameters, e.g.
     - an I-V or current-voltage _____ is the current in a circuit as a function of the applied voltage
     - Receiver-Operator _____
   - in fiction
     - in Dungeons ' Dragons, _____ is another name for ability score

   .

   a. Technocracy
   b. Russian financial crisis
   c. Demand
   d. Characteristic

4. _____ is the physical growth of rural or natural land into urban areas as a result of population immigration to an existing urban area. Effects include change in density and administration services. While the exact definition and population size of urbanized areas varies among different countries, _____ is attributed to growth of cities.
   a. Urban prairie
   b. ACCRA Cost of Living Index
   c. Urban renewal
   d. Urbanization

5. In microeconomics, _____ is quite simply the conversion of inputs into outputs. It is an economic process that uses resources to create a good or service that is suitable for exchange. This can include manufacturing, storing, shipping, and packaging.
   a. MET
   b. Production
   c. Solved
   d. Red Guards

Chapter 17. Industrialization and Urban Growth

6. The _____ was a sudden downturn in the economy of the United States that occurred in 1857. A general recession first emerged late in 1856, but the successive failure of banks and businesses that characterized the panic began in mid-1857. While the overall economic downturn was brief, the recovery was unequal, and the lasting impact was more political than economic.
   a. 130-30 fund
   b. 100-year flood
   c. 1921 recession
   d. Panic of 1857

7. The _____ was a serious economic depression in the United States that began in 1893. This panic is sometimes considered a part of the Long Depression which began with the Panic of 1873, and like that of earlier crashes, was caused by railroad overbuilding and shaky railroad financing; which set off a series of bank failures. Compounding market overbuilding and a railroad bubble was a run on the gold supply and a policy of using both gold and silver metals as a peg for the US Dollar value.
   a. 130-30 fund
   b. 1921 recession
   c. 100-year flood
   d. Panic of 1893

8. The _____ is a term used for industries primarily concerned with the design or manufacture of clothing as well as the distribution and use of textiles.

Prior to the manufacturing processes were mechanized, textiles were produced in the home, and excess sold for extra money. Most cloth was made from either wool, cotton, or flax, depending on the era and location.

   a. 130-30 fund
   b. 100-year flood
   c. Textile manufacture during the Industrial Revolution
   d. Textile industry

9. _____ is the term denoting either an entrance or changes which are inserted into a system and which activate/modify a process. It is an abstract concept, used in the modeling, system(s) design and system(s) exploitation. It is usually connected with other terms, e.g., _____ field, _____ variable, _____ parameter, _____ value, _____ signal, _____ device and _____ file.
   a. Input
   b. AD-IA Model
   c. ACCRA Cost of Living Index
   d. ACEA agreement

10. In economics, the people in the _____ are the suppliers of labor. The _____ is all the nonmilitary people who are employed or unemployed. In 2005, the worldwide _____ was over 3 billion people.
    a. Departmentalization
    b. Distributed workforce
    c. Labor force
    d. Grenelle agreements

11. _____, in microeconomics, are the cost advantages that a business obtains due to expansion. They are factors that cause a producere;s average cost per unit to fall as scale is increased. _____ is a long run concept and refers to reductions in unit cost as the size of a facility, or scale, increases.
    a. Economies of scale
    b. Economic production quantity
    c. Isoquant
    d. Underinvestment employment relationship

12. _____ in economics refers to metrics and measures of output from production processes, per unit of input. Labor _____, for example, is typically measured as a ratio of output per labor-hour, an input. _____ may be conceived of as a metrics of the technical or engineering efficiency of production.

Chapter 17. Industrialization and Urban Growth

a. Piece work
b. Production-possibility frontier
c. Fordism
d. Productivity

13. _____ is a term used to describe large corporations, in either an individual or collective sense. The term first came into use in a symbolic sense subsequent to the American Civil War, particularly after 1880, in connection with the combination movement that began in American business at that time. Organizations that fall into the category of '_____' include ExxonMobil, Wal-Mart, Google, Microsoft, General Motors, Citigroup and Arcelor Mittal.

a. First-mover advantage
b. Sole proprietorship
c. Big business
d. Brainsworking

14. _____ is a common concept in economics, and gives rise to derived concepts such as consumer debt. Generally _____ is defined by opposition to production. But the precise definition can vary because different schools of economists define production quite differently.

a. Cash or share options
b. Federal Reserve Bank Notes
c. Consumption
d. Foreclosure data providers

15. Competition law, known in the United States as _____ law, has three main elements:

- prohibiting agreements or practices that restrict free trading and competition between business entities. This includes in particular the repression of cartels.
- banning abusive behaviour by a firm dominating a market, or anti-competitive practices that tend to lead to such a dominant position. Practices controlled in this way may include predatory pricing, tying, price gouging, refusal to deal, and many others.
- supervising the mergers and acquisitions of large corporations, including some joint ventures. Transactions that are considered to threaten the competitive process can be prohibited altogether, or approved subject to 'remedies' such as an obligation to divest part of the merged business or to offer licences or access to facilities to enable other businesses to continue competing.

The substance and practice of competition law varies from jurisdiction to jurisdiction. Protecting the interests of consumers (consumer welfare) and ensuring that entrepreneurs have an opportunity to compete in the market economy are often treated as important objectives. Competition law is closely connected with law on deregulation of access to markets, state aids and subsidies, the privatisation of state owned assets and the establishment of independent sector regulators. In recent decades, competition law has been viewed as a way to provide better public services.

a. Intellectual property law
b. Anti-Inflation Act
c. United Kingdom competition law
d. Antitrust

16.

The _____ was the first United States Federal statute to limit cartels and monopolies. It falls under antitrust law.

Chapter 17. Industrialization and Urban Growth

The Act provides: 'Every contract, combination in the form of trust or otherwise, or conspiracy, in restraint of trade or commerce among the several States, or with foreign nations, is declared to be illegal'. The Act also provides: 'Every person who shall monopolize, or attempt to monopolize, or combine or conspire with any other person or persons, to monopolize any part of the trade or commerce among the several States, or with foreign nations, shall be deemed guilty of a felony [. . .]' The Act put responsibility upon government attorneys and district courts to pursue and investigate trusts, companies and organizations suspected of violating the Act. The Clayton Act extended the right to sue under the antitrust laws to 'any person who shall be injured in his business or property by reason of anything forbidden in the antitrust laws.' Under the Clayton Act, private parties may sue in U.S. district court and should they prevail, they may be awarded treble damages and the cost of suit, including reasonable attorney's fees.

a. 130-30 fund
b. 1921 recession
c. 100-year flood
d. Sherman Antitrust Act

17. _____ is the conformance of a residence or abode to the implied warranty of _____. A residence that complies is said to be 'habitable.' It is an implied warranty or contract, meaning it does not have to be an express contract, covenant, or provision of a contract. It is a common law right of a tenant or Legal doctrine.
a. Patent portfolio
b. Misappropriation
c. Clean Air Act Extension of 1970
d. Habitability

18. The notion of _____ is found in the writings of Mikhail Bakunin, Friedrich Nietzsche, and in Werner Sombart's Krieg und Kapitalismus (War and Capitalism) (1913, p. 207), where he wrote: 'again out of destruction a new spirit of creativity arises'. In Capitalism, Socialism and Democracy, the Austrian economist Joseph Schumpeter popularized and used the term to describe the process of transformation that accompanies radical innovation.
a. 1921 recession
b. 130-30 fund
c. 100-year flood
d. Creative destruction

19. _____s is the social science that studies the production, distribution, and consumption of goods and services. The term _____s comes from the Ancient Greek oá¼°κονομῖα from oá¼¶κος (oikos, 'house') + vŒμος (nomos, 'custom' or 'law'), hence 'rules of the house(hold)'. Current _____ models developed out of the broader field of political economy in the late 19th century, owing to a desire to use an empirical approach more akin to the physical sciences.
a. Energy economics
b. Opportunity cost
c. Inflation
d. Economic

20. _____ is the increase in the amount of the goods and services produced by an economy over time. It is conventionally measured as the percent rate of increase in real gross domestic product, or real GDP. Growth is usually calculated in real terms, i.e. inflation-adjusted terms, in order to net out the effect of inflation on the price of the goods and services produced.
a. ACEA agreement
b. ACCRA Cost of Living Index
c. AD-IA Model
d. Economic growth

Chapter 17. Industrialization and Urban Growth

21. The _____ was a worldwide economic downturn starting in most places in 1929 and ending at different times in the 1930s or early 1940s for different countries. It was the largest and most important economic depression in the 20th century, and is used in the 21st century as an example of how far the world's economy can fall. The _____ originated in the United States; historians most often use as a starting date the stock market crash on October 29, 1929, known as Black Tuesday.
   a. Wall Street Crash of 1929
   b. Jarrow March
   c. Great Depression
   d. British Empire Economic Conference

22. A variety of measures of national income and output are used in economics to estimate total economic activity in a country or region, including gross domestic product (GDP), _____ , and net national income (NNI.)

   There are three main ways of calculating these numbers; the output approach, the income approach and the expenditure approach. In theory, the three must yield the same, because total expenditures on goods and services must equal the total income paid to the producers (GNI), and that must also equal the total value of the output of goods and services (_____.)

   a. Household final consumption expenditure
   b. Gross world product
   c. Purchasing power parity
   d. Gross national product

23. _____ is the change in population over time, and can be quantified as the change in the number of individuals in a population using 'per unit time' for measurement. The term _____ can technically refer to any species, but almost always refers to humans, and it is often used informally for the more specific demographic term _____ rate, and is often used to refer specifically to the growth of the population of the world.

   Simple models of _____ include the Malthusian Growth Model and the logistic model.

   a. Population dynamics
   b. 130-30 fund
   c. Population growth
   d. 100-year flood

24. Economics:

   - _____, the desire to own something and the ability to pay for it
   - _____ curve, a graphic representation of a _____ schedule
   - _____ deposit, the money in checking accounts
   - _____ pull theory, the theory that inflation occurs when _____ for goods and services exceeds existing supplies
   - _____ schedule, a table that lists the quantity of a good a person will buy it each different price
   - _____ side economics, the school of economics at believes government spending and tax cuts open economy by raising _____

   a. McKesson ' Robbins scandal
   b. Production
   c. Variability
   d. Demand

Chapter 17. Industrialization and Urban Growth

25. _____ is a term in economics, where demand for one good or service occurs as a result of demand for another. This may occur as the former is a part of production of the second. For example, demand for coal leads to _____ for mining, as coal must be mined for coal to be consumed.
   - a. Rate risk
   - b. Days Sales Outstanding
   - c. Leontief production function
   - d. Derived demand

26. In economics, _____ is the ratio of the percent change in one variable to the percent change in another variable. It is a tool for measuring the responsiveness of a function to changes in parameters in a relative way. Commonly analyzed are _____ of substitution, price and wealth.
   - a. ACEA agreement
   - b. Elasticity of demand
   - c. Elasticity
   - d. ACCRA Cost of Living Index

27. Price _____ is defined as the measure of responsiveness in the quantity demanded for a commodity as a result of change in price of the same commodity. It is a measure of how consumers react to a change in price. In other words, it is percentage change in quantity demanded by the percentage change in price of the same commodity.
   - a. Elasticity of Demand
   - b. Elasticity
   - c. ACEA agreement
   - d. ACCRA Cost of Living Index

28. In economics, the _____ of demand measures the responsiveness of the demand of a good to the change in the income of the people demanding the good. It is calculated as the ratio of the percent change in demand to the percent change in income. For example, if, in response to a 10% increase in income, the demand of a good increased by 20%, the _____ of demand would be 20%/10% = 2.
   - a. ACEA agreement
   - b. ACCRA Cost of Living Index
   - c. Income elasticity
   - d. AD-IA Model

29. In economics, the _____ measures the responsiveness of the demand of a good to the change in the income of the people demanding the good. It is calculated as the ratio of the percent change in demand to the percent change in income. For example, if, in response to a 10% increase in income, the demand of a good increased by 20%, the _____ would be 20%/10% = 2.
   - a. Income elasticity of Demand
   - b. Indifference map
   - c. Elasticity of substitution
   - d. Expenditure minimization problem

30. The term '_____' refers to the concept of collecting information and attempting to spot a pattern in the information. In some fields of study, the term '_____' has more formally-defined meanings.

    In project management _____ is a mathematical technique that uses historical results to predict future outcome.

   - a. Trend analysis
   - b. Quantile regression
   - c. Coefficient of determination
   - d. Probit model

31. Network externalities resemble economies of scale, but they are not considered such because they are a function of the number of users of a good or service in an industry, not of the production efficiency within a business. _____ are only considered examples of network externalities if they are driven by demand side economies.

Chapter 17. Industrialization and Urban Growth

Formally, a production function $F(K, L)$ is defined to have:

- constant returns to scale if (for any constant a greater than or equal to 0) $F(aK, aL) = aF(K, L)$
- increasing returns to scale if (for any constant a greater than 1) $F(aK, aL) > aF(K, L)$,
- decreasing returns to scale if (for any constant a greater than 1) $F(aK, aL) < aF(K, L)$

where K and L are factors of production, capital and labour, respectively.

As an example, the Cobb-Douglas functional form has constant returns to scale when the sum of the exponents adds up to one.

a. ACEA agreement
b. Economies of scale external to the firm
c. AD-IA Model
d. ACCRA Cost of Living Index

32. The _____ was a period in the late 18th and early 19th centuries when major changes in agriculture, manufacturing, mining, and transportation had a profound effect on the socioeconomic and cultural conditions in Britain. The changes subsequently spread throughout Europe, North America, and eventually the world. The onset of the _____ marked a major turning point in human society; almost every aspect of daily life was eventually influenced in some way.

a. Adam Smith
b. Adolf Hitler
c. Industrial Revolution
d. Adolph Fischer

33. An _____ is a person who has possession of an enterprise and assumes significant accountability for the inherent risks and the outcome. It is an ambitious leader who combines land, labor, and capital to create and market new goods or services. The term is a loanword from French and was first defined by the Irish economist Richard Cantillon.

a. Expansionary policies
b. ACCRA Cost of Living Index
c. ACEA agreement
d. Entrepreneur

34. An _____ is described by a conglomerate of meta-physical dispositions meant to cause the innovative and energetic practice to identify or create an opportunity and take action aimed at realizing it. The philosophical themes - existentialism, axiology, pragmatism, ethics - are thereby understood to be strange attractors influencing the construction of the entitye;s persona as well as the concrete practices of the entity Figure 1:Conceptual Model of Philosophical Components of an _____

Important for entrepreneurship is the e;creative mindsete; that helps entrepreneurs to create new ideas and bring these to the market in a way appropriate to create value for an external audience.

a. Entrepreneurial mindset
b. Intrapreneurship
c. ACEA agreement
d. ACCRA Cost of Living Index

35. _____ is an economic theory named after the 20th century Austrian economist Joseph Schumpeter. Unlike modern economic growth theories, his approach explains growth by innovation and entrepreneurial spirit.

a. Fed model
b. Schumpeterian growth
c. Lipstick effect
d. Real prices and ideal prices

Chapter 18. Big Business and Government Intervention

1. _____ is a term used to describe large corporations, in either an individual or collective sense. The term first came into use in a symbolic sense subsequent to the American Civil War, particularly after 1880, in connection with the combination movement that began in American business at that time. Organizations that fall into the category of '_____' include ExxonMobil, Wal-Mart, Google, Microsoft, General Motors, Citigroup and Arcelor Mittal.
   - a. First-mover advantage
   - b. Brainsworking
   - c. Big business
   - d. Sole proprietorship

2. The _____ is a monetary system in which a region's common medium of exchange are paper notes that are normally freely convertible into pre-set, fixed quantities of gold. The _____ is not currently used by any government, having been replaced completely by fiat currency. Gold certificates were used as paper currency in the United States from 1882 to 1933, these certificates were freely convertable into gold coins.

   In the 1790s Britain suffered a massive shortage of silver coinage and ceased to mint larger silver coins.

   - a. 1921 recession
   - b. 100-year flood
   - c. 130-30 fund
   - d. Gold Standard

3. The _____ of the United States was passed in 1900 (ratified on March 14) and established gold as the only standard for redeeming paper money, stopping bimetallism (which had allowed silver in exchange for gold.) It was signed by President William McKinley.
   - a. Flex dollars
   - b. Fed Shreds
   - c. Gold Standard Act
   - d. Remonetisation

4. In economics, a _____ exists when a specific individual or enterprise has sufficient control over a particular product or service to determine significantly the terms on which other individuals shall have access to it. Monopolies are thus characterized by a lack of economic competition for the good or service that they provide and a lack of viable substitute goods. The verb 'monopolize' refers to the process by which a firm gains persistently greater market share than what is expected under perfect competition.
   - a. 100-year flood
   - b. 1921 recession
   - c. 130-30 fund
   - d. Monopoly

5. Competition law, known in the United States as _____ law, has three main elements:

   - prohibiting agreements or practices that restrict free trading and competition between business entities. This includes in particular the repression of cartels.
   - banning abusive behaviour by a firm dominating a market, or anti-competitive practices that tend to lead to such a dominant position. Practices controlled in this way may include predatory pricing, tying, price gouging, refusal to deal, and many others.
   - supervising the mergers and acquisitions of large corporations, including some joint ventures. Transactions that are considered to threaten the competitive process can be prohibited altogether, or approved subject to 'remedies' such as an obligation to divest part of the merged business or to offer licences or access to facilities to enable other businesses to continue competing.

The substance and practice of competition law varies from jurisdiction to jurisdiction. Protecting the interests of consumers (consumer welfare) and ensuring that entrepreneurs have an opportunity to compete in the market economy are often treated as important objectives. Competition law is closely connected with law on deregulation of access to markets, state aids and subsidies, the privatisation of state owned assets and the establishment of independent sector regulators. In recent decades, competition law has been viewed as a way to provide better public services.

a. Intellectual property law
b. Antitrust
c. Anti-Inflation Act
d. United Kingdom competition law

6. _____s is the social science that studies the production, distribution, and consumption of goods and services. The term _____s comes from the Ancient Greek oá¼°κονομῖα from oá¼¶κος (oikos, 'house') + vĺŒμος (nomos, 'custom' or 'law'), hence 'rules of the house(hold)'. Current _____ models developed out of the broader field of political economy in the late 19th century, owing to a desire to use an empirical approach more akin to the physical sciences.

a. Energy economics
b. Economic
c. Opportunity cost
d. Inflation

7. _____ is the increase in the amount of the goods and services produced by an economy over time. It is conventionally measured as the percent rate of increase in real gross domestic product, or real GDP. Growth is usually calculated in real terms, i.e. inflation-adjusted terms, in order to net out the effect of inflation on the price of the goods and services produced.

a. AD-IA Model
b. Economic growth
c. ACCRA Cost of Living Index
d. ACEA agreement

8.

The _____ was the first United States Federal statute to limit cartels and monopolies. It falls under antitrust law.

The Act provides: 'Every contract, combination in the form of trust or otherwise, or conspiracy, in restraint of trade or commerce among the several States, or with foreign nations, is declared to be illegal'. The Act also provides: 'Every person who shall monopolize, or attempt to monopolize, or combine or conspire with any other person or persons, to monopolize any part of the trade or commerce among the several States, or with foreign nations, shall be deemed guilty of a felony [. . .]' The Act put responsibility upon government attorneys and district courts to pursue and investigate trusts, companies and organizations suspected of violating the Act. The Clayton Act extended the right to sue under the antitrust laws to 'any person who shall be injured in his business or property by reason of anything forbidden in the antitrust laws.' Under the Clayton Act, private parties may sue in U.S. district court and should they prevail, they may be awarded treble damages and the cost of suit, including reasonable attorney's fees.

a. 1921 recession
b. 130-30 fund
c. 100-year flood
d. Sherman Antitrust Act

Chapter 18. Big Business and Government Intervention

9. The _____ consists of a number of economic theories which describe the nature of the firm, company including its existence, its behaviour, and its relationship with the market.

In simplified terms, the _____ aims to answer these questions:

1. Existence - why do firms emerge, why are not all transactions in the economy mediated over the market?
2. Boundaries - why the boundary between firms and the market is located exactly there? Which transactions are performed internally and which are negotiated on the market?
3. Organization - why are firms structured in such specific way? What is the interplay of formal and informal relationships?

Despite looking simple, these questions are not answered by the established economic theory, which usually views firms as given, and treats them as black boxes without any internal structure.

The First World War period saw a change of emphasis in economic theory away from industry-level analysis which mainly included analysing markets to analysis at the level of the firm, as it became increasingly clear that perfect competition was no longer an adequate model of how firms behaved. Economic theory till then had focussed on trying to understand markets alone and there had been little study on understanding why firms or organisations exist.

a. Theory of the firm
b. Technology gap
c. Policy Ineffectiveness Proposition
d. Khazzoom-Brookes postulate

10. An _____ is a person who has possession of an enterprise and assumes significant accountability for the inherent risks and the outcome. It is an ambitious leader who combines land, labor, and capital to create and market new goods or services. The term is a loanword from French and was first defined by the Irish economist Richard Cantillon.

a. ACCRA Cost of Living Index
b. Expansionary policies
c. ACEA agreement
d. Entrepreneur

11. _____, in microeconomics, are the cost advantages that a business obtains due to expansion. They are factors that cause a producere;s average cost per unit to fall as scale is increased. _____ is a long run concept and refers to reductions in unit cost as the size of a facility, or scale, increases.

a. Economic production quantity
b. Underinvestment employment relationship
c. Isoquant
d. Economies of scale

12. The phrase _____ and acquisitions refers to the aspect of corporate strategy, corporate finance and management dealing with the buying, selling and combining of different companies that can aid, finance, or help a growing company in a given industry grow rapidly without having to create another business entity.

An acquisition, also known as a takeover or a buyout, is the buying of one company (the 'target') by another. An acquisition may be friendly or hostile.

a. Peace dividend
b. Differential accumulation
c. Political economy
d. Mergers

Chapter 18. Big Business and Government Intervention

13. In economics, a _____ is a general slowdown in economic activity over a sustained period of time, or a business cycle contraction. During _____s, many macroeconomic indicators vary in a similar way. Production as measured by Gross Domestic Product (GDP), employment, investment spending, capacity utilization, household incomes and business profits all fall during _____s.

   a. Monetary economics
   b. Leading indicators
   c. Recession
   d. Treasury View

14. In economics, the _____ is the term used to refer to the environment in which bonds are bought and sold between a central bank ' its regulated banks. It is not a free market process.

   - To intervene in the 'business cycle', a central bank may choose to go into the _____ and buy or sell government bonds, which is known as _____ operations to increase reserves.

   a. Outside money
   b. ACCRA Cost of Living Index
   c. Inside money
   d. Open Market

15. Network externalities resemble economies of scale, but they are not considered such because they are a function of the number of users of a good or service in an industry, not of the production efficiency within a business. _____ are only considered examples of network externalities if they are driven by demand side economies.

   Formally, a production function $F(K, L)$ is defined to have:

   - constant returns to scale if (for any constant a greater than or equal to 0) $F(aK, aL) = aF(K, L)$
   - increasing returns to scale if (for any constant a greater than 1) $F(aK, aL) > aF(K, L)$,
   - decreasing returns to scale if (for any constant a greater than 1) $F(aK, aL) < aF(K, L)$

   where K and L are factors of production, capital and labour, respectively.

   As an example, the Cobb-Douglas functional form has constant returns to scale when the sum of the exponents adds up to one.

   a. AD-IA Model
   b. ACEA agreement
   c. ACCRA Cost of Living Index
   d. Economies of scale external to the firm

16. In economics, a _____ occurs when, due to the economies of scale of a particular industry, the maximum efficiency of production and distribution is realized through a single supplier.

   Natural monopolies arise where the largest supplier in an industry, often the first supplier in a market, has an overwhelming cost advantage over other actual or potential competitors. This tends to be the case in industries where capital costs predominate, creating economies of scale which are large in relation to the size of the market, and hence high barriers to entry; examples include water services and electricity.

Chapter 18. Big Business and Government Intervention

a. Privatizing profits and socializing losses
c. Collective goods
b. Common-pool resource
d. Natural Monopoly

17. The _____ was a regulatory body in the United States created by the Interstate Commerce Act of 1887, which was signed into law by President Grover Cleveland. The agency was abolished in 1995, and the agency's remaining functions were transferred to the Surface Transportation Board.

The Commission's five members were appointed by the President with the consent of the United States Senate.

a. Office of Thrift Supervision
c. ACCRA Cost of Living Index
b. ACEA agreement
d. Interstate Commerce Commission

18. The _____ was a worldwide economic downturn starting in most places in 1929 and ending at different times in the 1930s or early 1940s for different countries. It was the largest and most important economic depression in the 20th century, and is used in the 21st century as an example of how far the world's economy can fall. The _____ originated in the United States; historians most often use as a starting date the stock market crash on October 29, 1929, known as Black Tuesday.

a. Jarrow March
c. British Empire Economic Conference
b. Wall Street Crash of 1929
d. Great Depression

19. The _____ is an independent agency of the United States government, established in 1914 by the _____ Act. Its principal mission is the promotion of 'consumer protection' and the elimination and prevention of what regulators perceive to be harmfully 'anti-competitive' business practices, such as coercive monopoly.

The _____ Act was one of President Wilson's major acts against trusts.

a. Federal Trade Commission
c. 1921 recession
b. 100-year flood
d. 130-30 fund

20. _____ was a predominant American integrated oil producing, transporting, refining, and marketing company. Established in 1870 as an Ohio Corporation, it was the largest oil refiner in the world and operated as a major company trust and was one of the world's first and largest multinational corporations until it was broken up by the United States Supreme Court in 1911. John D. Rockefeller was a founder, chairman and major shareholder, and the company made him a billionaire and eventually the richest man in history.

a. 100-year flood
c. 130-30 fund
b. 1921 recession
d. Standard Oil

21. A _____ is a duty imposed on goods when they are moved across a political boundary. They are usually associated with protectionism, the economic policy of restraining trade between nations. For political reasons, _____s are usually imposed on imported goods, although they may also be imposed on exported goods.

a. 100-year flood
c. 1921 recession
b. 130-30 fund
d. Tariff

Chapter 19. Financial Developments (1863-1914)

1. _____ involves the 'matching' of lenders with savings to borrowers who need money by an agent or third party, such as a bank.

If this matching is successful, the lender obtains a positive rate of return, the borrower receives a return for risk taking and entrepeneurship and the banker receives a marginal return for making the successful match. If the borrower's speculative play with the depositor's funds does not pay off, the depositor can lose the savings borrowed by the borrower and the bank can face significant losses on its loan portfolio.

   a. Arranger
   b. Origination fee
   c. Annual percentage rate
   d. Intermediation

2. The _____ is the market for securities, where companies and governments can raise longterm funds. It is a market in which money is lent for periods longer than a year. The _____ includes the stock market and the bond market.
   a. Capital market
   b. Financial instrument
   c. Multi-family office
   d. Performance attribution

3. Competition law, known in the United States as _____ law, has three main elements:

   - prohibiting agreements or practices that restrict free trading and competition between business entities. This includes in particular the repression of cartels.
   - banning abusive behaviour by a firm dominating a market, or anti-competitive practices that tend to lead to such a dominant position. Practices controlled in this way may include predatory pricing, tying, price gouging, refusal to deal, and many others.
   - supervising the mergers and acquisitions of large corporations, including some joint ventures. Transactions that are considered to threaten the competitive process can be prohibited altogether, or approved subject to 'remedies' such as an obligation to divest part of the merged business or to offer licences or access to facilities to enable other businesses to continue competing.

The substance and practice of competition law varies from jurisdiction to jurisdiction. Protecting the interests of consumers (consumer welfare) and ensuring that entrepreneurs have an opportunity to compete in the market economy are often treated as important objectives. Competition law is closely connected with law on deregulation of access to markets, state aids and subsidies, the privatisation of state owned assets and the establishment of independent sector regulators. In recent decades, competition law has been viewed as a way to provide better public services.

   a. Antitrust
   b. Anti-Inflation Act
   c. United Kingdom competition law
   d. Intellectual property law

4. The _____ is the central bank of the United Kingdom and is the model on which most modern, large central banks have been based. Since 1946 it has been a state-owned institution. It was established in 1694 to act as the English Government's banker, and to this day it still acts as the banker for the UK Government.
   a. 1921 recession
   b. 100-year flood
   c. 130-30 fund
   d. Bank of England

5.

Chapter 19. Financial Developments (1863-1914)

The _____ was the first United States Federal statute to limit cartels and monopolies. It falls under antitrust law.

The Act provides: 'Every contract, combination in the form of trust or otherwise, or conspiracy, in restraint of trade or commerce among the several States, or with foreign nations, is declared to be illegal'. The Act also provides: 'Every person who shall monopolize, or attempt to monopolize, or combine or conspire with any other person or persons, to monopolize any part of the trade or commerce among the several States, or with foreign nations, shall be deemed guilty of a felony [. . .]' The Act put responsibility upon government attorneys and district courts to pursue and investigate trusts, companies and organizations suspected of violating the Act. The Clayton Act extended the right to sue under the antitrust laws to 'any person who shall be injured in his business or property by reason of anything forbidden in the antitrust laws.' Under the Clayton Act, private parties may sue in U.S. district court and should they prevail, they may be awarded treble damages and the cost of suit, including reasonable attorney's fees.

a. 1921 recession
b. Sherman Antitrust Act
c. 100-year flood
d. 130-30 fund

6. Economics:

- _____ ,the desire to own something and the ability to pay for it
- _____ curve, a graphic representation of a _____ schedule
- _____ deposit, the money in checking accounts
- _____ pull theory, the theory that inflation occurs when _____ for goods and services exceeds existing supplies
- _____ schedule, a table that lists the quantity of a good a person will buy it each different price
- _____ side economics, the school of economics at believes government spending and tax cuts open economy by raising _____

a. Demand
b. McKesson ' Robbins scandal
c. Variability
d. Production

7. _____ is a type of bank account where the money in the account is legally able to be withdrawn immediately upon demand (or 'at call'.) This type of bank account can also be referred to as a 'cheque' or 'checking' or transactional account.

This type of bank account, allowing immediate conversion of the account balance into cash or withdrawal to another account, can be contrasted with a time deposit (also known as a certificate of deposit or term deposit), where the funds are not legally available for immediate withdrawal by the depositor.

a. Debt rescheduling
b. Tangible Common Equity
c. Demand deposit
d. Clawbacks in economic development

8. _____ is money accepted for exchange of goods in an economy. The prevalence of one money over another arises, usually, when a government designates through decrees that the government shall accept only particular notes and coins in payment for taxes. Typically, money of _____ consists of stamped coins and minted paper bills.
   a. Currency
   b. Security thread
   c. Totnes pound
   d. Local currency

9. The _____ is a monetary system in which a region's common medium of exchange are paper notes that are normally freely convertible into pre-set, fixed quantities of gold. The _____ is not currently used by any government, having been replaced completely by fiat currency. Gold certificates were used as paper currency in the United States from 1882 to 1933, these certificates were freely convertable into gold coins.

In the 1790s Britain suffered a massive shortage of silver coinage and ceased to mint larger silver coins.

   a. Gold Standard
   b. 100-year flood
   c. 1921 recession
   d. 130-30 fund

10. The _____ of the United States was passed in 1900 (ratified on March 14) and established gold as the only standard for redeeming paper money, stopping bimetallism (which had allowed silver in exchange for gold.) It was signed by President William McKinley.
    a. Remonetisation
    b. Flex dollars
    c. Gold Standard Act
    d. Fed Shreds

11. The _____ is the central banking system of the United States. Created in 1913 by the enactment of the Federal Reserve Act (signed by Woodrow Wilson), it is a quasi-public and quasi-private (government entity with private components) banking system that comprises (1) the presidentially appointed Board of Governors of the _____ in Washington, D.C.; (2) the Federal Open Market Committee; (3) twelve regional Federal Reserve Banks located in major cities throughout the nation acting as fiscal agents for the U.S. Treasury, each with its own nine-member board of directors; (4) numerous other private U.S. member banks, which subscribe to required amounts of non-transferable stock in their regional Federal Reserve Banks; and (5) various advisory councils. Since February 2006, Ben Bernanke has served as the Chairman of the Board of Governors of the _____.

    a. Monetary Policy Report to the Congress
    b. Federal Reserve System Open Market Account
    c. Term auction facility
    d. Federal Reserve System

12. The _____ was a serious economic depression in the United States that began in 1893. This panic is sometimes considered a part of the Long Depression which began with the Panic of 1873, and like that of earlier crashes, was caused by railroad overbuilding and shaky railroad financing; which set off a series of bank failures. Compounding market overbuilding and a railroad bubble was a run on the gold supply and a policy of using both gold and silver metals as a peg for the US Dollar value.
    a. Panic of 1893
    b. 1921 recession
    c. 100-year flood
    d. 130-30 fund

13. The _____ was a financial crisis that occurred in the United States when the New York Stock Exchange fell close to 50% from its peak the previous year. Panic occurred, as this was during a time of economic recession, and there were numerous runs on banks and trust companies. The 1907 panic eventually spread throughout the nation when many state and local banks and businesses entered into bankruptcy.

Chapter 19. Financial Developments (1863-1914)

a. 100-year flood
b. 1921 recession
c. 130-30 fund
d. Panic of 1907

14. The term _____ refers to economy-wide fluctuations in production or economic activity over several months or years. These fluctuations occur around a long-term growth trend, and typically involve shifts over time between periods of relatively rapid economic growth (expansion or boom), and periods of relative stagnation or decline (contraction or recession.)

These fluctuations are often measured using the growth rate of real gross domestic product.

a. Business cycle
b. Tobit model
c. Nominal value
d. Consumer theory

15. In economics, the _____ measures the payments that flow between any individual country and all other countries. It is used to summarize all international economic transactions for that country during a specific time period, usually a year. The _____ is determined by the country's exports and imports of goods, services, and financial capital, as well as financial transfers.

a. Gross domestic product per barrel
b. Balance of payments
c. Gross world product
d. Skyscraper Index

16. _____s are a type of administrative division, in some countries managed by a local government. They vary greatly in size, spanning entire regions or counties, several municipalities, or subdivisions of municipalities.

In Austria, a _____ or Bezirk is an administrative division normally encompassing several municipalities, roughly equivalent to the Landkreis in Germany.

a. District
b. 100-year flood
c. 1921 recession
d. 130-30 fund

17. The term financial crisis is applied broadly to a variety of situations in which some financial institutions or assets suddenly lose a large part of their value. In the 19th and early 20th centuries, many _____ were associated with banking panics, and many recessions coincided with these panics. Other situations that are often called _____ include stock market crashes and the bursting of other financial bubbles, currency crises, and sovereign defaults.

a. Financial crises
b. Georgism
c. Microeconomics
d. General equilibrium

18. A _____ is the transfer of wealth from one party (such as a person or company) to another. A _____ is usually made in exchange for the provision of goods, services or both, or to fulfill a legal obligation.

The simplest and oldest form of _____ is barter, the exchange of one good or service for another.

a. Social gravity
b. Going concern
c. Soft count
d. Payment

19. The _____ consists of a number of economic theories which describe the nature of the firm, company including its existence, its behaviour, and its relationship with the market.

In simplified terms, the _____ aims to answer these questions:

1. Existence - why do firms emerge, why are not all transactions in the economy mediated over the market?
2. Boundaries - why the boundary between firms and the market is located exactly there? Which transactions are performed internally and which are negotiated on the market?
3. Organization - why are firms structured in such specific way? What is the interplay of formal and informal relationships?

Despite looking simple, these questions are not answered by the established economic theory, which usually views firms as given, and treats them as black boxes without any internal structure.

The First World War period saw a change of emphasis in economic theory away from industry-level analysis which mainly included analysing markets to analysis at the level of the firm, as it became increasingly clear that perfect competition was no longer an adequate model of how firms behaved. Economic theory till then had focussed on trying to understand markets alone and there had been little study on understanding why firms or organisations exist.

    a. Theory of the firm
    b. Policy Ineffectiveness Proposition
    c. Technology gap
    d. Khazzoom-Brookes postulate

20. The _____ is a United States government corporation created by the Glass-Steagall Act of 1933. It provides deposit insurance, which guarantees the safety of deposits in member banks, currently up to $250,000 per depositor per bank. Funds in non-interest bearing transaction accounts are fully insured, with no limit, under the temporary Transaction Account Guarantee Program.
    a. Foreign direct investment
    b. Luxembourg Income Study
    c. Great Leap Forward
    d. Federal Deposit Insurance Corporation

21. _____, in law and economics, is a form of risk management primarily used to hedge against the risk of a contingent loss. _____ is defined as the equitable transfer of the risk of a loss, from one entity to another, in exchange for a premium, and can be thought of as a guaranteed small loss to prevent a large, possibly devastating loss. An insurer is a company selling the _____; an insured or policyholder is the person or entity buying the _____.
    a. ACCRA Cost of Living Index
    b. Insurance
    c. AD-IA Model
    d. ACEA agreement

22. An _____ is a financial institution that raises capital, trades in securities and manages corporate mergers and acquisitions. _____s profit from companies and governments by raising money through issuing and selling securities in the capital markets (both equity, bond) and insuring bonds (selling credit default swaps), as well as providing advice on transactions such as mergers and acquisitions. To perform these services in the United States, an adviser must be a licensed broker-dealer, and is subject to SEC (FINRA) regulation see SEC.
    a. Annual percentage rate
    b. Investment bank
    c. Interbanca
    d. Anonymous internet banking

23. _____s are cash, evidence of an ownership interest in an entity or deliver, cash or another _____.

Chapter 19. Financial Developments (1863-1914)   95

_____s can be categorized by form depending on whether they are cash instruments or derivative instruments:

- Cash instruments are _____s whose value is determined directly by markets. They can be divided into securities, which are readily transferable, and other cash instruments such as loans and deposits, where both borrower and lender have to agree on a transfer.
- Derivative instruments are _____s which derive their value from the value and characteristics of one or more underlying assets. They can be divided into exchange-traded derivatives and over-the-counter (OTC) derivatives.

Alternatively, _____s can be categorized by 'asset class' depending on whether they are equity based (reflecting ownership of the issuing entity) or debt based (reflecting a loan the investor has made to the issuing entity.) If it is debt, it can be further categorised into short term (less than one year) or long term.

Foreign Exchange instruments and transactions are neither debt nor equity based and belong in their own category.

a. Municipal Bond Arbitrage
c. Fundamentally based indexes
b. Market liquidity
d. Financial instrument

24. _____s are financial contracts whose values are derived from the value of something else (known as the underlying.) The underlying value on which a _____ is based can be an asset (e.g., commodities, equities (stocks), residential mortgages, commercial real estate, loans, bonds), an index (e.g., interest rates, exchange rates, stock market indices, consumer price index (CPI) -- see inflation _____s), weather conditions bonds or other forms of credit.
a. Second derivative
c. 130-30 fund
b. 100-year flood
d. Derivative

25. _____ is an equity (stock) exchange located at 11 Wall Street in lower Manhattan, New York, USA. It is the largest stock exchange in the world by dollar value of its listed companies' securities. As of October 2008, the combined capitalization of all domestic _____ listed companies was US$10.1 trillion.
a. 130-30 fund
c. 100-year flood
b. 1921 recession
d. New York Stock Exchange

26. A _____ is a corporation or mutual organization which provides trading facilities for stock brokers and traders, to trade stocks and other securities. It may be a physical trading room where the traders gather, or a formalised communications network. Creation of a _____ is a strategy of economic development.
a. 100-year flood
c. Stock Exchange
b. SEAQ
d. Primary shares

27.

A _____ is a type of financial intermediary and a type of bank. Commercial banking is also known as business banking. It is a bank that provides checking accounts, savings accounts, and money market accounts and that accepts time deposits.

a. Bought deal
b. Lombard banking
c. Daylight overdraft
d. Commercial bank

28. The _____ was a worldwide economic downturn starting in most places in 1929 and ending at different times in the 1930s or early 1940s for different countries. It was the largest and most important economic depression in the 20th century, and is used in the 21st century as an example of how far the world's economy can fall. The _____ originated in the United States; historians most often use as a starting date the stock market crash on October 29, 1929, known as Black Tuesday.
   a. Wall Street Crash of 1929
   b. British Empire Economic Conference
   c. Great Depression
   d. Jarrow March

29. _____ is money declared by a government to be legal tender. The term derives from the Latin fiat, meaning 'let it be done'. _____ achieves value because a government accepts it in payment of taxes and says it can be used within the country as a 'tender' to pay all debts.
   a. Fiat money
   b. Devaluation
   c. World currency
   d. Currency board

30. _____ or financing is to provide capital (funds), which means money for a project, a person, a business or any other private or public institutions.

Those funds can be allocated for either short term or long term purposes. The health fund is a new way of _____ private healthcare centers.

   a. Customer retention
   b. Business transformation
   c. Funding
   d. No-bid contract

31. The _____ was the start of the Long Depression, a severe nationwide economic depression in the United States that lasted until 1879. It was precipitated by the bankruptcy of the Philadelphia banking firm Jay Cooke ' Company on September 18, 1873, following the crash on May 9, 1873 of the Vienna Stock Exchange in Austria (the so-called Gründerkrach or e;founders' crashe;.) It was one of a series of economic crises in the 19th and early 20th centuries.
   a. 130-30 fund
   b. 100-year flood
   c. 1921 recession
   d. Panic of 1873

32. The _____ was enacted in July 14, 1890 as a United States federal law. While not authorizing the free and unlimited coinage of silver that the Free Silver supporters wanted, it increased the amount of silver the government was required to purchase every month. The _____ had been passed in response to the growing complaints of farmers and mining interests.
   a. Sherman Silver Purchase Act
   b. Pure Food and Drug Act
   c. Security and Freedom Through Encryption Act
   d. 100-year flood

33. A _____ is a duty imposed on goods when they are moved across a political boundary. They are usually associated with protectionism, the economic policy of restraining trade between nations. For political reasons, _____s are usually imposed on imported goods, although they may also be imposed on exported goods.
   a. Tariff
   b. 1921 recession
   c. 100-year flood
   d. 130-30 fund

Chapter 19. Financial Developments (1863-1914)

34. In economics, a _____ is a general slowdown in economic activity over a sustained period of time, or a business cycle contraction. During _____s, many macroeconomic indicators vary in a similar way. Production as measured by Gross Domestic Product (GDP), employment, investment spending, capacity utilization, household incomes and business profits all fall during _____s.
   - a. Monetary economics
   - b. Leading indicators
   - c. Treasury View
   - d. Recession

35. _____s is the social science that studies the production, distribution, and consumption of goods and services. The term _____s comes from the Ancient Greek οἰκονομία from οἶκος (oikos, 'house') + νόμος (nomos, 'custom' or 'law'), hence 'rules of the house(hold)'. Current _____ models developed out of the broader field of political economy in the late 19th century, owing to a desire to use an empirical approach more akin to the physical sciences.
   - a. Inflation
   - b. Opportunity cost
   - c. Energy economics
   - d. Economic

36. A _____ is something for which there is demand, but which is supplied without qualitative differentiation across a market. It is a product that is the same no matter who produces it, such as petroleum, notebook paper, or milk. In other words, copper is copper.
   - a. Soft commodity
   - b. 100-year flood
   - c. Hard commodity
   - d. Commodity

37. A _____ refers to any type debt instrument, such as a loan, bond, mortgage that does not have a fixed rate of interest over the life of the instrument. Such debt typically uses an index or other base rate for establishing the interest rate for each relevant period. One of the most common rates to use as the basis for applying interest rates is the London Inter-bank Offered Rate, or LIBOR
   - a. Disposal tax effect
   - b. Money market
   - c. Moneylender
   - d. Floating interest rate

Chapter 20. The Giant Economy and Its International Relations

1. In economics, _____ refers to the ability of a person or a country to produce a particular good at a lower marginal cost and opportunity cost than another person or country. It is the ability to produce a product most efficiently given all the other products that could be produced. It can be contrasted with absolute advantage which refers to the ability of a person or a country to produce a particular good at a lower absolute cost than another.
   - a. Gravity model of trade
   - b. Hot money
   - c. Comparative advantage
   - d. Triffin dilemma

2. _____ or economic opportunity loss is the value of the next best alternative foregone as the result of making a decision. _____ analysis is an important part of a company's decision-making processes but is not treated as an actual cost in any financial statement. The next best thing that a person can engage in is referred to as the _____ of doing the best thing and ignoring the next best thing to be done.
   - a. Economic
   - b. Industrial organization
   - c. Economic ideology
   - d. Opportunity cost

3. In economics, the _____ measures the payments that flow between any individual country and all other countries. It is used to summarize all international economic transactions for that country during a specific time period, usually a year. The _____ is determined by the country's exports and imports of goods, services, and financial capital, as well as financial transfers.
   - a. Balance of payments
   - b. Skyscraper Index
   - c. Gross world product
   - d. Gross domestic product per barrel

4. A _____ is the transfer of wealth from one party (such as a person or company) to another. A _____ is usually made in exchange for the provision of goods, services or both, or to fulfill a legal obligation.

   The simplest and oldest form of _____ is barter, the exchange of one good or service for another.
   - a. Soft count
   - b. Going concern
   - c. Payment
   - d. Social gravity

5. The term '_____' refers to the concept of collecting information and attempting to spot a pattern in the information. In some fields of study, the term '_____' has more formally-defined meanings.

   In project management _____ is a mathematical technique that uses historical results to predict future outcome.
   - a. Trend analysis
   - b. Coefficient of determination
   - c. Quantile regression
   - d. Probit model

6. A variety of measures of national income and output are used in economics to estimate total economic activity in a country or region, including gross domestic product (GDP), _____ , and net national income (NNI.)

   There are three main ways of calculating these numbers; the output approach, the income approach and the expenditure approach. In theory, the three must yield the same, because total expenditures on goods and services must equal the total income paid to the producers (GNI), and that must also equal the total value of the output of goods and services (_____.)

Chapter 20. The Giant Economy and Its International Relations

a. Household final consumption expenditure
b. Purchasing power parity
c. Gross world product
d. Gross national product

7. In economics, the _____ of a good or of a service is the utility of the specific use to which an agent would put a given increase in that good or service, or of the specific use that would be abandoned in response to a given decrease. In other words, _____ is the utility of the marginal use -- which, on the assumption of economic rationality, would be the least urgent use of the good or service, from the best feasible combination of actions in which its use is included. Under the mainstream assumptions, the _____ of a good or service is the posited quantified change in utility obtained by increasing or by decreasing use of that good or service.

a. Marginal utility
b. 130-30 fund
c. 100-year flood
d. 1921 recession

8. In economics, _____ is a measure of the relative satisfaction from consumption of various goods and services. Given this measure, one may speak meaningfully of increasing or decreasing _____, and thereby explain economic behavior in terms of attempts to increase one's _____. For illustrative purposes, changes in _____ are sometimes expressed in units called utils.

a. Ordinal utility
b. Utility function
c. Utility
d. Expected utility hypothesis

9. A _____ is a duty imposed on goods when they are moved across a political boundary. They are usually associated with protectionism, the economic policy of restraining trade between nations. For political reasons, _____s are usually imposed on imported goods, although they may also be imposed on exported goods.

a. 100-year flood
b. 130-30 fund
c. 1921 recession
d. Tariff

10. The _____ is 'the basic residential unit in which economic production, consumption, inheritance, child rearing, and shelter are organized and carried out'; [the _____] 'may or may not be synonymous with family'.

The _____ is the basic unit of analysis in many social, microeconomic and government models. The term refers to all individuals who live in the same dwelling.

a. 130-30 fund
b. 100-year flood
c. Family economics
d. Household

11. _____ is the a method of technical and economic research of the systems for purpose to optimize a parity between system's consumer functions or properties and expenses to achieve those functions or properties.

This methodology for continuous perfection of production, industrial technologies, organizational structures was developed by Juryj Sobolev in 1948 at the 'Perm telephone factory'

- 1948 Juryj Sobolev - the first success in application of a method analysis at the 'Perm telephone factory' .
- 1949 - the first application for the invention as result of use of the new method.

Chapter 20. The Giant Economy and Its International Relations

Today in economically developed countries practically each enterprise or the company use methodology of the kind of functional-cost analysis as a practice of the quality management, most full satisfying to principles of standards of series ISO 9000.

- Interest of consumer not in products itself, but the advantage which it will receive from its usage.
- The consumer aspires to reduce his expenses
- Functions needed by consumer can be executed in the various ways, and, hence, with various efficiency and expenses. Among possible alternatives of realization of functions exist such in which the parity of quality and the price is the optimal for the consumer.

The goal of _____ is achievement of the highest consumer satisfaction of production at simultaneous decrease in all kinds of industrial expenses Classical _____ has three English synonyms - Value Engineering, Value Management, Value Analysis.

a. Willingness to pay
b. Monopoly wage
c. Staple financing
d. Function cost analysis

12. The _____ was a period in the late 18th and early 19th centuries when major changes in agriculture, manufacturing, mining, and transportation had a profound effect on the socioeconomic and cultural conditions in Britain. The changes subsequently spread throughout Europe, North America, and eventually the world. The onset of the _____ marked a major turning point in human society; almost every aspect of daily life was eventually influenced in some way.

a. Industrial Revolution
b. Adolf Hitler
c. Adam Smith
d. Adolph Fischer

13. _____ is the economic policy of restraining trade between states, through methods such as tariffs on imported goods, restrictive quotas, and a variety of other restrictive government regulations designed to discourage imports, and prevent foreign take-over of local markets and companies. This policy is closely aligned with anti-globalization, and contrasts with free trade, where government barriers to trade are kept to a minimum. The term is mostly used in the context of economics, where _____ refers to policies or doctrines which 'protect' businesses and workers within a country by restricting or regulating trade with foreign nations.

a. Protectionism
b. Google economy
c. Knowledge economy
d. Digital economy

14. The _____ was an act signed into law on June 17, 1930, that raised U.S. tariffs on over 20,000 imported goods to record levels. In the United States 1,028 economists signed a petition against this legislation, and after it was passed, many countries retaliated with their own increased tariffs on U.S. goods, and American exports and imports were reduced by more than half.

Although rated capacity had increased tremendously, actual output, income, and expenditure had not.

a. Judgment summons
b. Patent Law Treaty
c. Loss of use
d. Smoot-Hawley Tariff Act

Chapter 20. The Giant Economy and Its International Relations

15. _____s is the social science that studies the production, distribution, and consumption of goods and services. The term _____s comes from the Ancient Greek oá¼°κονομῖα from oá¼¶κος (oikos, 'house') + vΐŒμος (nomos, 'custom' or 'law'), hence 'rules of the house(hold)'. Current _____ models developed out of the broader field of political economy in the late 19th century, owing to a desire to use an empirical approach more akin to the physical sciences.
    a. Energy economics
    b. Inflation
    c. Economic
    d. Opportunity cost

16. The _____ is the central bank of the United Kingdom and is the model on which most modern, large central banks have been based. Since 1946 it has been a state-owned institution. It was established in 1694 to act as the English Government's banker, and to this day it still acts as the banker for the UK Government.
    a. Bank of England
    b. 1921 recession
    c. 130-30 fund
    d. 100-year flood

17. In economics, _____ is a monetary standard in which the value of the monetary unit is defined as equivalent either to a certain quantity of gold or to a certain quantity of silver. Such a system effectively establishes a fixed rate of exchange for the two metals. The merits of the system were the subject of debate in the late 19th century.
    a. 1921 recession
    b. Bimetallism
    c. 100-year flood
    d. 130-30 fund

18. In finance, the _____s between two currencies specifies how much one currency is worth in terms of the other. It is the value of a foreign natione;s currency in terms of the home natione;s currency. For example an _____ of 102 Japanese yen to the United States dollar means that JPY 102 is worth the same as USD 1.
    a. ACEA agreement
    b. ACCRA Cost of Living Index
    c. Interbank market
    d. Exchange rate

19. A _____, sometimes called a pegged exchange rate, is a type of exchange rate regime wherein a currency's value is matched to the value of another single currency or to a basket of other currencies such as gold.

    A _____ is usually used to stabilize the value of a currency, vis-a-vis the currency it is pegged to. This facilitates trade and investments between the two countries, and is especially useful for small economies where external trade forms a large part of their GDP.

    a. Leading indicators
    b. Fixed exchange rate
    c. Monetary economics
    d. Law of supply

20. The _____ was a worldwide economic downturn starting in most places in 1929 and ending at different times in the 1930s or early 1940s for different countries. It was the largest and most important economic depression in the 20th century, and is used in the 21st century as an example of how far the world's economy can fall. The _____ originated in the United States; historians most often use as a starting date the stock market crash on October 29, 1929, known as Black Tuesday.
    a. Great Depression
    b. Jarrow March
    c. British Empire Economic Conference
    d. Wall Street Crash of 1929

Chapter 20. The Giant Economy and Its International Relations

21. The _____ is a monetary system in which a region's common medium of exchange are paper notes that are normally freely convertible into pre-set, fixed quantities of gold. The _____ is not currently used by any government, having been replaced completely by fiat currency. Gold certificates were used as paper currency in the United States from 1882 to 1933, these certificates were freely convertable into gold coins.

In the 1790s Britain suffered a massive shortage of silver coinage and ceased to mint larger silver coins.

- a. 130-30 fund
- b. 100-year flood
- c. 1921 recession
- d. Gold standard

22. In economics, _____ is a sustained decrease in the general price level of goods and services. _____ occurs when the annual inflation rate falls below zero percent, resulting in an increase in the real value of money -- a negative inflation rate. This should not be confused with disinflation, a slow-down in the inflation rate (i.e. when the inflation decreases, but still remains positive.)

- a. Tobit model
- b. Literacy rate
- c. Price revolution
- d. Deflation

23. The _____ is an international financial institution that provides financial and technical assistance to developing countries for development programs (e.g. bridges, roads, schools, etc.) with the stated goal of reducing poverty.

The _____ differs from the _____ Group, in that the _____ comprises only two institutions:

- International Bank for Reconstruction and Development (IBRD)
- International Development Association (IDA)

Whereas the latter incorporates these two in addition to three more:

- International Finance Corporation (IFC)
- Multilateral Investment Guarantee Agency (MIGA)
- International Centre for Settlement of Investment Disputes (ICSID)

John Maynard Keynes (right) represented the UK at the conference, and Harry Dexter White represented the US.

The _____ is one of two major financial institutions created as a result of the Bretton Woods Conference in 1944. The International Monetary Fund, a related but separate institution, is the second.

- a. World Bank
- b. Flow to Equity-Approach
- c. Financial costs of the 2003 Iraq War
- d. Bank-State-Branch

24. _____ in its literal sense is the process of transformation of local or regional phenomena into global ones. It can be described as a process by which the people of the world are unified into a single society and function together.

This process is a combination of economic, technological, sociocultural and political forces.

Chapter 20. The Giant Economy and Its International Relations 103

a. Helsinki Process on Globalisation and Democracy
b. Globalization
c. Globally Integrated Enterprise
d. Global Cosmopolitanism

25. A _____ refers to any type debt instrument, such as a loan, bond, mortgage that does not have a fixed rate of interest over the life of the instrument. Such debt typically uses an index or other base rate for establishing the interest rate for each relevant period. One of the most common rates to use as the basis for applying interest rates is the London Inter-bank Offered Rate, or LIBOR
   a. Disposal tax effect
   b. Floating interest rate
   c. Money market
   d. Moneylender

26. _____ is a broad label that refers to any individuals or households that use goods and services generated within the economy. The concept of a _____ is used in different contexts, so that the usage and significance of the term may vary.

Typically when business people and economists talk of _____s they are talking about person as _____, an aggregated commodity item with little individuality other than that expressed in the buy/not-buy decision.

   a. 100-year flood
   b. 1921 recession
   c. Consumer
   d. 130-30 fund

27. _____ is an equity (stock) exchange located at 11 Wall Street in lower Manhattan, New York, USA. It is the largest stock exchange in the world by dollar value of its listed companies' securities. As of October 2008, the combined capitalization of all domestic _____ listed companies was US$10.1 trillion.
   a. 130-30 fund
   b. 100-year flood
   c. New York Stock Exchange
   d. 1921 recession

28. A _____ is a corporation or mutual organization which provides trading facilities for stock brokers and traders, to trade stocks and other securities. It may be a physical trading room where the traders gather, or a formalised communications network. Creation of a _____ is a strategy of economic development.
   a. SEAQ
   b. Primary shares
   c. Stock Exchange
   d. 100-year flood

29. A _____ is a public market for the trading of company stock and derivatives at an agreed price; these are securities listed on a stock exchange as well as those only traded privately.

The size of the world _____ was estimated at about $36.6 trillion US at the beginning of October 2008. The total world derivatives market has been estimated at about $791 trillion face or nominal value, 11 times the size of the entire world economy.

   a. Adam Smith
   b. Stock market
   c. Adolph Fischer
   d. Adolf Hitler

30. _____ are the prices that the factors of production of a finished item attract.

There has been some economic debate as to what determines these prices. Classical and Marxist economists argued that the _____ decided the value of a product and so value was intrinsic within the product.

a. Marginal product
c. Productivity model

b. Marginal product of labor
d. Factor prices

31. _____ is an economic theory, which states that the relative prices for two identical factors of production in the same market will eventually equal each other because of competition. The price for each single factor need not become equal, but relative factors will. Whichever factor receives the lowest price before two countries integrate economically and effectively become one market will therefore tend to become more expensive relative to other factors in the economy, while those with the highest price will tend to become cheaper.

a. Factor price equalization
c. Premium pricing

b. Big ticket item
d. Price book

32. _____ in economics and business is the result of an exchange and from that trade we assign a numerical monetary value to a good, service or asset. If Alice trades Bob 4 apples for an orange, the _____ of an orange is 4 apples. Inversely, the _____ of an apple is 1/4 oranges.

a. Price war
c. Premium pricing

b. Price book
d. Price

Chapter 21. Labor and the Law

1. In economics, the people in the _____ are the suppliers of labor. The _____ is all the nonmilitary people who are employed or unemployed. In 2005, the worldwide _____ was over 3 billion people.
   a. Grenelle agreements
   b. Departmentalization
   c. Distributed workforce
   d. Labor force

2. Competition law, known in the United States as _____ law, has three main elements:

   - prohibiting agreements or practices that restrict free trading and competition between business entities. This includes in particular the repression of cartels.
   - banning abusive behaviour by a firm dominating a market, or anti-competitive practices that tend to lead to such a dominant position. Practices controlled in this way may include predatory pricing, tying, price gouging, refusal to deal, and many others.
   - supervising the mergers and acquisitions of large corporations, including some joint ventures. Transactions that are considered to threaten the competitive process can be prohibited altogether, or approved subject to 'remedies' such as an obligation to divest part of the merged business or to offer licences or access to facilities to enable other businesses to continue competing.

   The substance and practice of competition law varies from jurisdiction to jurisdiction. Protecting the interests of consumers (consumer welfare) and ensuring that entrepreneurs have an opportunity to compete in the market economy are often treated as important objectives. Competition law is closely connected with law on deregulation of access to markets, state aids and subsidies, the privatisation of state owned assets and the establishment of independent sector regulators. In recent decades, competition law has been viewed as a way to provide better public services.

   a. United Kingdom competition law
   b. Anti-Inflation Act
   c. Intellectual property law
   d. Antitrust

3. The _____ was a landmark piece of legislation in the United States that outlawed racial segregation in schools, public places, and employment.
   a. Le Chapelier Law
   b. Civil Rights Act of 1964
   c. Patent portfolio
   d. Postcautionary principle

4. The _____ of 1938 (_____, ch. 676, 52 Stat. 1060, June 25, 1938, 29 U.S.C.ch.8), also called the Wages and Hours Bill, is United States federal law that applies to employees engaged in interstate commerce or employed by an enterprise engaged in commerce or in the production of goods for commerce, unless the employer can claim an exemption from coverage.
   a. Generalized System of Preferences
   b. Hostile work environment
   c. Habitability
   d. Fair Labor Standards Act

5. A trade union or _____ is an organization of workers who have banded together to achieve common goals in key areas and working conditions. The trade union, through its leadership, bargains with the employer on behalf of union members (rank and file members) and negotiates labor contracts (Collective bargaining) with employers. This may include the negotiation of wages, work rules, complaint procedures, rules governing hiring, firing and promotion of workers, benefits, workplace safety and policies.
   a. Demand-side technologies
   b. Labor union
   c. Basis of futures
   d. Business valuation standards

Chapter 21. Labor and the Law

6. _____ is a cross-disciplinary area concerned with protecting the safety, health and welfare of people engaged in work or employment. As a secondary effect, it may also protect co-workers, family members, employers, customers, suppliers, nearby communities, and other members of the public who are impacted by the workplace environment. It may involve interactions among many subject areas, including occupational medicine, occupational (or industrial) hygiene, public health, safety engineering, chemistry, health physics, ergonomics, toxicology, epidemiology, environmental health, industrial relations, public policy, sociology, and occupational health psychology.

   a. ACCRA Cost of Living Index
   b. ACEA agreement
   c. AD-IA Model
   d. Occupational Safety and Health

7. The _____ is the primary federal law which governs occupational health and safety in the private sector and federal government in the United States. It was enacted by Congress in 1970 and was signed by President Richard Nixon on December 29, 1970. Its main goal is to ensure that employers provide employees with an environment free from recognized hazards, such as exposure to toxic chemicals, excessive noise levels, mechanical dangers, heat or cold stress, or unsanitary conditions.

   a. Irish competition law
   b. Escalator clause
   c. Electronic Commerce Protection Act
   d. Occupational Safety and Health Act

8. _____, known in the United States as antitrust law, has three main elements:

   - prohibiting agreements or practices that restrict free trading and competition between business entities. This includes in particular the repression of cartels.
   - banning abusive behaviour by a firm dominating a market, or anti-competitive practices that tend to lead to such a dominant position. Practices controlled in this way may include predatory pricing, tying, price gouging, refusal to deal, and many others.
   - supervising the mergers and acquisitions of large corporations, including some joint ventures. Transactions that are considered to threaten the competitive process can be prohibited altogether, or approved subject to 'remedies' such as an obligation to divest part of the merged business or to offer licences or access to facilities to enable other businesses to continue competing.

   The substance and practice of _____ varies from jurisdiction to jurisdiction. Protecting the interests of consumers (consumer welfare) and ensuring that entrepreneurs have an opportunity to compete in the market economy are often treated as important objectives. _____ is closely connected with law on deregulation of access to markets, state aids and subsidies, the privatisation of state owned assets and the establishment of independent sector regulators. In recent decades, _____ has been viewed as a way to provide better public services.

   a. Hostile work environment
   b. Due diligence
   c. Fee simple
   d. Competition law

9. A _____ or labor union is an organization of workers who have banded together to achieve common goals in key areas and working conditions. The _____, through its leadership, bargains with the employer on behalf of union members (rank and file members) and negotiates labor contracts (Collective bargaining) with employers. This may include the negotiation of wages, work rules, complaint procedures, rules governing hiring, firing and promotion of workers, benefits, workplace safety and policies.

Chapter 21. Labor and the Law

a. Guaranteed investment contracts
b. Trade union
c. Consumer goods
d. Case-Shiller Home Price Indices

10. A _____ is the exclusive authority to determine how a resource is used, whether that resource is owned by government or by individuals. All economic goods have a _____s attribute. This attribute has three broad components

1. The right to use the good
2. The right to earn income from the good
3. The right to transfer the good to others

The concept of _____s as used by economists and legal scholars are related but distinct. The distinction is largely seen in the economists' focus on the ability of an individual or collective to control the use of the good.

a. Holder in due course
b. Property right
c. High-reeve
d. Post-sale restraint

11. The _____ proposed by John L. Lewis in 1932, was a federation of unions that organized workers in industrial unions in the United States and Canada from 1935 to 1955. The Taft-Hartley Act of 1947 required union leaders to swear that they were not Communists. Many CIO leaders refused to obey that requirement, later found unconstitutional.

a. Chinese correction
b. Foreign direct investment
c. Multinational corporation
d. Congress of Industrial Organizations

12. Economic _____ is defined as an excess distribution to any factor in a production process above that which is required to induce the factor into the process or any excess above that which is necessary to keep the factor in its current use..

Classical Factor _____ is primarily concerned with the fee paid for the use of fixed (e.g. natural) resources. The classical definition is expressed as any excess payment above that required to induce or provide for production.

a. 130-30 fund
b. 100-year flood
c. 1921 recession
d. Rent

13. The _____ was one of the first federations of labor unions in the United States. It was founded in Columbus, Ohio in 1886 by Samuel Gompers as a reorganization of its predecessor, the Federation of Organized Trades and Labor Unions. Gompers became president of the AFL in 1886 and was reelected every year except one until his death on December 13, 1924.

a. ACCRA Cost of Living Index
b. AD-IA Model
c. American Federation of Labor
d. ACEA agreement

14. _____ is a field of economics that studies the strategic behavior of firms, the structure of markets and their interactions. The study of _____ adds to the perfectly competitive model real-world frictions such as limited information, transaction cost, cost of adjusting prices, government actions, and barriers to entry by new firms into a market. It then considers how firms are organized and how they compete.

a. Economic
b. Inflation
c. Economic ideology
d. Industrial Organization

15. An _____ is an equitable remedy in the form of a court order, whereby a party is required to do certain acts. The party that fails to adhere to the _____ faces civil or criminal penalties and may have to pay damages or accept sanctions for failing to follow the court's order. In some cases, breaches of _____s are considered serious criminal offences that merit arrest and possible prison sentences.

a. ACEA agreement
b. Injunction
c. AD-IA Model
d. ACCRA Cost of Living Index

16.

The _____ was the first United States Federal statute to limit cartels and monopolies. It falls under antitrust law.

The Act provides: 'Every contract, combination in the form of trust or otherwise, or conspiracy, in restraint of trade or commerce among the several States, or with foreign nations, is declared to be illegal'. The Act also provides: 'Every person who shall monopolize, or attempt to monopolize, or combine or conspire with any other person or persons, to monopolize any part of the trade or commerce among the several States, or with foreign nations, shall be deemed guilty of a felony [. . .]' The Act put responsibility upon government attorneys and district courts to pursue and investigate trusts, companies and organizations suspected of violating the Act. The Clayton Act extended the right to sue under the antitrust laws to 'any person who shall be injured in his business or property by reason of anything forbidden in the antitrust laws.' Under the Clayton Act, private parties may sue in U.S. district court and should they prevail, they may be awarded treble damages and the cost of suit, including reasonable attorney's fees.

a. 100-year flood
b. 130-30 fund
c. 1921 recession
d. Sherman Antitrust Act

Chapter 22. The Command Economy Emerges: World War I

1. _____ the Great War, and the War to End All Wars, was a global military conflict which involved the majority of the world's great powers, organized into two opposing military alliances: the Entente Powers and the Central Powers. Over 70 million military personnel were mobilized in one of the largest wars in history. In a state of total war, the major combatants fully placed their scientific and industrial capabilities at the service of the war effort.
   a. 130-30 fund
   b. World War I
   c. 1921 recession
   d. 100-year flood

2. A _____ or directed economy is an economic system in which the government or workers' councils manages the economy. It is an economic system in which the central government makes all decisions on the production and consumption of goods and services. Its most extensive form is referred to as a _____, centrally planned economy, or command and control economy.
   a. Transition economy
   b. Subsistence economy
   c. Command economy
   d. Nutritional Economics

3. A _____ refers to any type debt instrument, such as a loan, bond, mortgage that does not have a fixed rate of interest over the life of the instrument. Such debt typically uses an index or other base rate for establishing the interest rate for each relevant period. One of the most common rates to use as the basis for applying interest rates is the London Inter-bank Offered Rate, or LIBOR
   a. Money market
   b. Floating interest rate
   c. Disposal tax effect
   d. Moneylender

4. The _____ was a worldwide economic downturn starting in most places in 1929 and ending at different times in the 1930s or early 1940s for different countries. It was the largest and most important economic depression in the 20th century, and is used in the 21st century as an example of how far the world's economy can fall. The _____ originated in the United States; historians most often use as a starting date the stock market crash on October 29, 1929, known as Black Tuesday.
   a. Jarrow March
   b. Wall Street Crash of 1929
   c. British Empire Economic Conference
   d. Great Depression

5. An _____ is a tax levied on the financial income of people, corporations, or other legal entities. Various _____ systems exist, with varying degrees of tax incidence. Income taxation can be progressive, proportional, or regressive.
   a. Income tax
   b. ACCRA Cost of Living Index
   c. ACEA agreement
   d. AD-IA Model

6. Competition law, known in the United States as _____ law, has three main elements:

   - prohibiting agreements or practices that restrict free trading and competition between business entities. This includes in particular the repression of cartels.
   - banning abusive behaviour by a firm dominating a market, or anti-competitive practices that tend to lead to such a dominant position. Practices controlled in this way may include predatory pricing, tying, price gouging, refusal to deal, and many others.
   - supervising the mergers and acquisitions of large corporations, including some joint ventures. Transactions that are considered to threaten the competitive process can be prohibited altogether, or approved subject to 'remedies' such as an obligation to divest part of the merged business or to offer licences or access to facilities to enable other businesses to continue competing.

The substance and practice of competition law varies from jurisdiction to jurisdiction. Protecting the interests of consumers (consumer welfare) and ensuring that entrepreneurs have an opportunity to compete in the market economy are often treated as important objectives. Competition law is closely connected with law on deregulation of access to markets, state aids and subsidies, the privatisation of state owned assets and the establishment of independent sector regulators. In recent decades, competition law has been viewed as a way to provide better public services.

a. Anti-Inflation Act
b. United Kingdom competition law
c. Intellectual property law
d. Antitrust

7. To _____ is to impose a financial charge or other levy upon a taxpayer by a state or the functional equivalent of a state.

_____es are also imposed by many subnational entities. _____es consist of direct _____ or indirect _____, and may be paid in money or as its labour equivalent (often but not always unpaid.)

a. 100-year flood
b. 1921 recession
c. 130-30 fund
d. Tax

8. In economics, the people in the _____ are the suppliers of labor. The _____ is all the nonmilitary people who are employed or unemployed. In 2005, the worldwide _____ was over 3 billion people.

a. Departmentalization
b. Grenelle agreements
c. Labor force
d. Distributed workforce

9. _____ involves the 'matching' of lenders with savings to borrowers who need money by an agent or third party, such as a bank.

If this matching is successful, the lender obtains a positive rate of return, the borrower receives a return for risk taking and entrepeneurship and the banker receives a marginal return for making the successful match. If the borrower's speculative play with the depositor's funds does not pay off, the depositor can lose the savings borrowed by the borrower and the bank can face significant losses on its loan portfolio.

a. Origination fee
b. Annual percentage rate
c. Arranger
d. Intermediation

10. In economics, _____ is a rise in the general level of prices of goods and services in an economy over a period of time. When the general price level rises, each unit of currency buys fewer goods and services; consequently, _____ is also a decline in the real value of money--a loss of purchasing power in the medium of exchange which is also the monetary unit of account in the economy. A chief measure of general price-level _____ is the general _____ rate, which is the percentage change in a general price index (normally the Consumer Price Index) over time.

a. Economic
b. Inflation
c. Energy economics
d. Opportunity cost

11. A _____ is a customs union with common policies on product regulation, and freedom of movement of the factors of production (capital and labour) and of enterprise. The goal is that the movement of capital, labour, goods, and services between the members is as easy as within them. This is the fourth stage of economic integration.
   a. Mutual recognition agreement
   b. Common market
   c. Grey market
   d. Competitiveness

12. The _____ consists of a number of economic theories which describe the nature of the firm, company including its existence, its behaviour, and its relationship with the market.

In simplified terms, the _____ aims to answer these questions:

1. Existence - why do firms emerge, why are not all transactions in the economy mediated over the market?
2. Boundaries - why the boundary between firms and the market is located exactly there? Which transactions are performed internally and which are negotiated on the market?
3. Organization - why are firms structured in such specific way? What is the interplay of formal and informal relationships?

Despite looking simple, these questions are not answered by the established economic theory, which usually views firms as given, and treats them as black boxes without any internal structure.

The First World War period saw a change of emphasis in economic theory away from industry-level analysis which mainly included analysing markets to analysis at the level of the firm, as it became increasingly clear that perfect competition was no longer an adequate model of how firms behaved. Economic theory till then had focussed on trying to understand markets alone and there had been little study on understanding why firms or organisations exist.

   a. Theory of the firm
   b. Policy Ineffectiveness Proposition
   c. Technology gap
   d. Khazzoom-Brookes postulate

13. A trade union or _____ is an organization of workers who have banded together to achieve common goals in key areas and working conditions. The trade union, through its leadership, bargains with the employer on behalf of union members (rank and file members) and negotiates labor contracts (Collective bargaining) with employers. This may include the negotiation of wages, work rules, complaint procedures, rules governing hiring, firing and promotion of workers, benefits, workplace safety and policies.
   a. Demand-side technologies
   b. Business valuation standards
   c. Labor union
   d. Basis of futures

14. _____, known in the United States as antitrust law, has three main elements:

- prohibiting agreements or practices that restrict free trading and competition between business entities. This includes in particular the repression of cartels.
- banning abusive behaviour by a firm dominating a market, or anti-competitive practices that tend to lead to such a dominant position. Practices controlled in this way may include predatory pricing, tying, price gouging, refusal to deal, and many others.
- supervising the mergers and acquisitions of large corporations, including some joint ventures. Transactions that are considered to threaten the competitive process can be prohibited altogether, or approved subject to 'remedies' such as an obligation to divest part of the merged business or to offer licences or access to facilities to enable other businesses to continue competing.

The substance and practice of _____ varies from jurisdiction to jurisdiction. Protecting the interests of consumers (consumer welfare) and ensuring that entrepreneurs have an opportunity to compete in the market economy are often treated as important objectives. _____ is closely connected with law on deregulation of access to markets, state aids and subsidies, the privatisation of state owned assets and the establishment of independent sector regulators. In recent decades, _____ has been viewed as a way to provide better public services.

a. Hostile work environment
b. Competition law
c. Due diligence
d. Fee simple

15. A _____ or labor union is an organization of workers who have banded together to achieve common goals in key areas and working conditions. The _____, through its leadership, bargains with the employer on behalf of union members (rank and file members) and negotiates labor contracts (Collective bargaining) with employers. This may include the negotiation of wages, work rules, complaint procedures, rules governing hiring, firing and promotion of workers, benefits, workplace safety and policies.

a. Guaranteed investment contracts
b. Case-Shiller Home Price Indices
c. Consumer goods
d. Trade union

16. _____ refers to the employment of children at regular and sustained labour. This practice is considered exploitative by many international organizations and is illegal in many countries. _____ was utilized to varying extents through most of history, but entered public dispute with the beginning of universal schooling, with changes in working conditions during industrialization, and with the emergence of the concepts of workers' and children's rights.

a. National Action Plan on the Elimination of Child Labour
b. Child labour
c. Global march against child labor
d. Debt bondage

17. A _____ is something for which there is demand, but which is supplied without qualitative differentiation across a market. It is a product that is the same no matter who produces it, such as petroleum, notebook paper, or milk. In other words, copper is copper.

a. Commodity
b. Soft commodity
c. Hard commodity
d. 100-year flood

18. The field of _____ looks at the relationship between management and workers, particularly groups of workers represented by a union.

Labor relations is an important factor in analyzing 'varieties of capitalism', such as neocorporatism, social democracy, and neoliberalism

Labor relations can take place on many levels, such as the 'shop-floor', the regional level, and the national level.

a. ACEA agreement
b. ACCRA Cost of Living Index
c. Industrial Relations
d. AD-IA Model

Chapter 23. Normalcy (1919-1929)

1. In economics, a _____ or a hard good is a good which does not quickly wear out it yields services or utility over time rather than being completely used up when used once. Most goods are therefore _____s to a certain degree. These are goods that can last for a relatively long time, such as refrigerators, cars, and DVD players.
   - a. Superior goods
   - b. Luxury good
   - c. Search good
   - d. Durable good

2. The _____ or gross domestic income (GDI), a basic measure of an economy's economic performance, is the market value of all final goods and services produced within the borders of a nation in a year. _____ can be defined in three ways, all of which are conceptually identical. First, it is equal to the total expenditures for all final goods and services produced within the country in a stipulated period of time (usually a 365-day year.)
   - a. Monopolistic competition
   - b. Market structure
   - c. Gross domestic product
   - d. Countercyclical

3. In economics, _____ is how a natione;s total economy is distributed among its population. . _____ has always been a central concern of economic theory and economic policy. Classical economists such as Adam Smith, Thomas Malthus and David Ricardo were mainly concerned with factor _____, that is, the distribution of income between the main factors of production, land, labour and capital.
   - a. Eco commerce
   - b. Income distribution
   - c. Authorised capital
   - d. Equipment trust certificate

4. A _____ is an object whose consumption increases the utility of the consumer, for which the quantity demanded exceeds the quantity supplied at zero price. _____s are usually modeled as having diminishing marginal utility. The first individual purchase has high utility; the second has less.
   - a. Pie method
   - b. Composite good
   - c. Good
   - d. Merit good

5. A _____ or labor union is an organization of workers who have banded together to achieve common goals in key areas and working conditions. The _____, through its leadership, bargains with the employer on behalf of union members (rank and file members) and negotiates labor contracts (Collective bargaining) with employers. This may include the negotiation of wages, work rules, complaint procedures, rules governing hiring, firing and promotion of workers, benefits, workplace safety and policies.
   - a. Consumer goods
   - b. Case-Shiller Home Price Indices
   - c. Guaranteed investment contracts
   - d. Trade union

6. _____ is a broad label that refers to any individuals or households that use goods and services generated within the economy. The concept of a _____ is used in different contexts, so that the usage and significance of the term may vary.

   Typically when business people and economists talk of _____s they are talking about person as _____, an aggregated commodity item with little individuality other than that expressed in the buy/not-buy decision.
   - a. 130-30 fund
   - b. 100-year flood
   - c. 1921 recession
   - d. Consumer

Chapter 23. Normalcy (1919-1929)

7. A _____ refers to any type debt instrument, such as a loan, bond, mortgage that does not have a fixed rate of interest over the life of the instrument. Such debt typically uses an index or other base rate for establishing the interest rate for each relevant period. One of the most common rates to use as the basis for applying interest rates is the London Inter-bank Offered Rate, or LIBOR
   a. Money market
   b. Disposal tax effect
   c. Moneylender
   d. Floating interest rate

8. The _____ is the central banking system of the United States. Created in 1913 by the enactment of the Federal Reserve Act (signed by Woodrow Wilson), it is a quasi-public and quasi-private (government entity with private components) banking system that comprises (1) the presidentially appointed Board of Governors of the _____ in Washington, D.C.; (2) the Federal Open Market Committee; (3) twelve regional Federal Reserve Banks located in major cities throughout the nation acting as fiscal agents for the U.S. Treasury, each with its own nine-member board of directors; (4) numerous other private U.S. member banks, which subscribe to required amounts of non-transferable stock in their regional Federal Reserve Banks; and (5) various advisory councils. Since February 2006, Ben Bernanke has served as the Chairman of the Board of Governors of the _____.
   a. Federal Reserve System Open Market Account
   b. Term auction facility
   c. Monetary Policy Report to the Congress
   d. Federal Reserve System

9. _____ in economics and business is the result of an exchange and from that trade we assign a numerical monetary value to a good, service or asset. If Alice trades Bob 4 apples for an orange, the _____ of an orange is 4 apples. Inversely, the _____ of an apple is 1/4 oranges.
   a. Price
   b. Price book
   c. Price war
   d. Premium pricing

10. The _____ was a worldwide economic downturn starting in most places in 1929 and ending at different times in the 1930s or early 1940s for different countries. It was the largest and most important economic depression in the 20th century, and is used in the 21st century as an example of how far the world's economy can fall. The _____ originated in the United States; historians most often use as a starting date the stock market crash on October 29, 1929, known as Black Tuesday.
    a. Jarrow March
    b. British Empire Economic Conference
    c. Wall Street Crash of 1929
    d. Great Depression

11. A variety of measures of national income and output are used in economics to estimate total economic activity in a country or region, including gross domestic product (GDP), _____ , and net national income (NNI.)

There are three main ways of calculating these numbers; the output approach, the income approach and the expenditure approach. In theory, the three must yield the same, because total expenditures on goods and services must equal the total income paid to the producers (GNI), and that must also equal the total value of the output of goods and services (_____.)

   a. Gross world product
   b. Purchasing power parity
   c. Gross national product
   d. Household final consumption expenditure

12. In economics, _____ is a sustained decrease in the general price level of goods and services. _____ occurs when the annual inflation rate falls below zero percent, resulting in an increase in the real value of money -- a negative inflation rate. This should not be confused with disinflation, a slow-down in the inflation rate (i.e. when the inflation decreases, but still remains positive.)

    a. Price revolution
    b. Literacy rate
    c. Tobit model
    d. Deflation

13. The _____ of the United States (Ex-Im Bank) is the official export credit agency of the United States federal government. It was established in 1934 by an executive order, and made an independent agency in the Executive branch by Congress in 1945, for the purposes of financing and insuring foreign purchases of United States goods for customers unable or unwilling to accept credit risk. The mission of the Bank is to create and sustain U.S. jobs by financing sales of U.S. exports to international buyers.

    a. ACCRA Cost of Living Index
    b. Export-Import Bank
    c. AD-IA Model
    d. ACEA agreement

14. The _____ was actually created in 1929, before the stock market crash on Black Tuesday, 1929, but its powers were later enlarged to meet the economic crisis farmers faced during the Great Depression. It was established by the Agricultural Marketing Act to stabilize prices and to promote the sale of agricultural products. The board would help farmers stabilize prices by holding surplus grain and cotton in storage.

    a. Great Depression in the United Kingdom
    b. Great Depression
    c. Great Contraction
    d. Federal Farm Board

15. The term _____ refers to government debt, expenditures and revenues, or to finance (particularly financial revenue) in general.

- _____ deficit is the budget deficit of federal or local government
- _____ policy is the discretionary spending of governments. Contrasts with monetary policy.
- _____ year and _____ quarter are reporting periods for firms and other agencies.

    a. Drawdown
    b. Fiscal
    c. Procter ' Gamble
    d. Bucket shop

16. In economics, _____ is the use of government spending and revenue collection to influence the economy.

_____ can be contrasted with the other main type of economic policy, monetary policy, which attempts to stabilize the economy by controlling interest rates and the supply of money. The two main instruments of _____ are government spending and taxation.

    a. Fiscalism
    b. Sustainable investment rule
    c. 100-year flood
    d. Fiscal policy

17. _____ the Great War, and the War to End All Wars, was a global military conflict which involved the majority of the world's great powers, organized into two opposing military alliances: the Entente Powers and the Central Powers. Over 70 million military personnel were mobilized in one of the largest wars in history. In a state of total war, the major combatants fully placed their scientific and industrial capabilities at the service of the war effort.
    a. World War I
    b. 1921 recession
    c. 100-year flood
    d. 130-30 fund

18. _____ involves the 'matching' of lenders with savings to borrowers who need money by an agent or third party, such as a bank.

If this matching is successful, the lender obtains a positive rate of return, the borrower receives a return for risk taking and entrepeneurship and the banker receives a marginal return for making the successful match. If the borrower's speculative play with the depositor's funds does not pay off, the depositor can lose the savings borrowed by the borrower and the bank can face significant losses on its loan portfolio.

    a. Intermediation
    b. Annual percentage rate
    c. Arranger
    d. Origination fee

19. In finance, a _____ is a debt security, in which the authorized issuer owes the holders a debt and, depending on the terms of the _____, is obliged to pay interest (the coupon) and/or to repay the principal at a later date, termed maturity. A _____ is a formal contract to repay borrowed money with interest at fixed intervals.

Thus a _____ is like a loan: the issuer is the borrower (debtor), the holder is the lender (creditor), and the coupon is the interest.

    a. Prize Bond
    b. Zero-coupon
    c. Callable
    d. Bond

20. A _____ is a customs union with common policies on product regulation, and freedom of movement of the factors of production (capital and labour) and of enterprise. The goal is that the movement of capital, labour, goods, and services between the members is as easy as within them. This is the fourth stage of economic integration.
    a. Competitiveness
    b. Mutual recognition agreement
    c. Grey market
    d. Common market

21. In economics, a _____ is a general slowdown in economic activity over a sustained period of time, or a business cycle contraction. During _____s, many macroeconomic indicators vary in a similar way. Production as measured by Gross Domestic Product (GDP), employment, investment spending, capacity utilization, household incomes and business profits all fall during _____s.
    a. Monetary economics
    b. Leading indicators
    c. Treasury View
    d. Recession

22. A _____ is a public market for the trading of company stock and derivatives at an agreed price; these are securities listed on a stock exchange as well as those only traded privately.

The size of the world _____ was estimated at about $36.6 trillion US at the beginning of October 2008 . The total world derivatives market has been estimated at about $791 trillion face or nominal value, 11 times the size of the entire world economy.

a. Stock market
b. Adam Smith
c. Adolph Fischer
d. Adolf Hitler

23. A _____ is a sudden dramatic decline of stock prices across a significant cross-section of a stock market. Crashes are driven by panic as much as by underlying economic factors. They often follow speculative stock market bubbles.

a. 1921 recession
b. 130-30 fund
c. 100-year flood
d. Stock market crash

24. The _____ is the central bank of the United Kingdom and is the model on which most modern, large central banks have been based. Since 1946 it has been a state-owned institution. It was established in 1694 to act as the English Government's banker, and to this day it still acts as the banker for the UK Government.

a. 100-year flood
b. 130-30 fund
c. Bank of England
d. 1921 recession

25. _____ was a predominant American integrated oil producing, transporting, refining, and marketing company. Established in 1870 as an Ohio Corporation, it was the largest oil refiner in the world and operated as a major company trust and was one of the world's first and largest multinational corporations until it was broken up by the United States Supreme Court in 1911. John D. Rockefeller was a founder, chairman and major shareholder, and the company made him a billionaire and eventually the richest man in history.

a. 1921 recession
b. Standard Oil
c. 130-30 fund
d. 100-year flood

26. A _____ is a form of collective investment found mostly in the United Kingdom. _____s are closed-end funds and are constituted as public limited companies.

Investors' money is pooled together from the sale of a fixed number of shares a trust issues when it launches.

a. Enterprise Investment Scheme
b. Investment trust
c. Index fund
d. Insurance broker

Chapter 24. The Great Depression

1. _____ is an economic system in which wealth, and the means of producing wealth, are privately owned. Through _____, the land, labor, and capital are owned, operated, and traded for the purpose of generating profits, without force or fraud, by private individuals either singly or jointly, and investments, distribution, income, production, pricing and supply of goods, commodities and services are determined by voluntary private decision in a market economy. A distinguishing feature of _____ is that each person owns his or her own labor and therefore is allowed to sell the use of it to employers.

   a. Late capitalism
   b. Creative capitalism
   c. Socialism for the rich and capitalism for the poor
   d. Capitalism

2. The _____ was a worldwide economic downturn starting in most places in 1929 and ending at different times in the 1930s or early 1940s for different countries. It was the largest and most important economic depression in the 20th century, and is used in the 21st century as an example of how far the world's economy can fall. The _____ originated in the United States; historians most often use as a starting date the stock market crash on October 29, 1929, known as Black Tuesday.

   a. Wall Street Crash of 1929
   b. Jarrow March
   c. British Empire Economic Conference
   d. Great Depression

3. _____ and Keynesian Theory) is a macroeconomic theory based on the ideas of 20th-century British economist John Maynard Keynes. _____ argues that private sector decisions sometimes lead to inefficient macroeconomic outcomes and therefore advocates active policy responses by the public sector, including monetary policy actions by the central bank and fiscal policy actions by the government to stabilize output over the business cycle.

The theories forming the basis of _____ were first presented in The General Theory of Employment, Interest and Money, published in 1936.

   a. Keynesian economics
   b. Deflation
   c. Market failure
   d. Rational choice theory

4. A _____ is an economic system that incorporates a mixture of private and government ownership or control, or a mixture of capitalism and socialism.

There is not one single definition for a _____, but relevant aspects include: a degree of private economic freedom (including privately owned industry) intermingled with centralized economic planning and government regulation (which may include regulation of the market for environmental concerns and social welfare, or state ownership and management of some of the means of production for national or social objectives.)

For some states, there is not a consensus on whether they are capitalist, socialist, or mixed economies.

   a. Hunter-gatherer
   b. Planned liberalism
   c. Dual economy
   d. Mixed economy

5. Crude _____ is the nativity or childbirths per 1,000 people per year.

It can be represented by number of childbirths in that year, and p is the current population. This figure is combined with the crude death rate to produce the rate of natural population growth (natural in that it does not take into account net migration.)

a. Malthusian equilibrium
b. Depensation
c. Birth rate
d. Neo-Malthusianism

6. The term _____ refers to economy-wide fluctuations in production or economic activity over several months or years. These fluctuations occur around a long-term growth trend, and typically involve shifts over time between periods of relatively rapid economic growth (expansion or boom), and periods of relative stagnation or decline (contraction or recession.)

These fluctuations are often measured using the growth rate of real gross domestic product.

a. Consumer theory
b. Nominal value
c. Business cycle
d. Tobit model

7. The _____ or gross domestic income (GDI), a basic measure of an economy's economic performance, is the market value of all final goods and services produced within the borders of a nation in a year. _____ can be defined in three ways, all of which are conceptually identical. First, it is equal to the total expenditures for all final goods and services produced within the country in a stipulated period of time (usually a 365-day year.)

a. Countercyclical
b. Market structure
c. Monopolistic competition
d. Gross domestic product

8. In economics, the _____ measures the payments that flow between any individual country and all other countries. It is used to summarize all international economic transactions for that country during a specific time period, usually a year. The _____ is determined by the country's exports and imports of goods, services, and financial capital, as well as financial transfers.

a. Gross world product
b. Gross domestic product per barrel
c. Skyscraper Index
d. Balance of payments

9. A _____ is the transfer of wealth from one party (such as a person or company) to another. A _____ is usually made in exchange for the provision of goods, services or both, or to fulfill a legal obligation.

The simplest and oldest form of _____ is barter, the exchange of one good or service for another.

a. Going concern
b. Payment
c. Social gravity
d. Soft count

10. In economics, the people in the _____ are the suppliers of labor. The _____ is all the nonmilitary people who are employed or unemployed. In 2005, the worldwide _____ was over 3 billion people.

a. Grenelle agreements
b. Distributed workforce
c. Departmentalization
d. Labor force

Chapter 24. The Great Depression

11. The _____ is the central banking system of the United States. Created in 1913 by the enactment of the Federal Reserve Act (signed by Woodrow Wilson), it is a quasi-public and quasi-private (government entity with private components) banking system that comprises (1) the presidentially appointed Board of Governors of the _____ in Washington, D.C.; (2) the Federal Open Market Committee; (3) twelve regional Federal Reserve Banks located in major cities throughout the nation acting as fiscal agents for the U.S. Treasury, each with its own nine-member board of directors; (4) numerous other private U.S. member banks, which subscribe to required amounts of non-transferable stock in their regional Federal Reserve Banks; and (5) various advisory councils. Since February 2006, Ben Bernanke has served as the Chairman of the Board of Governors of the _____.

    a. Federal Reserve System Open Market Account
    b. Federal Reserve System
    c. Monetary Policy Report to the Congress
    d. Term auction facility

12. The phrase _____ and acquisitions refers to the aspect of corporate strategy, corporate finance and management dealing with the buying, selling and combining of different companies that can aid, finance, or help a growing company in a given industry grow rapidly without having to create another business entity.

    An acquisition, also known as a takeover or a buyout, is the buying of one company (the 'target') by another. An acquisition may be friendly or hostile.

    a. Mergers
    b. Peace dividend
    c. Political economy
    d. Differential accumulation

13. A _____ is a public market for the trading of company stock and derivatives at an agreed price; these are securities listed on a stock exchange as well as those only traded privately.

    The size of the world _____ was estimated at about $36.6 trillion US at the beginning of October 2008 . The total world derivatives market has been estimated at about $791 trillion face or nominal value, 11 times the size of the entire world economy.

    a. Adolf Hitler
    b. Adam Smith
    c. Adolph Fischer
    d. Stock market

14. _____ is a broad label that refers to any individuals or households that use goods and services generated within the economy. The concept of a _____ is used in different contexts, so that the usage and significance of the term may vary.

    Typically when business people and economists talk of _____s they are talking about person as _____, an aggregated commodity item with little individuality other than that expressed in the buy/not-buy decision.

    a. 100-year flood
    b. 1921 recession
    c. Consumer
    d. 130-30 fund

15. The _____ was actually created in 1929, before the stock market crash on Black Tuesday, 1929, but its powers were later enlarged to meet the economic crisis farmers faced during the Great Depression. It was established by the Agricultural Marketing Act to stabilize prices and to promote the sale of agricultural products. The board would help farmers stabilize prices by holding surplus grain and cotton in storage.

Chapter 24. The Great Depression

a. Great Depression
c. Great Contraction
b. Federal Farm Board
d. Great Depression in the United Kingdom

16. _____ in economics and business is the result of an exchange and from that trade we assign a numerical monetary value to a good, service or asset. If Alice trades Bob 4 apples for an orange, the _____ of an orange is 4 apples. Inversely, the _____ of an apple is 1/4 oranges.

a. Price book
c. Premium pricing
b. Price war
d. Price

17. _____s are a type of administrative division, in some countries managed by a local government. They vary greatly in size, spanning entire regions or counties, several municipalities, or subdivisions of municipalities.

In Austria, a _____ or Bezirk is an administrative division normally encompassing several municipalities, roughly equivalent to the Landkreis in Germany.

a. 100-year flood
c. 130-30 fund
b. 1921 recession
d. District

18. _____ is the physical growth of rural or natural land into urban areas as a result of population immigration to an existing urban area. Effects include change in density and administration services. While the exact definition and population size of urbanized areas varies among different countries, _____ is attributed to growth of cities.

a. Urbanization
c. ACCRA Cost of Living Index
b. Urban prairie
d. Urban renewal

19. _____ is a common concept in economics, and gives rise to derived concepts such as consumer debt. Generally _____ is defined by opposition to production. But the precise definition can vary because different schools of economists define production quite differently.

a. Federal Reserve Bank Notes
c. Foreclosure data providers
b. Cash or share options
d. Consumption

20. The term _____ refers to government debt, expenditures and revenues, or to finance (particularly financial revenue) in general.

- _____ deficit is the budget deficit of federal or local government
- _____ policy is the discretionary spending of governments. Contrasts with monetary policy.
- _____ year and _____ quarter are reporting periods for firms and other agencies.

a. Drawdown
c. Procter ' Gamble
b. Bucket shop
d. Fiscal

21. In economics, _____ is the use of government spending and revenue collection to influence the economy.

Chapter 24. The Great Depression

_____ can be contrasted with the other main type of economic policy, monetary policy, which attempts to stabilize the economy by controlling interest rates and the supply of money. The two main instruments of _____ are government spending and taxation.

a. Fiscalism
c. Sustainable investment rule

b. 100-year flood
d. Fiscal policy

22. _____ or government expenditure is classified by economists into three main types. Government purchases of goods and services for current use are classed as government consumption. Government purchases of goods and services intended to create future benefits, such as infrastructure investment or research spending, are classed as government investment.

a. 130-30 fund
c. 100-year flood

b. Government spending
d. 1921 recession

23. The _____ was an act signed into law on June 17, 1930, that raised U.S. tariffs on over 20,000 imported goods to record levels. In the United States 1,028 economists signed a petition against this legislation, and after it was passed, many countries retaliated with their own increased tariffs on U.S. goods, and American exports and imports were reduced by more than half.

Although rated capacity had increased tremendously, actual output, income, and expenditure had not.

a. Smoot-Hawley Tariff Act
c. Loss of use

b. Judgment summons
d. Patent Law Treaty

24. A _____ is a duty imposed on goods when they are moved across a political boundary. They are usually associated with protectionism, the economic policy of restraining trade between nations. For political reasons, _____s are usually imposed on imported goods, although they may also be imposed on exported goods.

a. 130-30 fund
c. 1921 recession

b. 100-year flood
d. Tariff

25. In economics, an _____ is any good or commodity, transported from one country to another country in a legitimate fashion, typically for use in trade. _____ goods or services are provided to foreign consumers by domestic producers. _____ is an important part of international trade.

a. AD-IA Model
c. ACEA agreement

b. ACCRA Cost of Living Index
d. Export

26. In economics, _____ is a sustained decrease in the general price level of goods and services. _____ occurs when the annual inflation rate falls below zero percent, resulting in an increase in the real value of money -- a negative inflation rate. This should not be confused with disinflation, a slow-down in the inflation rate (i.e. when the inflation decreases, but still remains positive.)

a. Literacy rate
c. Tobit model

b. Price revolution
d. Deflation

27. _____s is the social science that studies the production, distribution, and consumption of goods and services. The term _____s comes from the Ancient Greek οἰκονομία from οἶκος (oikos, 'house') + νόμος (nomos, 'custom' or 'law'), hence 'rules of the house(hold)'. Current _____ models developed out of the broader field of political economy in the late 19th century, owing to a desire to use an empirical approach more akin to the physical sciences.

   a. Inflation
   b. Economic
   c. Energy economics
   d. Opportunity cost

28. The _____ is a monetary system in which a region's common medium of exchange are paper notes that are normally freely convertible into pre-set, fixed quantities of gold. The _____ is not currently used by any government, having been replaced completely by fiat currency. Gold certificates were used as paper currency in the United States from 1882 to 1933, these certificates were freely convertible into gold coins.

In the 1790s Britain suffered a massive shortage of silver coinage and ceased to mint larger silver coins.

   a. 130-30 fund
   b. 100-year flood
   c. Gold standard
   d. 1921 recession

Chapter 25. The New Deal

1. The _____ is the central banking system of the United States. Created in 1913 by the enactment of the Federal Reserve Act (signed by Woodrow Wilson), it is a quasi-public and quasi-private (government entity with private components) banking system that comprises (1) the presidentially appointed Board of Governors of the _____ in Washington, D.C.; (2) the Federal Open Market Committee; (3) twelve regional Federal Reserve Banks located in major cities throughout the nation acting as fiscal agents for the U.S. Treasury, each with its own nine-member board of directors; (4) numerous other private U.S. member banks, which subscribe to required amounts of non-transferable stock in their regional Federal Reserve Banks; and (5) various advisory councils. Since February 2006, Ben Bernanke has served as the Chairman of the Board of Governors of the _____.

   a. Federal Reserve System Open Market Account
   b. Federal Reserve System
   c. Term auction facility
   d. Monetary Policy Report to the Congress

2. The _____ was a worldwide economic downturn starting in most places in 1929 and ending at different times in the 1930s or early 1940s for different countries. It was the largest and most important economic depression in the 20th century, and is used in the 21st century as an example of how far the world's economy can fall. The _____ originated in the United States; historians most often use as a starting date the stock market crash on October 29, 1929, known as Black Tuesday.

   a. Wall Street Crash of 1929
   b. British Empire Economic Conference
   c. Jarrow March
   d. Great Depression

3. The _____ consists of a number of economic theories which describe the nature of the firm, company including its existence, its behaviour, and its relationship with the market.

   In simplified terms, the _____ aims to answer these questions:

   1. Existence - why do firms emerge, why are not all transactions in the economy mediated over the market?
   2. Boundaries - why the boundary between firms and the market is located exactly there? Which transactions are performed internally and which are negotiated on the market?
   3. Organization - why are firms structured in such specific way? What is the interplay of formal and informal relationships?

   Despite looking simple, these questions are not answered by the established economic theory, which usually views firms as given, and treats them as black boxes without any internal structure.

   The First World War period saw a change of emphasis in economic theory away from industry-level analysis which mainly included analysing markets to analysis at the level of the firm, as it became increasingly clear that perfect competition was no longer an adequate model of how firms behaved. Economic theory till then had focussed on trying to understand markets alone and there had been little study on understanding why firms or organisations exist.

   a. Theory of the firm
   b. Technology gap
   c. Policy Ineffectiveness Proposition
   d. Khazzoom-Brookes postulate

4. _____ and Keynesian Theory) is a macroeconomic theory based on the ideas of 20th-century British economist John Maynard Keynes. _____ argues that private sector decisions sometimes lead to inefficient macroeconomic outcomes and therefore advocates active policy responses by the public sector, including monetary policy actions by the central bank and fiscal policy actions by the government to stabilize output over the business cycle.

The theories forming the basis of _____ were first presented in The General Theory of Employment, Interest and Money, published in 1936.

a. Rational choice theory
b. Market failure
c. Deflation
d. Keynesian economics

5. In economics, the people in the _____ are the suppliers of labor. The _____ is all the nonmilitary people who are employed or unemployed. In 2005, the worldwide _____ was over 3 billion people.

a. Labor force
b. Grenelle agreements
c. Departmentalization
d. Distributed workforce

6. A _____ is something for which there is demand, but which is supplied without qualitative differentiation across a market. It is a product that is the same no matter who produces it, such as petroleum, notebook paper, or milk. In other words, copper is copper.

a. Commodity
b. Soft commodity
c. Hard commodity
d. 100-year flood

7. A _____ refers to any type debt instrument, such as a loan, bond, mortgage that does not have a fixed rate of interest over the life of the instrument. Such debt typically uses an index or other base rate for establishing the interest rate for each relevant period. One of the most common rates to use as the basis for applying interest rates is the London Inter-bank Offered Rate, or LIBOR

a. Floating interest rate
b. Moneylender
c. Disposal tax effect
d. Money market

8. The _____ or the Dirty Thirties was a period of severe dust storms causing major ecological and agricultural damage to American and Canadian prairie lands from 1930 to 1936 (in some areas until 1940.) The phenomenon was caused by severe drought coupled with decades of extensive farming without crop rotation or other techniques to prevent erosion. Deep plowing of the virgin topsoil of the Great Plains had killed the natural grasses that normally kept the soil in place and trapped moisture even during periods of drought and high winds.

a. 100-year flood
b. 1921 recession
c. Dust Bowl
d. 130-30 fund

9. The _____ is a federally owned corporation in the United States created by congressional charter in May 1933 to provide navigation, flood control, electricity generation, fertilizer manufacturing, and economic development in the Tennessee Valley, a region particularly impacted by the Great Depression. The _____ was envisioned not only as an electricity provider, but also as a regional economic development agency that would use federal experts and electricity to rapidly modernize the region's economy and society.

The _____'s jurisdiction covers most of Tennessee, parts of Alabama, Mississippi, and Kentucky, and small slices of Georgia, North Carolina, and Virginia.

a. 130-30 fund
b. 100-year flood
c. 1921 recession
d. Tennessee Valley Authority

Chapter 25. The New Deal

10. The _____ is a United States government corporation created by the Glass-Steagall Act of 1933. It provides deposit insurance, which guarantees the safety of deposits in member banks, currently up to $250,000 per depositor per bank. Funds in non-interest bearing transaction accounts are fully insured, with no limit, under the temporary Transaction Account Guarantee Program.
    a. Great Leap Forward
    b. Foreign direct investment
    c. Luxembourg Income Study
    d. Federal Deposit Insurance Corporation

11. The _____ , a component of the Federal Reserve System, is charged under United States law with overseeing the nation's open market operations. It is the Federal Reserve Committee that makes key decisions about interest rates and the growth jam of the United States money supply. It is the principal organ of United States national monetary policy.
    a. Primary Dealer Credit Facility
    b. Federal Open Market Committee
    c. Fed Funds Probability
    d. Federal Reserve Transparency Act

12. The _____ established the Federal Deposit Insurance Corporation (FDIC) in the United States and included banking reforms, some of which were designed to control speculation. Some provisions such as Regulation Q, which allowed the Federal Reserve to regulate interest rates in savings accounts, were repealed by the Depository Institutions Deregulation and Monetary Control Act of 1980. Provisions that prohibit a bank holding company from owning other financial companies were repealed on November 12, 1999, by the Gramm-Leach-Bliley Act.
    a. 100-year flood
    b. Glass-Steagall Act of 1933
    c. 130-30 fund
    d. 1921 recession

13. _____ , in law and economics, is a form of risk management primarily used to hedge against the risk of a contingent loss. _____ is defined as the equitable transfer of the risk of a loss, from one entity to another, in exchange for a premium, and can be thought of as a guaranteed small loss to prevent a large, possibly devastating loss. An insurer is a company selling the _____ ; an insured or policyholder is the person or entity buying the _____ .
    a. Insurance
    b. ACEA agreement
    c. AD-IA Model
    d. ACCRA Cost of Living Index

14. In economics, the _____ is the term used to refer to the environment in which bonds are bought and sold between a central bank ' its regulated banks. It is not a free market process.

- To intervene in the 'business cycle', a central bank may choose to go into the _____ and buy or sell government bonds, which is known as _____ operations to increase reserves.

    a. Inside money
    b. Outside money
    c. Open Market
    d. ACCRA Cost of Living Index

15. A public utility (usually just utility) is an organization that maintains the infrastructure for a public service (often also providing a service using that infrastructure.) _____ are subject to forms of public control and regulation ranging from local community-based groups to state-wide government monopolies. Common arguments in favor of regulation include the desire to control market power, facilitate competition, promote investment or system expansion, or stabilize markets.
    a. 130-30 fund
    b. 1921 recession
    c. 100-year flood
    d. Public Utilities

16. A security is a fungible, negotiable instrument representing financial value. _____ are broadly categorized into debt _____; equity _____, e.g., common stocks; and derivative (finance) contracts such as forwards, futures, options and swaps. The company or other entity issuing the security is called the issuer.
   a. Red herring prospectus
   b. Settlement risk
   c. Pass-Through Certificates
   d. Securities

17. Congress enacted the _____, in the aftermath of the stock market crash of 1929 and during the ensuing Great Depression.
   a. 130-30 fund
   b. 100-year flood
   c. National Housing Act of 1934
   d. Securities Act of 1933

18. The U.S. _____ is an independent agency of the United States government which holds primary responsibility for enforcing the federal securities laws and regulating the securities industry, the nation's stock and options exchanges, and other electronic securities markets. The SEC was created by section 4 of the Securities Exchange Act of 1934 (now codified as 15 U.S.C. § 78d and commonly referred to as the 1934 Act.)
   a. 130-30 fund
   b. 100-year flood
   c. 1921 recession
   d. Securities and Exchange Commission

19. Competition law, known in the United States as _____ law, has three main elements:

   - prohibiting agreements or practices that restrict free trading and competition between business entities. This includes in particular the repression of cartels.
   - banning abusive behaviour by a firm dominating a market, or anti-competitive practices that tend to lead to such a dominant position. Practices controlled in this way may include predatory pricing, tying, price gouging, refusal to deal, and many others.
   - supervising the mergers and acquisitions of large corporations, including some joint ventures. Transactions that are considered to threaten the competitive process can be prohibited altogether, or approved subject to 'remedies' such as an obligation to divest part of the merged business or to offer licences or access to facilities to enable other businesses to continue competing.

   The substance and practice of competition law varies from jurisdiction to jurisdiction. Protecting the interests of consumers (consumer welfare) and ensuring that entrepreneurs have an opportunity to compete in the market economy are often treated as important objectives. Competition law is closely connected with law on deregulation of access to markets, state aids and subsidies, the privatisation of state owned assets and the establishment of independent sector regulators. In recent decades, competition law has been viewed as a way to provide better public services.

   a. United Kingdom competition law
   b. Anti-Inflation Act
   c. Intellectual property law
   d. Antitrust

20. _____ is a field of economics that studies the strategic behavior of firms, the structure of markets and their interactions. The study of _____ adds to the perfectly competitive model real-world frictions such as limited information, transaction cost, cost of adjusting prices, government actions, and barriers to entry by new firms into a market. It then considers how firms are organized and how they compete.

Chapter 25. The New Deal

a. Industrial Organization
c. Economic ideology
b. Inflation
d. Economic

21. _____ refers to the employment of children at regular and sustained labour. This practice is considered exploitative by many international organizations and is illegal in many countries. _____ was utilized to varying extents through most of history, but entered public dispute with the beginning of universal schooling, with changes in working conditions during industrialization, and with the emergence of the concepts of workers' and children's rights.

a. National Action Plan on the Elimination of Child Labour
b. Global march against child labor
c. Debt bondage
d. Child labour

22. The _____ of 1938 (_____, ch. 676, 52 Stat. 1060, June 25, 1938, 29 U.S.C.ch.8), also called the Wages and Hours Bill, is United States federal law that applies to employees engaged in interstate commerce or employed by an enterprise engaged in commerce or in the production of goods for commerce, unless the employer can claim an exemption from coverage.

a. Generalized System of Preferences
b. Hostile work environment
c. Habitability
d. Fair Labor Standards Act

23. A _____ is the lowest hourly, daily or monthly wage that employers may legally pay to employees or workers. Equivalently, it is the lowest wage at which workers may sell their labor. Although _____ laws are in effect in a great many jurisdictions, there are differences of opinion about the benefits and drawbacks of a _____.

a. Marginal propensity to consume
b. Microfoundations
c. Permanent war economy
d. Minimum wage

24. _____s is the social science that studies the production, distribution, and consumption of goods and services. The term _____s comes from the Ancient Greek οἰκονομῖα from οἶκος (oikos, 'house') + νόμος (nomos, 'custom' or 'law'), hence 'rules of the house(hold)'. Current _____ models developed out of the broader field of political economy in the late 19th century, owing to a desire to use an empirical approach more akin to the physical sciences.

a. Economic
b. Inflation
c. Energy economics
d. Opportunity cost

25. The term _____ refers to government debt, expenditures and revenues, or to finance (particularly financial revenue) in general.

- _____ deficit is the budget deficit of federal or local government
- _____ policy is the discretionary spending of governments. Contrasts with monetary policy.
- _____ year and _____ quarter are reporting periods for firms and other agencies.

a. Bucket shop
b. Fiscal
c. Drawdown
d. Procter ' Gamble

26. _____ refers to the process where tax thresholds are either not adjusted for inflation causing in either case an automatic rise in tax revenues.

Suppose a person earns $20,000 per year and is liable to 20% tax on earnings above a threshold of $5,000 per year. Then they pay (20000-5000)*0.2 = $3000 in tax, or 15% of income.

a. Tax sale
b. Fiscal drag
c. Tax law
d. Taxation as slavery

27. In 1940, President Franklin Roosevelt split the authority into two agencies, the Civil Aeronautics Administration (CAA) and the _____ The CAA was responsible for air traffic control, safety programs, and airway development. The _____ was entrusted with safety rulemaking, accident investigation, and economic regulation of the airlines.

a. 100-year flood
b. 130-30 fund
c. 1921 recession
d. Civil Aeronautics Board

28. The _____ was a regulatory body in the United States created by the Interstate Commerce Act of 1887, which was signed into law by President Grover Cleveland. The agency was abolished in 1995, and the agency's remaining functions were transferred to the Surface Transportation Board.

The Commission's five members were appointed by the President with the consent of the United States Senate.

a. Office of Thrift Supervision
b. ACEA agreement
c. ACCRA Cost of Living Index
d. Interstate Commerce Commission

Chapter 26. The Prosperity of Wartime

1. _____ was a global military conflict which involved a majority of the world's nations, including all of the great powers, organized into two opposing military alliances: the Allies and the Axis. The war involved the mobilization of over 100 million military personnel, making it the most widespread war in history. In a state of 'total war', the major participants placed their entire economic, industrial, and scientific capabilities at the service of the war effort, erasing the distinction between civilian and military resources.

   a. 100-year flood
   b. World War II
   c. 1921 recession
   d. 130-30 fund

2. _____ in economics and business is the result of an exchange and from that trade we assign a numerical monetary value to a good, service or asset. If Alice trades Bob 4 apples for an orange, the _____ of an orange is 4 apples. Inversely, the _____ of an apple is 1/4 oranges.

   a. Price book
   b. Price
   c. Price war
   d. Premium pricing

3. In microeconomics, _____ is quite simply the conversion of inputs into outputs. It is an economic process that uses resources to create a good or service that is suitable for exchange. This can include manufacturing, storing, shipping, and packaging.

   a. Production
   b. Solved
   c. MET
   d. Red Guards

4. _____ is a broad label that refers to any individuals or households that use goods and services generated within the economy. The concept of a _____ is used in different contexts, so that the usage and significance of the term may vary.

   Typically when business people and economists talk of _____s they are talking about person as _____, an aggregated commodity item with little individuality other than that expressed in the buy/not-buy decision.

   a. 1921 recession
   b. 100-year flood
   c. 130-30 fund
   d. Consumer

5. In economics, a _____ or a hard good is a good which does not quickly wear out it yields services or utility over time rather than being completely used up when used once. Most goods are therefore _____s to a certain degree. These are goods that can last for a relatively long time, such as refrigerators, cars, and DVD players.

   a. Luxury good
   b. Search good
   c. Superior goods
   d. Durable good

6. In economics, the _____ is the term used to refer to the environment in which bonds are bought and sold between a central bank ' its regulated banks. It is not a free market process.

   - To intervene in the 'business cycle', a central bank may choose to go into the _____ and buy or sell government bonds, which is known as _____ operations to increase reserves.

   a. Inside money
   b. Outside money
   c. ACCRA Cost of Living Index
   d. Open Market

Chapter 26. The Prosperity of Wartime

7. A United States Treasury security is a government debt issued by the United States Department of the Treasury through the Bureau of the Public Debt. Treasury securities are the debt financing instruments of the United States Federal government, and they are often referred to simply as Treasuries. There are four types of marketable treasury securities: _____, Treasury notes, Treasury bonds, and Treasury Inflation Protected Securities (TIPS.)
    a. Labour battalions
    b. Lawcards
    c. Debt to Assets
    d. Treasury bills

8. A _____ is an object whose consumption increases the utility of the consumer, for which the quantity demanded exceeds the quantity supplied at zero price. _____s are usually modeled as having diminishing marginal utility. The first individual purchase has high utility; the second has less.
    a. Composite good
    b. Pie method
    c. Merit good
    d. Good

9. _____s is the social science that studies the production, distribution, and consumption of goods and services. The term _____s comes from the Ancient Greek οἰκονομία from οἶκος (oikos, 'house') + νόμος (nomos, 'custom' or 'law'), hence 'rules of the house(hold)'. Current _____ models developed out of the broader field of political economy in the late 19th century, owing to a desire to use an empirical approach more akin to the physical sciences.
    a. Economic
    b. Inflation
    c. Energy economics
    d. Opportunity cost

10. The _____ was a worldwide economic downturn starting in most places in 1929 and ending at different times in the 1930s or early 1940s for different countries. It was the largest and most important economic depression in the 20th century, and is used in the 21st century as an example of how far the world's economy can fall. The _____ originated in the United States; historians most often use as a starting date the stock market crash on October 29, 1929, known as Black Tuesday.
    a. Wall Street Crash of 1929
    b. British Empire Economic Conference
    c. Jarrow March
    d. Great Depression

11. An _____ is a tax levied on the financial income of people, corporations, or other legal entities. Various _____ systems exist, with varying degrees of tax incidence. Income taxation can be progressive, proportional, or regressive.
    a. ACCRA Cost of Living Index
    b. AD-IA Model
    c. Income tax
    d. ACEA agreement

12. In economics, the people in the _____ are the suppliers of labor. The _____ is all the nonmilitary people who are employed or unemployed. In 2005, the worldwide _____ was over 3 billion people.
    a. Labor force
    b. Distributed workforce
    c. Departmentalization
    d. Grenelle agreements

13. To _____ is to impose a financial charge or other levy upon a taxpayer by a state or the functional equivalent of a state.

_____es are also imposed by many subnational entities. _____es consist of direct _____ or indirect _____, and may be paid in money or as its labour equivalent (often but not always unpaid.)

Chapter 26. The Prosperity of Wartime

a. Tax
b. 130-30 fund
c. 1921 recession
d. 100-year flood

14. To tax is to impose a financial charge or other levy upon a taxpayer by a state or the functional equivalent of a state. _____ are also imposed by many subnational entities. _____ consist of direct tax or indirect tax, and may be paid in money or as its labour equivalent (often but not always unpaid.)

a. 130-30 fund
b. Taxes
c. 100-year flood
d. 1921 recession

15. _____ the Great War, and the War to End All Wars, was a global military conflict which involved the majority of the world's great powers, organized into two opposing military alliances: the Entente Powers and the Central Powers. Over 70 million military personnel were mobilized in one of the largest wars in history. In a state of total war, the major combatants fully placed their scientific and industrial capabilities at the service of the war effort.

a. 130-30 fund
b. 100-year flood
c. World War I
d. 1921 recession

16. _____ are final goods specifically intended for the mass market. For instance, _____ do not include investment assets, like precious antiques, even though these antiques are final goods.

Manufactured goods are goods that have been processed by way of machinery.

a. Consumer goods
b. Fiscal stimulus plans
c. Bulgarian-American trade
d. G-20 Leaders Summit on Financial Markets and the World Economy

17. _____ is a common concept in economics, and gives rise to derived concepts such as consumer debt. Generally _____ is defined by opposition to production. But the precise definition can vary because different schools of economists define production quite differently.

a. Foreclosure data providers
b. Federal Reserve Bank Notes
c. Cash or share options
d. Consumption

18. In economics, _____ is how a natione;s total economy is distributed among its population. . _____ has always been a central concern of economic theory and economic policy. Classical economists such as Adam Smith, Thomas Malthus and David Ricardo were mainly concerned with factor _____, that is, the distribution of income between the main factors of production, land, labour and capital.

a. Equipment trust certificate
b. Eco commerce
c. Authorised capital
d. Income distribution

19. The _____ was the continuing state of conflict, tension, and competition that existed after World War II between the Soviet Union and its satellites and the powers of the Western world under the leadership of the United States from the mid-1940s to the early 1990s. Throughout this period, the conflict was expressed through military coalitions, espionage, weapons development, invasions, propaganda, and competitive technological development, which included the space race. The conflict included costly defense spending, a massive conventional and nuclear arms race, and numerous proxy wars; the two superpowers never fought one another directly.

a. Mutual assured destruction
b. Reagan Doctrine
c. Cold War
d. Sino-Soviet split

Chapter 27. Before the New Frontier: The Postwar Economy

1. The _____ or gross domestic income (GDI), a basic measure of an economy's economic performance, is the market value of all final goods and services produced within the borders of a nation in a year. _____ can be defined in three ways, all of which are conceptually identical. First, it is equal to the total expenditures for all final goods and services produced within the country in a stipulated period of time (usually a 365-day year.)
    a. Market structure
    b. Countercyclical
    c. Gross domestic product
    d. Monopolistic competition

2. _____ the Great War, and the War to End All Wars, was a global military conflict which involved the majority of the world's great powers, organized into two opposing military alliances: the Entente Powers and the Central Powers. Over 70 million military personnel were mobilized in one of the largest wars in history. In a state of total war, the major combatants fully placed their scientific and industrial capabilities at the service of the war effort.
    a. World War I
    b. 100-year flood
    c. 1921 recession
    d. 130-30 fund

3. _____ was a global military conflict which involved a majority of the world's nations, including all of the great powers, organized into two opposing military alliances: the Allies and the Axis. The war involved the mobilization of over 100 million military personnel, making it the most widespread war in history. In a state of 'total war', the major participants placed their entire economic, industrial, and scientific capabilities at the service of the war effort, erasing the distinction between civilian and military resources.
    a. World War II
    b. 1921 recession
    c. 100-year flood
    d. 130-30 fund

4. In economics, the _____ measures the payments that flow between any individual country and all other countries. It is used to summarize all international economic transactions for that country during a specific time period, usually a year. The _____ is determined by the country's exports and imports of goods, services, and financial capital, as well as financial transfers.
    a. Skyscraper Index
    b. Gross world product
    c. Balance of payments
    d. Gross domestic product per barrel

5. The _____ is a group of three respected economists who advise the President of the United States on economic policy. It is a part of the Executive Office of the President of the United States, and provides much of the economic policy of the White House. The council prepares the annual Economic Report of the President.
    a. Federal Reserve Bank Notes
    b. Hybrid renewable energy systems
    c. Constrained Pareto optimality
    d. Council of Economic Advisers

6. _____s is the social science that studies the production, distribution, and consumption of goods and services. The term _____s comes from the Ancient Greek οἰκονομῖα from οἶκος (oikos, 'house') + νόμος (nomos, 'custom' or 'law'), hence 'rules of the house(hold)'. Current _____ models developed out of the broader field of political economy in the late 19th century, owing to a desire to use an empirical approach more akin to the physical sciences.
    a. Inflation
    b. Energy economics
    c. Economic
    d. Opportunity cost

7. A _____ is the transfer of wealth from one party (such as a person or company) to another. A _____ is usually made in exchange for the provision of goods, services or both, or to fulfill a legal obligation.

The simplest and oldest form of _____ is barter, the exchange of one good or service for another.

a. Social gravity	b. Going concern
c. Soft count	d. Payment

8. _____ is the increase in the amount of the goods and services produced by an economy over time. It is conventionally measured as the percent rate of increase in real gross domestic product, or real GDP. Growth is usually calculated in real terms, i.e. inflation-adjusted terms, in order to net out the effect of inflation on the price of the goods and services produced.

a. ACEA agreement	b. ACCRA Cost of Living Index
c. AD-IA Model	d. Economic growth

9. The _____ was actually created in 1929, before the stock market crash on Black Tuesday, 1929, but its powers were later enlarged to meet the economic crisis farmers faced during the Great Depression. It was established by the Agricultural Marketing Act to stabilize prices and to promote the sale of agricultural products. The board would help farmers stabilize prices by holding surplus grain and cotton in storage.

a. Great Contraction	b. Federal Farm Board
c. Great Depression in the United Kingdom	d. Great Depression

10. In economics, _____ is a sustained decrease in the general price level of goods and services. _____ occurs when the annual inflation rate falls below zero percent, resulting in an increase in the real value of money -- a negative inflation rate. This should not be confused with disinflation, a slow-down in the inflation rate (i.e. when the inflation decreases, but still remains positive.)

a. Tobit model	b. Deflation
c. Price revolution	d. Literacy rate

11. The term _____ refers to government debt, expenditures and revenues, or to finance (particularly financial revenue) in general.

- _____ deficit is the budget deficit of federal or local government
- _____ policy is the discretionary spending of governments. Contrasts with monetary policy.
- _____ year and _____ quarter are reporting periods for firms and other agencies.

a. Fiscal	b. Procter ' Gamble
c. Drawdown	d. Bucket shop

12. In economics, _____ is the use of government spending and revenue collection to influence the economy.

_____ can be contrasted with the other main type of economic policy, monetary policy, which attempts to stabilize the economy by controlling interest rates and the supply of money. The two main instruments of _____ are government spending and taxation.

a. 100-year flood	b. Sustainable investment rule
c. Fiscal policy	d. Fiscalism

Chapter 27. Before the New Frontier: The Postwar Economy

13. The _____ was the primary plan of the United States for rebuilding and creating a stronger foundation for the countries of Western Europe, and repelling communism after World War II. The initiative was named for Secretary of State George Marshall and was largely the creation of State Department officials, especially William L. Clayton and George F. Kennan. George Marshall spoke of the administration's want to help European recovery in his address at Harvard University in June 1947.

   a. 130-30 fund
   b. Marshall Plan
   c. 100-year flood
   d. 1921 recession

14. _____ is an economic theory named after the 20th century Austrian economist Joseph Schumpeter. Unlike modern economic growth theories, his approach explains growth by innovation and entrepreneurial spirit.

   a. Fed model
   b. Lipstick effect
   c. Real prices and ideal prices
   d. Schumpeterian growth

15. In economics, the _____ is the term used to refer to the environment in which bonds are bought and sold between a central bank ' its regulated banks. It is not a free market process.

   - To intervene in the 'business cycle', a central bank may choose to go into the _____ and buy or sell government bonds, which is known as _____ operations to increase reserves.

   a. Outside money
   b. Inside money
   c. ACCRA Cost of Living Index
   d. Open Market

16. The _____ was the continuing state of conflict, tension, and competition that existed after World War II between the Soviet Union and its satellites and the powers of the Western world under the leadership of the United States from the mid-1940s to the early 1990s. Throughout this period, the conflict was expressed through military coalitions, espionage, weapons development, invasions, propaganda, and competitive technological development, which included the space race. The conflict included costly defense spending, a massive conventional and nuclear arms race, and numerous proxy wars; the two superpowers never fought one another directly.

   a. Sino-Soviet split
   b. Reagan Doctrine
   c. Mutual assured destruction
   d. Cold War

17. The _____ was a worldwide economic downturn starting in most places in 1929 and ending at different times in the 1930s or early 1940s for different countries. It was the largest and most important economic depression in the 20th century, and is used in the 21st century as an example of how far the world's economy can fall. The _____ originated in the United States; historians most often use as a starting date the stock market crash on October 29, 1929, known as Black Tuesday.

   a. Jarrow March
   b. Great Depression
   c. British Empire Economic Conference
   d. Wall Street Crash of 1929

18. _____ is a voluntary transfer of resources from one country to another, given at least partly with the objective of benefiting the recipient country. It may have other functions as well: it may be given as a signal of diplomatic approval, or to strengthen a military ally, to reward a government for behaviour desired by the donor, to extend the donor's cultural influence, to provide infrastructure needed by the donor for resource extraction from the recipient country, or to gain other kinds of commercial access. Humanitarianism and altruism are, nevertheless, significant motivations for the giving of _____.

Chapter 27. Before the New Frontier: The Postwar Economy

a. AD-IA Model
b. ACCRA Cost of Living Index
c. Aid
d. ACEA agreement

19. In finance, the _____s between two currencies specifies how much one currency is worth in terms of the other. It is the value of a foreign natione;s currency in terms of the home natione;s currency. For example an _____ of 102 Japanese yen to the United States dollar means that JPY 102 is worth the same as USD 1.
   a. ACCRA Cost of Living Index
   b. Interbank market
   c. ACEA agreement
   d. Exchange rate

20. A _____, sometimes called a pegged exchange rate, is a type of exchange rate regime wherein a currency's value is matched to the value of another single currency or to a basket of other currencies such as gold.

A _____ is usually used to stabilize the value of a currency, vis-a-vis the currency it is pegged to. This facilitates trade and investments between the two countries, and is especially useful for small economies where external trade forms a large part of their GDP.

   a. Law of supply
   b. Fixed exchange rate
   c. Monetary economics
   d. Leading indicators

21. In economics, _____ is a monetary standard in which the value of the monetary unit is defined as equivalent either to a certain quantity of gold or to a certain quantity of silver. Such a system effectively establishes a fixed rate of exchange for the two metals. The merits of the system were the subject of debate in the late 19th century.
   a. 130-30 fund
   b. 100-year flood
   c. 1921 recession
   d. Bimetallism

22. The American Federation of Labor and Congress of Industrial Organizations, commonly _____, is a national trade union center, the largest federation of unions in the United States, made up of 65 national and international unions (including Canadian), together representing more than 10 million workers. It was formed in 1955 when the AFL and the CIO merged after a long estrangement. From 1955 until 2005, the _____'s member unions represented nearly all unionized workers in the United States.
   a. ACCRA Cost of Living Index
   b. AD-IA Model
   c. ACEA agreement
   d. AFL-CIO

23. The _____ was the outcome of the failure of negotiating governments to create the International Trade Organization (ITO.) GATT was formed in 1947 and lasted until 1994, when it was replaced by the World Trade Organization. The Bretton Woods Conference had introduced the idea for an organization to regulate trade as part of a larger plan for economic recovery after World War II.
   a. GATT
   b. General Agreement on Trade in Services
   c. General Agreement on Tariffs and Trade
   d. Dutch-Scandinavian Economic Pact

24. The _____ is an international organization that oversees the global financial system by following the macroeconomic policies of its member countries, in particular those with an impact on exchange rates and the balance of payments. It is an organization formed to stabilize international exchange rates and facilitate development. It also offers financial and technical assistance to its members, making it an international lender of last resort.

Chapter 27. Before the New Frontier: The Postwar Economy

a. ACEA agreement
b. ACCRA Cost of Living Index
c. International Monetary Fund
d. Office of Thrift Supervision

25. _____ is exchange of capital, goods, and services across international borders or territories. In most countries, it represents a significant share of gross domestic product (GDP.) While _____ has been present throughout much of history, its economic, social, and political importance has been on the rise in recent centuries.

a. Import license
b. International Trade
c. Incoterms
d. Intra-industry trade

26. A _____ is a duty imposed on goods when they are moved across a political boundary. They are usually associated with protectionism, the economic policy of restraining trade between nations. For political reasons, _____s are usually imposed on imported goods, although they may also be imposed on exported goods.

a. 1921 recession
b. 100-year flood
c. 130-30 fund
d. Tariff

27. The _____ is an international financial institution that provides financial and technical assistance to developing countries for development programs (e.g. bridges, roads, schools, etc.) with the stated goal of reducing poverty.

The _____ differs from the _____ Group, in that the _____ comprises only two institutions:

- International Bank for Reconstruction and Development (IBRD)
- International Development Association (IDA)

Whereas the latter incorporates these two in addition to three more:

- International Finance Corporation (IFC)
- Multilateral Investment Guarantee Agency (MIGA)
- International Centre for Settlement of Investment Disputes (ICSID)

John Maynard Keynes (right) represented the UK at the conference, and Harry Dexter White represented the US.

The _____ is one of two major financial institutions created as a result of the Bretton Woods Conference in 1944. The International Monetary Fund, a related but separate institution, is the second.

a. Financial costs of the 2003 Iraq War
b. Bank-State-Branch
c. Flow to Equity-Approach
d. World Bank

28. The _____ is an important selective, mainly private, international organization designed by its founders to supervise and liberalize international trade. The organization officially commenced on 1 January 1995, under the Marrakesh Agreement, succeeding the 1947 General Agreement on Tariffs and Trade (GATT.)

The _____ deals with regulation of trade between participating countries; it provides a framework for negotiating and formalising trade agreements, and a dispute resolution process aimed at enforcing participants' adherence to _____ agreements which are signed by representatives of member governments and ratified by their parliaments.

a. Bio-energy village
b. 2009 G-20 London summit protests
c. Backus-Kehoe-Kydland consumption correlation puzzle
d. World Trade Organization

29. The _____ is an international organization of central banks which 'fosters international monetary and financial cooperation and serves as a bank for central banks.' It is not accountable to any national government. The BIS carries out its work through subcommittees, the secretariats it hosts, and through its annual General Meeting of all members. It also provides banking services, but only to central banks, or to international organizations like itself.

a. 130-30 fund
b. Bank for International Settlements
c. 100-year flood
d. 1921 recession

30. A _____ is a customs union with common policies on product regulation, and freedom of movement of the factors of production (capital and labour) and of enterprise. The goal is that the movement of capital, labour, goods, and services between the members is as easy as within them. This is the fourth stage of economic integration.

a. Grey market
b. Competitiveness
c. Mutual recognition agreement
d. Common Market

31. _____ is the practice within the banking industry of authorizing electronic transactions done with a debit card or credit card and holding this balance as unavailable either until the merchant clears the transaction _____s can fall off the account anywhere from 1-5 days after the transaction date depending on the bank's policy; in the case of credit cards, holds may last as long as 30 days, depending on the issuing bank.

Signature-based credit and debit card transactions are a two-step process, consisting of an authorization and a settlement.

When a merchant swipes a customer's credit card, the credit card terminal connects to the merchant's acquirer which verifies that the customer's account is valid and that sufficient funds are available to cover the transaction's cost.

a. Interbank network
b. Authorization hold
c. Issuing bank
d. Electronic funds transfer

32. The _____ are two of the treaties of the European Union signed on March 25, 1957. Both treaties were signed by The Six: Belgium, France, Italy, Luxembourg, the Netherlands and West Germany.

The first established the European Economic Community and the second established the European Atomic Energy Community (EAEC or Euratom.)

Chapter 27. Before the New Frontier: The Postwar Economy

a. Maastricht Treaty
b. Treaty of Amsterdam
c. 100-year flood
d. Treaties of Rome

33. _____ is that which is owed; usually referencing assets owed, but the term can also cover moral obligations and other interactions not requiring money. In the case of assets, _____ is a means of using future purchasing power in the present before a summation has been earned. Some companies and corporations use _____ as a part of their overall corporate finance strategy.
   a. Hard money loan
   b. Collateral Management
   c. Debenture
   d. Debt

34. A _____ is an expression that compares quantities relative to each other. The most common examples involve two quantities, but any number of quantities can be compared. _____s are represented mathematically by separating each quantity with a colon, for example the _____ 2:3, which is read as the _____ 'two to three'.
   a. 130-30 fund
   b. Y-intercept
   c. 100-year flood
   d. Ratio

Chapter 28. Population, Labor, and the Tertiary Sector

1. A _____ is any period of greatly increased birth rate during a certain period, and usually within certain geographical bounds and when the birth rate exceeds 2% of the population. People born during such a period are sometimes called _____ers, but note the difference between a demographic boom in births and the cultural generations born during such a birth boom. Some contest the general conventional wisdom that _____s signify good times and periods of general economic growth, and stability.
   a. Demographic analysis
   b. Demographic warfare
   c. Rate of natural increase
   d. Baby Boom

2. The _____ was a worldwide economic downturn starting in most places in 1929 and ending at different times in the 1930s or early 1940s for different countries. It was the largest and most important economic depression in the 20th century, and is used in the 21st century as an example of how far the world's economy can fall. The _____ originated in the United States; historians most often use as a starting date the stock market crash on October 29, 1929, known as Black Tuesday.
   a. British Empire Economic Conference
   b. Wall Street Crash of 1929
   c. Great Depression
   d. Jarrow March

3. _____ was a global military conflict which involved a majority of the world's nations, including all of the great powers, organized into two opposing military alliances: the Allies and the Axis. The war involved the mobilization of over 100 million military personnel, making it the most widespread war in history. In a state of 'total war', the major participants placed their entire economic, industrial, and scientific capabilities at the service of the war effort, erasing the distinction between civilian and military resources.
   a. 1921 recession
   b. 130-30 fund
   c. 100-year flood
   d. World War II

4. _____ to the arrival of new individuals into a habitat or population. It is a biological concept and is important in population ecology, differentiated from emigration and migration.

   _____ is a modern phenomenon.
   a. AD-IA Model
   b. ACEA agreement
   c. ACCRA Cost of Living Index
   d. Immigration

5. _____ is a measure of the number of deaths (in general scaled to the size of that population, per unit time. _____ is typically expressed in units of deaths per 1000 individuals per year; thus, a _____ of 9.5 in a population of 100,000 would mean 950 deaths per year in that entire population. It is distinct from morbidity rate, which refers to the number of individuals in poor health during a given time period (the prevalence rate) or the number who currently have that disease (the incidence rate), scaled to the size of the population.
   a. 100-year flood
   b. 130-30 fund
   c. Mortality rate
   d. 1921 recession

6. In economics, the people in the _____ are the suppliers of labor. The _____ is all the nonmilitary people who are employed or unemployed. In 2005, the worldwide _____ was over 3 billion people.
   a. Grenelle agreements
   b. Labor force
   c. Distributed workforce
   d. Departmentalization

Chapter 28. Population, Labor, and the Tertiary Sector

7. _____ is a term in economics, where demand for one good or service occurs as a result of demand for another. This may occur as the former is a part of production of the second. For example, demand for coal leads to _____ for mining, as coal must be mined for coal to be consumed.

   a. Derived demand
   b. Days Sales Outstanding
   c. Leontief production function
   d. Rate risk

8. Economics:

   - _____,the desire to own something and the ability to pay for it
   - _____ curve,a graphic representation of a _____ schedule
   - _____ deposit, the money in checking accounts
   - _____ pull theory,the theory that inflation occurs when _____ for goods and services exceeds existing supplies
   - _____ schedule,a table that lists the quantity of a good a person will buy it each different price
   - _____ side economics,the school of economics at believes government spending and tax cuts open economy by raising _____

   a. Variability
   b. McKesson ' Robbins scandal
   c. Production
   d. Demand

9. In mathematics, an _____ is a statement about the relative size or order of two objects, or about whether they are the same or not

   - The notation a < b means that a is less than b.
   - The notation a > b means that a is greater than b.
   - The notation a ≠ b means that a is not equal to b, but does not say that one is greater than the other or even that they can be compared in size.

   In each statement above, a is not equal to b. These relations are known as strict inequalities. The notation a < b may also be read as 'a is strictly less than b'.

   a. ACEA agreement
   b. ACCRA Cost of Living Index
   c. Inequality
   d. AD-IA Model

10. The _____ or gross domestic income (GDI), a basic measure of an economy's economic performance, is the market value of all final goods and services produced within the borders of a nation in a year. _____ can be defined in three ways, all of which are conceptually identical. First, it is equal to the total expenditures for all final goods and services produced within the country in a stipulated period of time (usually a 365-day year.)

    a. Market structure
    b. Countercyclical
    c. Monopolistic competition
    d. Gross domestic product

11. In microeconomics, _____ is quite simply the conversion of inputs into outputs. It is an economic process that uses resources to create a good or service that is suitable for exchange. This can include manufacturing, storing, shipping, and packaging.

a. Red Guards
b. Solved
c. MET
d. Production

12. The _____ is the number of total hours that workers wish to work at a given real wage rate.

Labor supply curves are derived from the 'labor-leisure' trade-off. More hours worked earn higher incomes but necessitate a cut in the amount of leisure that workers enjoy.

a. Supply of Labor
b. Dual labor market
c. Compound interest
d. De minimis fringe benefits

13. _____ or economic opportunity loss is the value of the next best alternative foregone as the result of making a decision. _____ analysis is an important part of a company's decision-making processes but is not treated as an actual cost in any financial statement. The next best thing that a person can engage in is referred to as the _____ of doing the best thing and ignoring the next best thing to be done.

a. Industrial organization
b. Economic
c. Economic ideology
d. Opportunity cost

14. _____ or information industries is a loosely defined term for industries that are information intensive in one way or the other. It is considered one of the most important economic sectors for a variety of reasons.

There are many different kinds of information industries, and many different ways to classify them.

a. ACCRA Cost of Living Index
b. AD-IA Model
c. Information industry
d. ACEA agreement

15. _____ refers to the stock of skills and knowledge embodied in the ability to perform labor so as to produce economic value. It is the skills and knowledge gained by a worker through education and experience. Many early economic theories refer to it simply as labor, one of three factors of production, and consider it to be a fungible resource -- homogeneous and easily interchangeable. Other conceptions of labor dispense with these assumptions.

a. General equilibrium
b. Price theory
c. Law of increasing costs
d. Human capital

16. _____ refers to discriminatory employment practices such as bias in hiring, promotion, job assignment, termination, and compensation, and various types of harassment.

In many countries, laws prohibit employers from discriminating on the basis of race, color, sex, religion, national origin, physical or mental disability, or age. There is also a growing body of law preventing or occasionally justifying _____ based on sexual orientation or gender identity.

a. Irish competition law
b. Impotent poor
c. Energy Independence and Security Act of 2007
d. Employment discrimination

Chapter 28. Population, Labor, and the Tertiary Sector

17. _____ the Great War, and the War to End All Wars, was a global military conflict which involved the majority of the world's great powers, organized into two opposing military alliances: the Entente Powers and the Central Powers. Over 70 million military personnel were mobilized in one of the largest wars in history. In a state of total war, the major combatants fully placed their scientific and industrial capabilities at the service of the war effort.

   a. 1921 recession
   b. World War I
   c. 100-year flood
   d. 130-30 fund

18. _____ is a pejorative term for the practice of hiring more workers than are needed to perform a given job complex and time-consuming merely to employ additional workers. The term 'make-work' is sometimes used as a synonym for _____.

   The term '_____' is usually used by management to describe behaviors and rules sought by workers.

   a. Channel coordination
   b. Cultural synergy
   c. Foreign ownership
   d. Featherbedding

19. A trade union or _____ is an organization of workers who have banded together to achieve common goals in key areas and working conditions. The trade union, through its leadership, bargains with the employer on behalf of union members (rank and file members) and negotiates labor contracts (Collective bargaining) with employers. This may include the negotiation of wages, work rules, complaint procedures, rules governing hiring, firing and promotion of workers, benefits, workplace safety and policies.

   a. Basis of futures
   b. Demand-side technologies
   c. Labor union
   d. Business valuation standards

20. Competition law, known in the United States as _____ law, has three main elements:

   - prohibiting agreements or practices that restrict free trading and competition between business entities. This includes in particular the repression of cartels.
   - banning abusive behaviour by a firm dominating a market, or anti-competitive practices that tend to lead to such a dominant position. Practices controlled in this way may include predatory pricing, tying, price gouging, refusal to deal, and many others.
   - supervising the mergers and acquisitions of large corporations, including some joint ventures. Transactions that are considered to threaten the competitive process can be prohibited altogether, or approved subject to 'remedies' such as an obligation to divest part of the merged business or to offer licences or access to facilities to enable other businesses to continue competing.

   The substance and practice of competition law varies from jurisdiction to jurisdiction. Protecting the interests of consumers (consumer welfare) and ensuring that entrepreneurs have an opportunity to compete in the market economy are often treated as important objectives. Competition law is closely connected with law on deregulation of access to markets, state aids and subsidies, the privatisation of state owned assets and the establishment of independent sector regulators. In recent decades, competition law has been viewed as a way to provide better public services.

   a. United Kingdom competition law
   b. Antitrust
   c. Anti-Inflation Act
   d. Intellectual property law

Chapter 28. Population, Labor, and the Tertiary Sector

21. _____, known in the United States as antitrust law, has three main elements:

- prohibiting agreements or practices that restrict free trading and competition between business entities. This includes in particular the repression of cartels.
- banning abusive behaviour by a firm dominating a market, or anti-competitive practices that tend to lead to such a dominant position. Practices controlled in this way may include predatory pricing, tying, price gouging, refusal to deal, and many others.
- supervising the mergers and acquisitions of large corporations, including some joint ventures. Transactions that are considered to threaten the competitive process can be prohibited altogether, or approved subject to 'remedies' such as an obligation to divest part of the merged business or to offer licences or access to facilities to enable other businesses to continue competing.

The substance and practice of _____ varies from jurisdiction to jurisdiction. Protecting the interests of consumers (consumer welfare) and ensuring that entrepreneurs have an opportunity to compete in the market economy are often treated as important objectives. _____ is closely connected with law on deregulation of access to markets, state aids and subsidies, the privatisation of state owned assets and the establishment of independent sector regulators. In recent decades, _____ has been viewed as a way to provide better public services.

a. Competition law
b. Fee simple
c. Hostile work environment
d. Due diligence

22. A _____ or labor union is an organization of workers who have banded together to achieve common goals in key areas and working conditions. The _____, through its leadership, bargains with the employer on behalf of union members (rank and file members) and negotiates labor contracts (Collective bargaining) with employers. This may include the negotiation of wages, work rules, complaint procedures, rules governing hiring, firing and promotion of workers, benefits, workplace safety and policies.

a. Case-Shiller Home Price Indices
b. Trade union
c. Guaranteed investment contracts
d. Consumer goods

23. The American Federation of Labor and Congress of Industrial Organizations, commonly _____, is a national trade union center, the largest federation of unions in the United States, made up of 65 national and international unions (including Canadian), together representing more than 10 million workers. It was formed in 1955 when the AFL and the CIO merged after a long estrangement. From 1955 until 2005, the _____'s member unions represented nearly all unionized workers in the United States.

a. AD-IA Model
b. AFL-CIO
c. ACEA agreement
d. ACCRA Cost of Living Index

24. _____ is a type of trade policy that allows traders to act and transact without interference from government. Thus, the policy permits trading partners mutual gains from trade, with goods and services produced according to the theory of comparative advantage.

Under a _____ policy, prices are a reflection of true supply and demand, and are the sole determinant of resource allocation.

a. 130-30 fund
b. 100-year flood
c. Free Trade
d. 1921 recession

25. The _____ was a period in the late 18th and early 19th centuries when major changes in agriculture, manufacturing, mining, and transportation had a profound effect on the socioeconomic and cultural conditions in Britain. The changes subsequently spread throughout Europe, North America, and eventually the world. The onset of the _____ marked a major turning point in human society; almost every aspect of daily life was eventually influenced in some way.
   a. Industrial Revolution
   b. Adam Smith
   c. Adolf Hitler
   d. Adolph Fischer

26. The _____ is a trilateral trade bloc in North America created by the governments of the United States, Canada, and Mexico. The agreement creating the trade bloc came into force on January 1, 1994. It superseded the Canada-United States Free Trade Agreement between the U.S. and Canada.
   a. Case-Shiller Home Price Indices
   b. North American Free Trade Agreement
   c. Federal Reserve Bank Notes
   d. Demand-side technologies

27. _____ in economics refers to metrics and measures of output from production processes, per unit of input. Labor _____, for example, is typically measured as a ratio of output per labor-hour, an input. _____ may be conceived of as a metrics of the technical or engineering efficiency of production.
   a. Production-possibility frontier
   b. Piece work
   c. Fordism
   d. Productivity

28. The _____ was one of the first federations of labor unions in the United States. It was founded in Columbus, Ohio in 1886 by Samuel Gompers as a reorganization of its predecessor, the Federation of Organized Trades and Labor Unions. Gompers became president of the AFL in 1886 and was reelected every year except one until his death on December 13, 1924.
   a. American Federation of Labor
   b. ACCRA Cost of Living Index
   c. AD-IA Model
   d. ACEA agreement

29. _____ is a field of economics that studies the strategic behavior of firms, the structure of markets and their interactions. The study of _____ adds to the perfectly competitive model real-world frictions such as limited information, transaction cost, cost of adjusting prices, government actions, and barriers to entry by new firms into a market. It then considers how firms are organized and how they compete.
   a. Inflation
   b. Economic
   c. Economic ideology
   d. Industrial Organization

30. _____ is the shortage of common things such as food, clothing, shelter and safe drinking water, all of which determine the quality of life. It may also include the lack of access to opportunities such as education and employment which aid the escape from _____ and/or allow one to enjoy the respect of fellow citizens. According to Mollie Orshansky who developed the _____ measurements used by the U.S. government, 'to be poor is to be deprived of those goods and services and pleasures which others around us take for granted.' Ongoing debates over causes, effects and best ways to measure _____, directly influence the design and implementation of _____-reduction programs and are therefore relevant to the fields of public administration and international development.
   a. Growth Elasticity of Poverty
   b. Poverty map
   c. Poverty
   d. Liberal welfare reforms

Chapter 28. Population, Labor, and the Tertiary Sector

31. The _____ is a measure of statistical dispersion, commonly used as a measure of inequality of income distribution or inequality of wealth distribution. It is defined as a ratio with values between 0 and 1: A low _____ indicates more equal income or wealth distribution, while a high _____ indicates more unequal distribution. 0 corresponds to perfect equality (everyone having exactly the same income) and 1 corresponds to perfect inequality (where one person has all the income, while everyone else has zero income.)
    a. Suits index
    c. Compensating variation
    b. Leapfrogging
    d. Gini coefficient

32. In economics, a _____ is a general slowdown in economic activity over a sustained period of time, or a business cycle contraction. During _____s, many macroeconomic indicators vary in a similar way. Production as measured by Gross Domestic Product (GDP), employment, investment spending, capacity utilization, household incomes and business profits all fall during _____s.
    a. Leading indicators
    c. Monetary economics
    b. Treasury View
    d. Recession

33. In mathematics, a _____ is a constant multiplicative factor of a certain object. For example, in the expression $9x^2$, the _____ of x^2 is 9.

The object can be such things as a variable, a vector, a function, etc.

    a. 1921 recession
    c. 100-year flood
    b. Coefficient
    d. 130-30 fund

34. The _____ is the apparent contradiction that although water is on the whole more useful, in terms of survival, than diamonds, diamonds command a higher price in the market. The economist Adam Smith is often considered to be the classic presenter of this paradox. Nicolaus Copernicus, John Locke, John Law and others had previously tried to explain the disparity.
    a. 130-30 fund
    c. St. Petersburg paradox
    b. 100-year flood
    d. Paradox of value

Chapter 29. Postwar Industry and Agriculture

1. In economics, the people in the _____ are the suppliers of labor. The _____ is all the nonmilitary people who are employed or unemployed. In 2005, the worldwide _____ was over 3 billion people.
   a. Grenelle agreements
   b. Distributed workforce
   c. Labor force
   d. Departmentalization

2. _____ in economics refers to metrics and measures of output from production processes, per unit of input. Labor _____, for example, is typically measured as a ratio of output per labor-hour, an input. _____ may be conceived of as a metrics of the technical or engineering efficiency of production.
   a. Productivity
   b. Piece work
   c. Fordism
   d. Production-possibility frontier

3. In microeconomics, _____ is quite simply the conversion of inputs into outputs. It is an economic process that uses resources to create a good or service that is suitable for exchange. This can include manufacturing, storing, shipping, and packaging.
   a. MET
   b. Red Guards
   c. Solved
   d. Production

4. _____s is the social science that studies the production, distribution, and consumption of goods and services. The term _____s comes from the Ancient Greek οἰκονομία from οἶκος (oikos, 'house') + νόμος (nomos, 'custom' or 'law'), hence 'rules of the house(hold)'. Current _____ models developed out of the broader field of political economy in the late 19th century, owing to a desire to use an empirical approach more akin to the physical sciences.
   a. Energy economics
   b. Inflation
   c. Economic
   d. Opportunity cost

5. _____ is the increase in the amount of the goods and services produced by an economy over time. It is conventionally measured as the percent rate of increase in real gross domestic product, or real GDP. Growth is usually calculated in real terms, i.e. inflation-adjusted terms, in order to net out the effect of inflation on the price of the goods and services produced.
   a. ACEA agreement
   b. AD-IA Model
   c. Economic growth
   d. ACCRA Cost of Living Index

6. _____ is the change in population over time, and can be quantified as the change in the number of individuals in a population using 'per unit time' for measurement. The term _____ can technically refer to any species, but almost always refers to humans, and it is often used informally for the more specific demographic term _____ rate, and is often used to refer specifically to the growth of the population of the world.

   Simple models of _____ include the Malthusian Growth Model and the logistic model.

   a. 100-year flood
   b. 130-30 fund
   c. Population dynamics
   d. Population growth

7. _____ in its literal sense is the process of transformation of local or regional phenomena into global ones. It can be described as a process by which the people of the world are unified into a single society and function together.

This process is a combination of economic, technological, sociocultural and political forces.

a. Global Cosmopolitanism
b. Helsinki Process on Globalisation and Democracy
c. Globalization
d. Globally Integrated Enterprise

8. The _____ was the continuing state of conflict, tension, and competition that existed after World War II between the Soviet Union and its satellites and the powers of the Western world under the leadership of the United States from the mid-1940s to the early 1990s. Throughout this period, the conflict was expressed through military coalitions, espionage, weapons development, invasions, propaganda, and competitive technological development, which included the space race. The conflict included costly defense spending, a massive conventional and nuclear arms race, and numerous proxy wars; the two superpowers never fought one another directly.

a. Mutual assured destruction
b. Cold War
c. Reagan Doctrine
d. Sino-Soviet split

9. A trade union or _____ is an organization of workers who have banded together to achieve common goals in key areas and working conditions. The trade union, through its leadership, bargains with the employer on behalf of union members (rank and file members) and negotiates labor contracts (Collective bargaining) with employers. This may include the negotiation of wages, work rules, complaint procedures, rules governing hiring, firing and promotion of workers, benefits, workplace safety and policies.

a. Business valuation standards
b. Demand-side technologies
c. Basis of futures
d. Labor union

10. Competition law, known in the United States as _____ law, has three main elements:

- prohibiting agreements or practices that restrict free trading and competition between business entities. This includes in particular the repression of cartels.
- banning abusive behaviour by a firm dominating a market, or anti-competitive practices that tend to lead to such a dominant position. Practices controlled in this way may include predatory pricing, tying, price gouging, refusal to deal, and many others.
- supervising the mergers and acquisitions of large corporations, including some joint ventures. Transactions that are considered to threaten the competitive process can be prohibited altogether, or approved subject to 'remedies' such as an obligation to divest part of the merged business or to offer licences or access to facilities to enable other businesses to continue competing.

The substance and practice of competition law varies from jurisdiction to jurisdiction. Protecting the interests of consumers (consumer welfare) and ensuring that entrepreneurs have an opportunity to compete in the market economy are often treated as important objectives. Competition law is closely connected with law on deregulation of access to markets, state aids and subsidies, the privatisation of state owned assets and the establishment of independent sector regulators. In recent decades, competition law has been viewed as a way to provide better public services.

a. Anti-Inflation Act
b. Intellectual property law
c. United Kingdom competition law
d. Antitrust

Chapter 29. Postwar Industry and Agriculture

11. _____, known in the United States as antitrust law, has three main elements:

- prohibiting agreements or practices that restrict free trading and competition between business entities. This includes in particular the repression of cartels.
- banning abusive behaviour by a firm dominating a market, or anti-competitive practices that tend to lead to such a dominant position. Practices controlled in this way may include predatory pricing, tying, price gouging, refusal to deal, and many others.
- supervising the mergers and acquisitions of large corporations, including some joint ventures. Transactions that are considered to threaten the competitive process can be prohibited altogether, or approved subject to 'remedies' such as an obligation to divest part of the merged business or to offer licences or access to facilities to enable other businesses to continue competing.

The substance and practice of _____ varies from jurisdiction to jurisdiction. Protecting the interests of consumers (consumer welfare) and ensuring that entrepreneurs have an opportunity to compete in the market economy are often treated as important objectives. _____ is closely connected with law on deregulation of access to markets, state aids and subsidies, the privatisation of state owned assets and the establishment of independent sector regulators. In recent decades, _____ has been viewed as a way to provide better public services.

a. Competition law
b. Fee simple
c. Due diligence
d. Hostile work environment

12. A _____ or labor union is an organization of workers who have banded together to achieve common goals in key areas and working conditions. The _____, through its leadership, bargains with the employer on behalf of union members (rank and file members) and negotiates labor contracts (Collective bargaining) with employers. This may include the negotiation of wages, work rules, complaint procedures, rules governing hiring, firing and promotion of workers, benefits, workplace safety and policies.

a. Consumer goods
b. Guaranteed investment contracts
c. Case-Shiller Home Price Indices
d. Trade union

13. The _____ consists of a number of economic theories which describe the nature of the firm, company including its existence, its behaviour, and its relationship with the market.

In simplified terms, the _____ aims to answer these questions:

1. Existence - why do firms emerge, why are not all transactions in the economy mediated over the market?
2. Boundaries - why the boundary between firms and the market is located exactly there? Which transactions are performed internally and which are negotiated on the market?
3. Organization - why are firms structured in such specific way? What is the interplay of formal and informal relationships?

Despite looking simple, these questions are not answered by the established economic theory, which usually views firms as given, and treats them as black boxes without any internal structure.

Chapter 29. Postwar Industry and Agriculture

The First World War period saw a change of emphasis in economic theory away from industry-level analysis which mainly included analysing markets to analysis at the level of the firm, as it became increasingly clear that perfect competition was no longer an adequate model of how firms behaved. Economic theory till then had focussed on trying to understand markets alone and there had been little study on understanding why firms or organisations exist.

- a. Theory of the firm
- b. Khazzoom-Brookes postulate
- c. Policy Ineffectiveness Proposition
- d. Technology gap

14. _____ in economics and business is the result of an exchange and from that trade we assign a numerical monetary value to a good, service or asset. If Alice trades Bob 4 apples for an orange, the _____ of an orange is 4 apples. Inversely, the _____ of an apple is 1/4 oranges.

- a. Price war
- b. Price
- c. Price book
- d. Premium pricing

15. A _____ or market-based mechanism is any of a wide variety of ways to match up buyers and sellers.

An example of a _____ uses announced bid and ask prices. Generally speaking, when two parties wish to engage in a trade, the purchaser will announce a price he is willing to pay (the bid price) and seller will announce a price he is willing to accept (the ask price.)

- a. Price Mechanism
- b. Market equilibrium
- c. Horizontal market
- d. Marketization

16. Economics:

- _____ ,the desire to own something and the ability to pay for it
- _____ curve,a graphic representation of a _____ schedule
- _____ deposit, the money in checking accounts
- _____ pull theory,the theory that inflation occurs when _____ for goods and services exceeds existing supplies
- _____ schedule,a table that lists the quantity of a good a person will buy it each different price
- _____ side economics,the school of economics at believes government spending and tax cuts open economy by raising _____

- a. Production
- b. McKesson ' Robbins scandal
- c. Demand
- d. Variability

17. _____ is a term in economics, where demand for one good or service occurs as a result of demand for another. This may occur as the former is a part of production of the second. For example, demand for coal leads to _____ for mining, as coal must be mined for coal to be consumed.

- a. Days Sales Outstanding
- b. Derived demand
- c. Leontief production function
- d. Rate risk

Chapter 29. Postwar Industry and Agriculture

18. In economics, _____ is the ratio of the percent change in one variable to the percent change in another variable. It is a tool for measuring the responsiveness of a function to changes in parameters in a relative way. Commonly analyzed are _____ of substitution, price and wealth.
    a. ACCRA Cost of Living Index
    b. Elasticity of demand
    c. Elasticity
    d. ACEA agreement

19. Price _____ is defined as the measure of responsiveness in the quantity demanded for a commodity as a result of change in price of the same commodity. It is a measure of how consumers react to a change in price. In other words, it is percentage change in quantity demanded by the percentage change in price of the same commodity.
    a. Elasticity
    b. ACCRA Cost of Living Index
    c. ACEA agreement
    d. Elasticity of Demand

20. In economics, the _____ of demand measures the responsiveness of the demand of a good to the change in the income of the people demanding the good. It is calculated as the ratio of the percent change in demand to the percent change in income. For example, if, in response to a 10% increase in income, the demand of a good increased by 20%, the _____ of demand would be 20%/10% = 2.
    a. ACCRA Cost of Living Index
    b. ACEA agreement
    c. AD-IA Model
    d. Income elasticity

21. In economics, the _____ measures the responsiveness of the demand of a good to the change in the income of the people demanding the good. It is calculated as the ratio of the percent change in demand to the percent change in income. For example, if, in response to a 10% increase in income, the demand of a good increased by 20%, the _____ would be 20%/10% = 2.
    a. Elasticity of substitution
    b. Indifference map
    c. Expenditure minimization problem
    d. Income elasticity of Demand

22. _____ is defined as the measure of responsiveness in the quantity demanded for a commodity as a result of change in price of the same commodity. It is a measure of how consumers react to a change in price. In other words, it is percentage change in quantity demanded as per the percentage change in price of the same commodity.
    a. 130-30 fund
    b. Price elasticity of Demand
    c. 1921 recession
    d. 100-year flood

23. An _____ is any great bottleneck (or price rise) in the supply of energy resources to an economy. It usually refers to the shortage of oil and additionally to electricity or other natural resources. An _____ may be referred to as an oil crisis, petroleum crisis, energy shortage, electricity shortage or electricity crisis.
    a. Olduvai theory
    b. Oil depletion
    c. Oil reserves in the United States
    d. Energy crisis

24. In finance, _____ is investment originating from other countries.See Foreign direct investment.
    a. Horizontal merger
    b. Preclusive purchasing
    c. Demand side economics
    d. Foreign investment

25. The phrase _____, according to the Organization for Economic Co-operation and Development, refers to 'creative work undertaken on a systematic basis in order to increase the stock of knowledge, including knowledge of man, culture and society, and the use of this stock of knowledge to devise new applications [sic]'

New product design and development is more than often a crucial factor in the survival of a company. In an industry that is fast changing, firms must continually revise their design and range of products. This is necessary due to continuous technology change and development as well as other competitors and the changing preference of customers.

a. 1921 recession
b. 100-year flood
c. 130-30 fund
d. Research and development

26. _____ refers to the stock of skills and knowledge embodied in the ability to perform labor so as to produce economic value. It is the skills and knowledge gained by a worker through education and experience. Many early economic theories refer to it simply as labor, one of three factors of production, and consider it to be a fungible resource -- homogeneous and easily interchangeable. Other conceptions of labor dispense with these assumptions.

a. General equilibrium
b. Price theory
c. Law of increasing costs
d. Human capital

27. _____ usually refers to the transformation of agriculture that began in 1945. One significant factor in this revolution was the Mexican government's request to establish an agricultural research station to develop more varieties of wheat that could be used to feed the rapidly growing population of the country.

In 1943, Mexico imported half its wheat, but by 1956, the _____ had made Mexico self-sufficient; by 1964, Mexico exported half a million tons of wheat.

a. 1921 recession
b. 130-30 fund
c. 100-year flood
d. Green Revolution

28. The U.S. _____ is the primary agricultural and food policy tool of the Federal government of the United States. The comprehensive omnibus bill is passed every several years by the United States Congress and deals with both agriculture and all other affairs under the purview of the United States Department of Agriculture.

The current _____, known as the Food, Conservation, and Energy Act of 2008, replaces the last _____ which expired in September 2007.

a. 1921 recession
b. Farm Bill
c. 130-30 fund
d. 100-year flood

Chapter 30. To the New Millennium and Beyond

1. _____s is the social science that studies the production, distribution, and consumption of goods and services. The term _____s comes from the Ancient Greek οἰκονομία from οἶκος (oikos, 'house') + νόμος (nomos, 'custom' or 'law'), hence 'rules of the house(hold)'. Current _____ models developed out of the broader field of political economy in the late 19th century, owing to a desire to use an empirical approach more akin to the physical sciences.
   a. Inflation
   b. Energy economics
   c. Opportunity cost
   d. Economic

2. _____ is the increase in the amount of the goods and services produced by an economy over time. It is conventionally measured as the percent rate of increase in real gross domestic product, or real GDP. Growth is usually calculated in real terms, i.e. inflation-adjusted terms, in order to net out the effect of inflation on the price of the goods and services produced.
   a. ACEA agreement
   b. Economic growth
   c. ACCRA Cost of Living Index
   d. AD-IA Model

3. _____ is a fee paid on borrowed assets. It is the price paid for the use of borrowed money , or, money earned by deposited funds . Assets that are sometimes lent with _____ include money, shares, consumer goods through hire purchase, major assets such as aircraft, and even entire factories in finance lease arrangements.
   a. Internal debt
   b. Interest
   c. Insolvency
   d. Asset protection

4. An _____ is the price a borrower pays for the use of money they do not own, for instance a small company might borrow from a bank to kick start their business, and the return a lender receives for deferring the use of funds, by lending it to the borrower. _____s are normally expressed as a percentage rate over the period of one year.

   _____s targets are also a vital tool of monetary policy and are used to control variables like investment, inflation, and unemployment.

   a. ACCRA Cost of Living Index
   b. Enterprise value
   c. Arrow-Debreu model
   d. Interest rate

5. _____ is that which is owed; usually referencing assets owed, but the term can also cover moral obligations and other interactions not requiring money. In the case of assets, _____ is a means of using future purchasing power in the present before a summation has been earned. Some companies and corporations use _____ as a part of their overall corporate finance strategy.
   a. Debenture
   b. Collateral Management
   c. Hard money loan
   d. Debt

6.

The _____ is an independent agency of the United States government, created, directed, and empowered by Congressional statute , and with the majority of its commissioners appointed by the current President. The _____ works towards six strategic goals in the areas of broadband, competition, the spectrum, the media, public safety and homeland security, and modernizing the _____.

   a. 1921 recession
   b. 100-year flood
   c. Federal Communications Commission
   d. 130-30 fund

7. The _____ is a protocol to the United Nations Framework Convention on Climate Change (UNFCCC or FCCC), an international environmental treaty produced at the United Nations Conference on treaty is intended to achieve 'stabilization of greenhouse gas concentrations in the atmosphere at a level that would prevent dangerous anthropogenic interference with the climate system.' The _____ establishes legally binding commitments for the reduction of four greenhouse gases (carbon dioxide, methane, nitrous oxide, sulphur hexafluoride), and two groups of gases (hydrofluorocarbons and perfluorocarbons) produced by 'Annex I' (industrialized) nations, as well as general commitments for all member countries. As of January 14 2009, 183 parties have ratified the protocol, which was initially adopted for use on 11 December 1997 in Kyoto, Japan and which entered into force on 16 February 2005. Under Kyoto, industrialized countries agreed to reduce their collective GHG emissions by 5.2% compared to the year 1990.

   a. Green New Deal
   b. Carbon offset
   c. Kyoto Protocol
   d. Greenhouse gases

8. In economics, a _____ is a general slowdown in economic activity over a sustained period of time, or a business cycle contraction. During _____s, many macroeconomic indicators vary in a similar way. Production as measured by Gross Domestic Product (GDP), employment, investment spending, capacity utilization, household incomes and business profits all fall during _____s.

   a. Recession
   b. Leading indicators
   c. Treasury View
   d. Monetary economics

9. The _____ was a worldwide economic downturn starting in most places in 1929 and ending at different times in the 1930s or early 1940s for different countries. It was the largest and most important economic depression in the 20th century, and is used in the 21st century as an example of how far the world's economy can fall. The _____ originated in the United States; historians most often use as a starting date the stock market crash on October 29, 1929, known as Black Tuesday.

   a. British Empire Economic Conference
   b. Jarrow March
   c. Great Depression
   d. Wall Street Crash of 1929

10. The _____ was a regulatory body in the United States created by the Interstate Commerce Act of 1887, which was signed into law by President Grover Cleveland. The agency was abolished in 1995, and the agency's remaining functions were transferred to the Surface Transportation Board.

    The Commission's five members were appointed by the President with the consent of the United States Senate.

    a. Office of Thrift Supervision
    b. ACEA agreement
    c. Interstate Commerce Commission
    d. ACCRA Cost of Living Index

11. _____ is a school of macroeconomic thought that argues that economic growth can be most effectively created using incentives for people to produce (supply) goods and services, such as adjusting income tax and capital gains tax rates, and by allowing greater flexibility by reducing regulation. Consumers will then benefit from a greater supply of goods and services at lower prices.

The term _____ was coined by journalist Jude Wanniski in 1975, and popularized the ideas of economists Robert Mundell and Arthur Laffer.

a. Commodity trading advisors
b. Clap note
c. Fiscal stimulus plans
d. Supply-side economics

12. The _____ Index or Pollutant Standard Index) is a number used by government agencies to characterize the quality of the air at a given location. As the Air qualityI increases, an increasingly large percentage of the population is likely to experience increasingly severe adverse health effects. To compute the Air qualityI requires an air pollutant concentration from a monitor or model.
    a. Air Quality
    b. AD-IA Model
    c. ACCRA Cost of Living Index
    d. ACEA agreement

13. The _____ was a landmark piece of legislation in the United States that outlawed racial segregation in schools, public places, and employment.
    a. Postcautionary principle
    b. Patent portfolio
    c. Le Chapelier Law
    d. Civil Rights Act of 1964

14. A _____ describes one of a number of pieces of legislation relating to the reduction of smog and air pollution in general. The use by governments to enforce clean air standards has contributed to an improvement in human health and longer life spans. Critics argue it has also sapped corporate profits and contributed to outsourcing, while defenders counter that improved environmental air quality has generated more jobs than it has eliminated.
    a. 100-year flood
    b. Smog
    c. 130-30 fund
    d. Clean Air Act

15. The _____ is a United States federal law that requires the Environmental Protection Agency (EPA) to develop and enforce regulations to protect the general public from exposure to airborne contaminants that are known to be hazardous to human health. This law is an amendment to the Clean Air Act (CAA) originally passed in 1963.
    a. Meat Inspection Act
    b. Competition law
    c. Clean Air Act Extension of 1970
    d. Beneficial ownership

16. _____ is a broad label that refers to any individuals or households that use goods and services generated within the economy. The concept of a _____ is used in different contexts, so that the usage and significance of the term may vary.

Typically when business people and economists talk of _____s they are talking about person as _____, an aggregated commodity item with little individuality other than that expressed in the buy/not-buy decision.

   a. 1921 recession
   b. 130-30 fund
   c. 100-year flood
   d. Consumer

17. _____ is any (course of) action deliberately taken (or not taken) to manage human activities with a view to prevent, reduce or mitigate harmful effects on nature and natural resources, and ensuring that man-made changes to the environment do not have harmful effects on humans.

It is useful to consider that _____ comprises two major terms: environment and policy. Environment primarily refers to the ecological (ecosystems) dimension, but can also take account of social (quality of life) dimension and an economic (resource management) dimension.

Chapter 30. To the New Millennium and Beyond

    a. ACCRA Cost of Living Index
    b. ACEA agreement
    c. AD-IA Model
    d. Environmental Policy

18. _____ is a practice of protecting the environment, on individual, organisational or governmental level, for the benefit of the natural environment and (or) humans.

Due to the pressures of population and technology the biophysical environment is being degraded, sometimes permanently. This has been recognised and governments began placing restraints on activities that caused environmental degradation.

    a. ACEA agreement
    b. AD-IA Model
    c. ACCRA Cost of Living Index
    d. Environmental Protection

19. The U.S. _____ is a federal agency whose goal is ending employment discrimination. The _____ investigates discrimination complaints based on an individual's race, color, national origin, religion, sex, age, disability and retaliation for reporting and/or opposing a discriminatory practice. The Commission is also tasked with filing suits on behalf of alleged victim(s) of discrimination against employers and as an adjudicatory for claims of discrimination brought against federal agencies.

    a. ACEA agreement
    b. ACCRA Cost of Living Index
    c. Equal Employment Opportunity Commission
    d. AD-IA Model

20. _____ is a cross-disciplinary area concerned with protecting the safety, health and welfare of people engaged in work or employment. As a secondary effect, it may also protect co-workers, family members, employers, customers, suppliers, nearby communities, and other members of the public who are impacted by the workplace environment. It may involve interactions among many subject areas, including occupational medicine, occupational (or industrial) hygiene, public health, safety engineering, chemistry, health physics, ergonomics, toxicology, epidemiology, environmental health, industrial relations, public policy, sociology, and occupational health psychology.

    a. Occupational Safety and Health
    b. AD-IA Model
    c. ACEA agreement
    d. ACCRA Cost of Living Index

21. The _____ is the primary federal law which governs occupational health and safety in the private sector and federal government in the United States. It was enacted by Congress in 1970 and was signed by President Richard Nixon on December 29, 1970. Its main goal is to ensure that employers provide employees with an environment free from recognized hazards, such as exposure to toxic chemicals, excessive noise levels, mechanical dangers, heat or cold stress, or unsanitary conditions.

    a. Electronic Commerce Protection Act
    b. Escalator clause
    c. Irish competition law
    d. Occupational Safety and Health Act

22. A security is a fungible, negotiable instrument representing financial value. _____ are broadly categorized into debt _____; equity _____, e.g., common stocks; and derivative (finance) contracts such as forwards, futures, options and swaps. The company or other entity issuing the security is called the issuer.

    a. Settlement risk
    b. Red herring prospectus
    c. Pass-Through Certificates
    d. Securities

Chapter 30. To the New Millennium and Beyond

23. In 1940, President Franklin Roosevelt split the authority into two agencies, the Civil Aeronautics Administration (CAA) and the _____ The CAA was responsible for air traffic control, safety programs, and airway development. The _____ was entrusted with safety rulemaking, accident investigation, and economic regulation of the airlines.
    a. 100-year flood
    b. 1921 recession
    c. 130-30 fund
    d. Civil Aeronautics Board

24. _____ is a term used to describe large corporations, in either an individual or collective sense. The term first came into use in a symbolic sense subsequent to the American Civil War, particularly after 1880, in connection with the combination movement that began in American business at that time. Organizations that fall into the category of '_____' include ExxonMobil, Wal-Mart, Google, Microsoft, General Motors, Citigroup and Arcelor Mittal.
    a. Brainsworking
    b. First-mover advantage
    c. Sole proprietorship
    d. Big business

25. A _____ is a measure of the average price of consumer goods and services purchased by households. A _____ measures a price change for a constant market basket of goods and services from one period to the next within the same area (city, region, or nation.) It is a price index determined by measuring the price of a standard group of goods meant to represent the typical market basket of a typical urban consumer.
    a. CPI
    b. Lipstick index
    c. Cost-of-living index
    d. Consumer price index

26. In economics, _____ is the total amount of money available in an economy at a particular point in time. There are several ways to define 'money', but standard measures usually include currency in circulation and demand deposits.

    _____ data are recorded and published, usually by the government or the central bank of the country.

    a. Neutrality of money
    b. Veil of money
    c. Velocity of money
    d. Money supply

27. _____ in economics and business is the result of an exchange and from that trade we assign a numerical monetary value to a good, service or asset. If Alice trades Bob 4 apples for an orange, the _____ of an orange is 4 apples. Inversely, the _____ of an apple is 1/4 oranges.
    a. Price book
    b. Price war
    c. Premium pricing
    d. Price

28. A _____ is a normalized average (typically a weighted average) of prices for a given class of goods or services in a given region, during a given interval of time. It is a statistic designed to help to compare how these prices, taken as a whole, differ between time periods or geographical locations.

    Price indices have several potential uses.

    a. Product sabotage
    b. Transactional Net Margin Method
    c. Two-part tariff
    d. Price index

29. An _____ is any great bottleneck (or price rise) in the supply of energy resources to an economy. It usually refers to the shortage of oil and additionally to electricity or other natural resources. An _____ may be referred to as an oil crisis, petroleum crisis, energy shortage, electricity shortage or electricity crisis.

Chapter 30. To the New Millennium and Beyond

a. Olduvai theory
b. Oil depletion
c. Oil reserves in the United States
d. Energy crisis

30. The _____ is the central banking system of the United States. Created in 1913 by the enactment of the Federal Reserve Act (signed by Woodrow Wilson), it is a quasi-public and quasi-private (government entity with private components) banking system that comprises (1) the presidentially appointed Board of Governors of the _____ in Washington, D.C.; (2) the Federal Open Market Committee; (3) twelve regional Federal Reserve Banks located in major cities throughout the nation acting as fiscal agents for the U.S. Treasury, each with its own nine-member board of directors; (4) numerous other private U.S. member banks, which subscribe to required amounts of non-transferable stock in their regional Federal Reserve Banks; and (5) various advisory councils. Since February 2006, Ben Bernanke has served as the Chairman of the Board of Governors of the _____.

a. Monetary Policy Report to the Congress
b. Federal Reserve System
c. Term auction facility
d. Federal Reserve System Open Market Account

31. A _____ is a customs union with common policies on product regulation, and freedom of movement of the factors of production (capital and labour) and of enterprise. The goal is that the movement of capital, labour, goods, and services between the members is as easy as within them. This is the fourth stage of economic integration.

a. Grey market
b. Mutual recognition agreement
c. Competitiveness
d. Common market

32. The _____ is an international organization that oversees the global financial system by following the macroeconomic policies of its member countries, in particular those with an impact on exchange rates and the balance of payments. It is an organization formed to stabilize international exchange rates and facilitate development. It also offers financial and technical assistance to its members, making it an international lender of last resort.

a. ACEA agreement
b. Office of Thrift Supervision
c. ACCRA Cost of Living Index
d. International Monetary Fund

33. A _____ is a public market for the trading of company stock and derivatives at an agreed price; these are securities listed on a stock exchange as well as those only traded privately.

The size of the world _____ was estimated at about $36.6 trillion US at the beginning of October 2008. The total world derivatives market has been estimated at about $791 trillion face or nominal value, 11 times the size of the entire world economy.

a. Adam Smith
b. Adolph Fischer
c. Adolf Hitler
d. Stock market

34. The _____ is an international financial institution that provides financial and technical assistance to developing countries for development programs (e.g. bridges, roads, schools, etc.) with the stated goal of reducing poverty.

The _____ differs from the _____ Group, in that the _____ comprises only two institutions:

- International Bank for Reconstruction and Development (IBRD)
- International Development Association (IDA)

Chapter 30. To the New Millennium and Beyond 161

Whereas the latter incorporates these two in addition to three more:

- International Finance Corporation (IFC)
- Multilateral Investment Guarantee Agency (MIGA)
- International Centre for Settlement of Investment Disputes (ICSID)

John Maynard Keynes (right) represented the UK at the conference, and Harry Dexter White represented the US.

The _____ is one of two major financial institutions created as a result of the Bretton Woods Conference in 1944. The International Monetary Fund, a related but separate institution, is the second.

a. Bank-State-Branch
c. Flow to Equity-Approach

b. Financial costs of the 2003 Iraq War
d. World Bank

35.

A _____ is a type of financial intermediary and a type of bank. Commercial banking is also known as business banking. It is a bank that provides checking accounts, savings accounts, and money market accounts and that accepts time deposits.

a. Daylight overdraft
c. Bought deal

b. Commercial bank
d. Lombard banking

36. The _____, a United States federal financial statute law passed in 1980, gave the Federal Reserve greater control over non-member banks.

- It forced all banks to abide by the Fed's rules.
- It allowed banks to merge.
- It removed the power of the Federal Reserve Board of Governors under the Glass-Steagall Act and Regulation Q to set the interest rates of savings accounts.
- It raised the deposit insurance of US banks and credit unions from $40,000 to $100,000.
- It allowed credit unions and savings and loans to offer checkable deposits.
- Allowed institutions to charge any interest rates they chose.

a. Cash flow loan
c. Market-based instruments

b. Capital guarantee
d. Depository Institutions Deregulation and Monetary Control Act

37. _____ is the removal or simplification of government rules and regulations that constrain the operation of market forces. _____ does not mean elimination of laws against fraud, but eliminating or reducing government control of how business is done, thereby moving toward a more free market.

The stated rationale for '_____' is often that fewer and simpler regulations will lead to a raised level of competitiveness, therefore higher productivity, more efficiency and lower prices overall.

- a. Macroeconomic policy instruments
- b. Secular basis
- c. Fundamental psychological law
- d. Deregulation

38. In economics, _____ is the removal of intermediaries in a supply chain: 'cutting out the middleman'. Instead of going through traditional distribution channels, which had some type of intermediate (such as a distributor, wholesaler, broker, or agent), companies may now deal with every customer directly, for example via the Internet. One important factor is a drop in the cost of servicing customers directly.
- a. Cluetrain Manifesto
- b. Disintermediation
- c. Business-to-government
- d. Consumer-to-consumer

39. A _____ association is a financial institution that specializes in accepting savings deposits and making mortgage and other loans. The S'L or thrift term is mainly used in the United States; similar institutions in the United Kingdom, Ireland and some Commonwealth countries include building societies and trustee savings banks.

They are often mutually held, meaning that the depositors and borrowers are members with voting rights, and have the ability to direct the financial and managerial goals of the organization, similar to the policyholders of a mutual insurance company.

- a. Participating policy
- b. Fonds commun de placement
- c. Collective investment scheme
- d. Savings and loan

40. A _____ is a sudden dramatic decline of stock prices across a significant cross-section of a stock market. Crashes are driven by panic as much as by underlying economic factors. They often follow speculative stock market bubbles.
- a. Stock market crash
- b. 130-30 fund
- c. 100-year flood
- d. 1921 recession

41. In economics, _____ is a rise in the general level of prices of goods and services in an economy over a period of time. When the general price level rises, each unit of currency buys fewer goods and services; consequently, _____ is also a decline in the real value of money--a loss of purchasing power in the medium of exchange which is also the monetary unit of account in the economy. A chief measure of general price-level _____ is the general _____ rate, which is the percentage change in a general price index (normally the Consumer Price Index) over time.
- a. Opportunity cost
- b. Economic
- c. Energy economics
- d. Inflation

42. The _____ consists of a number of economic theories which describe the nature of the firm, company including its existence, its behaviour, and its relationship with the market.

Chapter 30. To the New Millennium and Beyond

In simplified terms, the _____ aims to answer these questions:

1. Existence - why do firms emerge, why are not all transactions in the economy mediated over the market?
2. Boundaries - why the boundary between firms and the market is located exactly there? Which transactions are performed internally and which are negotiated on the market?
3. Organization - why are firms structured in such specific way? What is the interplay of formal and informal relationships?

Despite looking simple, these questions are not answered by the established economic theory, which usually views firms as given, and treats them as black boxes without any internal structure.

The First World War period saw a change of emphasis in economic theory away from industry-level analysis which mainly included analysing markets to analysis at the level of the firm, as it became increasingly clear that perfect competition was no longer an adequate model of how firms behaved. Economic theory till then had focussed on trying to understand markets alone and there had been little study on understanding why firms or organisations exist.

a. Policy Ineffectiveness Proposition
b. Khazzoom-Brookes postulate
c. Technology gap
d. Theory of the firm

43. The _____ is a United States government corporation created by the Glass-Steagall Act of 1933. It provides deposit insurance, which guarantees the safety of deposits in member banks, currently up to $250,000 per depositor per bank. Funds in non-interest bearing transaction accounts are fully insured, with no limit, under the temporary Transaction Account Guarantee Program.

a. Federal Deposit Insurance Corporation
b. Luxembourg Income Study
c. Great Leap Forward
d. Foreign direct investment

44. The _____ was an institution that administered deposit insurance for savings and loan institutions in the United States. It was abolished in 1989 by the Financial Institutions Reform, Recovery and Enforcement Act, which passed responsibility for savings and loan deposit insurance to the Federal Deposit Insurance Corporation (FDIC.)

The FSLIC was created as part of the National Housing Act of 1934 in order to insure deposits in savings and loans, a year after the FDIC was created to insure deposits in commercial banks.

a. Federal Savings and Loan Insurance Corporation
b. Federal Financial Institutions Examination Council
c. Net capital rule
d. Covered security

45. The _____ or gross domestic income (GDI), a basic measure of an economy's economic performance, is the market value of all final goods and services produced within the borders of a nation in a year. _____ can be defined in three ways, all of which are conceptually identical. First, it is equal to the total expenditures for all final goods and services produced within the country in a stipulated period of time (usually a 365-day year.)

a. Market structure
b. Countercyclical
c. Monopolistic competition
d. Gross domestic product

Chapter 30. To the New Millennium and Beyond

46. A _____ is a place of residence or refuge and comfort. It is usually a place in which an individual or a family can rest and be able to store personal property. Most modern-day households contain sanitary facilities and a means of preparing food.
    a. 100-year flood
    b. 130-30 fund
    c. 1921 recession
    d. Home

47. _____, in law and economics, is a form of risk management primarily used to hedge against the risk of a contingent loss. _____ is defined as the equitable transfer of the risk of a loss, from one entity to another, in exchange for a premium, and can be thought of as a guaranteed small loss to prevent a large, possibly devastating loss. An insurer is a company selling the _____; an insured or policyholder is the person or entity buying the _____.
    a. AD-IA Model
    b. Insurance
    c. ACCRA Cost of Living Index
    d. ACEA agreement

48. The _____ was a United States Government-owned asset management company charged with liquidating assets (primarily real estate-related assets, including mortgage loans) that had been assets of savings and loan associations (S'Ls) declared insolvent by the Office of Thrift Supervision, as a consequence of the savings and loan crisis of the 1980s. It also took over the insurance functions of the former Federal Home Loan Bank Board. It was created by the Financial Institutions Reform Recovery and Enforcement Act (FIRREA), adopted in 1989.
    a. 130-30 fund
    b. 1921 recession
    c. 100-year flood
    d. Resolution Trust Corporation

49. In economics, the people in the _____ are the suppliers of labor. The _____ is all the nonmilitary people who are employed or unemployed. In 2005, the worldwide _____ was over 3 billion people.
    a. Distributed workforce
    b. Grenelle agreements
    c. Departmentalization
    d. Labor force

50. _____ is the change in population over time, and can be quantified as the change in the number of individuals in a population using 'per unit time' for measurement. The term _____ can technically refer to any species, but almost always refers to humans, and it is often used informally for the more specific demographic term _____ rate , and is often used to refer specifically to the growth of the population of the world.

    Simple models of _____ include the Malthusian Growth Model and the logistic model.

    a. 100-year flood
    b. 130-30 fund
    c. Population dynamics
    d. Population growth

51. _____ in economics refers to metrics and measures of output from production processes, per unit of input. Labor _____, for example, is typically measured as a ratio of output per labor-hour, an input. _____ may be conceived of as a metrics of the technical or engineering efficiency of production.
    a. Productivity
    b. Fordism
    c. Piece work
    d. Production-possibility frontier

Chapter 30. To the New Millennium and Beyond

52. _____ is an economic situation in which inflation and economic stagnation occur simultaneously and remain unchecked for a period of time. The portmanteau _____ is generally attributed to British politician Iain Macleod, who coined the term in a speech to Parliament in 1965. The concept is notable partly because, in postwar macroeconomic theory, inflation and recession were regarded as mutually exclusive, and also because _____ has generally proven to be difficult and costly to eradicate once it gets started.
    a. Price/wage spiral
    b. Stagflation
    c. Real interest rate
    d. Chronic inflation

53. In economics, the _____ measures the payments that flow between any individual country and all other countries. It is used to summarize all international economic transactions for that country during a specific time period, usually a year. The _____ is determined by the country's exports and imports of goods, services, and financial capital, as well as financial transfers.
    a. Gross domestic product per barrel
    b. Skyscraper Index
    c. Balance of payments
    d. Gross world product

54. The _____ was actually created in 1929, before the stock market crash on Black Tuesday, 1929, but its powers were later enlarged to meet the economic crisis farmers faced during the Great Depression. It was established by the Agricultural Marketing Act to stabilize prices and to promote the sale of agricultural products. The board would help farmers stabilize prices by holding surplus grain and cotton in storage.
    a. Federal Farm Board
    b. Great Depression in the United Kingdom
    c. Great Contraction
    d. Great Depression

55. A _____ is the transfer of wealth from one party (such as a person or company) to another. A _____ is usually made in exchange for the provision of goods, services or both, or to fulfill a legal obligation.

The simplest and oldest form of _____ is barter, the exchange of one good or service for another.

    a. Social gravity
    b. Going concern
    c. Soft count
    d. Payment

56. In finance, _____ is investment originating from other countries.See Foreign direct investment.
    a. Demand side economics
    b. Horizontal merger
    c. Foreign investment
    d. Preclusive purchasing

57. _____ refers to the economic policies promoted by United States President Ronald Reagan during the 1980s. The four pillars of Reagan's economic policy were to:

    1. reduce the growth of government spending,
    2. reduce income and capital gains marginal tax rates,
    3. reduce government regulation of the economy,
    4. control the money supply to reduce inflation.

In attempting to cut back on domestic spending while lowering taxes, Reagan's approach was a departure from his immediate predecessors.

Chapter 30. To the New Millennium and Beyond

Reagan became president during a period of high inflation and unemployment (commonly referred to as stagflation), which had largely abated by the time he left office eight years later.

Prior to the Reagan Administration was a roughly ten year period of economic stagnation and inflation, known as stagflation.

a. Social savings
b. Business sector
c. Reaganomics
d. Happiness economics

58. To _____ is to impose a financial charge or other levy upon a taxpayer by a state or the functional equivalent of a state.

_____es are also imposed by many subnational entities. _____es consist of direct _____ or indirect _____, and may be paid in money or as its labour equivalent (often but not always unpaid.)

a. 1921 recession
b. 100-year flood
c. 130-30 fund
d. Tax

59. _____ is the process of changing the way taxes are collected or managed by the government.

_____ers have different goals. Some seek to reduce the level of taxation of all people by the government.

a. Special-purpose local-option sales tax
b. Nil-rate band
c. Tax break
d. Tax Reform

60. The _____ hypothesis is a concept from macroeconomics that contends that there is a strong link between a national economy's current account balance and its government budget balance. As an example, it is hypothesized that a large budget deficit leads to a large current account deficit. The theory goes as follows:

$Y = C + I + G + NX$

where Y represents National Income or GDP, C is consumption, I is investment, G is government spending and NX stands for net exports.

a. Power of the purse
b. Public-private partnership
c. 100-year flood
d. Twin deficits

61. _____ forms part of the public sector deficit. _____ differs from cyclical deficit in that it exists even when the economy is at its potential.

_____ issues can only be addressed by explicit and direct government policies: reducing spending (including entitlements), increasing the tax base, and/or increasing tax rates.

a. Sovereign credit
b. Tax increment financing
c. Minimum Municipal Obligation
d. Structural deficit

62. _____ the Great War, and the War to End All Wars, was a global military conflict which involved the majority of the world's great powers, organized into two opposing military alliances: the Entente Powers and the Central Powers. Over 70 million military personnel were mobilized in one of the largest wars in history. In a state of total war, the major combatants fully placed their scientific and industrial capabilities at the service of the war effort.
   a. 130-30 fund
   b. World War I
   c. 100-year flood
   d. 1921 recession

63. _____ is the income of individuals or nations after adjusting for inflation. It is calculated by subtracting inflation from the nominal income. Real variables, such as _____, real GDP, and real interest rate are variables that are measured in physical units, while nominal variables such as nominal income, nominal GDP, and nominal interest rate are measured in monetary units.
   a. Family income
   b. Net national income
   c. Windfall gain
   d. Real income

64. The notion of _____ is found in the writings of Mikhail Bakunin, Friedrich Nietzsche, and in Werner Sombart's Krieg und Kapitalismus (War and Capitalism) (1913, p. 207), where he wrote: 'again out of destruction a new spirit of creativity arises'. In Capitalism, Socialism and Democracy, the Austrian economist Joseph Schumpeter popularized and used the term to describe the process of transformation that accompanies radical innovation.
   a. 1921 recession
   b. 130-30 fund
   c. 100-year flood
   d. Creative destruction

65. _____ is a type of trade policy that allows traders to act and transact without interference from government. Thus, the policy permits trading partners mutual gains from trade, with goods and services produced according to the theory of comparative advantage.

Under a _____ policy, prices are a reflection of true supply and demand, and are the sole determinant of resource allocation.

   a. 100-year flood
   b. 1921 recession
   c. 130-30 fund
   d. Free Trade

66. The _____ is a trilateral trade bloc in North America created by the governments of the United States, Canada, and Mexico. The agreement creating the trade bloc came into force on January 1, 1994. It superseded the Canada-United States Free Trade Agreement between the U.S. and Canada.
   a. Federal Reserve Bank Notes
   b. Case-Shiller Home Price Indices
   c. Demand-side technologies
   d. North American Free Trade Agreement

Chapter 31. Does Our Past Have a Future?

1. Competition law, known in the United States as _____ law, has three main elements:

   - prohibiting agreements or practices that restrict free trading and competition between business entities. This includes in particular the repression of cartels.
   - banning abusive behaviour by a firm dominating a market, or anti-competitive practices that tend to lead to such a dominant position. Practices controlled in this way may include predatory pricing, tying, price gouging, refusal to deal, and many others.
   - supervising the mergers and acquisitions of large corporations, including some joint ventures. Transactions that are considered to threaten the competitive process can be prohibited altogether, or approved subject to 'remedies' such as an obligation to divest part of the merged business or to offer licences or access to facilities to enable other businesses to continue competing.

   The substance and practice of competition law varies from jurisdiction to jurisdiction. Protecting the interests of consumers (consumer welfare) and ensuring that entrepreneurs have an opportunity to compete in the market economy are often treated as important objectives. Competition law is closely connected with law on deregulation of access to markets, state aids and subsidies, the privatisation of state owned assets and the establishment of independent sector regulators. In recent decades, competition law has been viewed as a way to provide better public services.

   a. Antitrust
   b. United Kingdom competition law
   c. Anti-Inflation Act
   d. Intellectual property law

2. A _____ is the exclusive authority to determine how a resource is used, whether that resource is owned by government or by individuals. All economic goods have a _____s attribute. This attribute has three broad components

   1. The right to use the good
   2. The right to earn income from the good
   3. The right to transfer the good to others

   The concept of _____s as used by economists and legal scholars are related but distinct. The distinction is largely seen in the economists' focus on the ability of an individual or collective to control the use of the good.

   a. High-reeve
   b. Post-sale restraint
   c. Holder in due course
   d. Property right

3. _____ is a term used to describe large corporations, in either an individual or collective sense. The term first came into use in a symbolic sense subsequent to the American Civil War, particularly after 1880, in connection with the combination movement that began in American business at that time. Organizations that fall into the category of '_____' include ExxonMobil, Wal-Mart, Google, Microsoft, General Motors, Citigroup and Arcelor Mittal.

   a. First-mover advantage
   b. Sole proprietorship
   c. Big business
   d. Brainsworking

4. A _____ is a group of people who share or are motivated by at least one common issue or interest, or work together on a specific project(s) to achieve a common objective. _____s are also characterised by attempts to share and exercise political and social power and to make decisions on a consensus-driven and egalitarian basis. _____s differ from cooperatives in that they are not necessarily focused upon an economic benefit or saving (but can be that as well.)

Chapter 31. Does Our Past Have a Future? 169

a. 1921 recession
b. 100-year flood
c. Collective
d. 130-30 fund

5. _____ are defined as public goods that could be delivered as private goods, but are usually delivered by the government for various reasons, including social policy, and finances from public funds like taxes.

Common examples of public goods include: defense and law enforcement (including the system of property rights), public fireworks, lighthouses, clean air and other environmental goods, and information goods, such as software development, authorship, and invention.

a. Common property
b. Government monopoly
c. Collective goods
d. Privatizing profits and socializing losses

6. A _____ is an object whose consumption increases the utility of the consumer, for which the quantity demanded exceeds the quantity supplied at zero price. _____s are usually modeled as having diminishing marginal utility. The first individual purchase has high utility; the second has less.

a. Good
b. Pie method
c. Merit good
d. Composite good

7. There are two main interpretations of the idea of a _____:

- A model in which the state assumes primary responsibility for the welfare of its citizens. This responsibility in theory ought to be comprehensive, because all aspects of welfare are considered and universally applied to citizens as a 'right'. _____ can also mean the creation of a 'social safety net' of minimum standards of varying forms of welfare. Here is found some confusion between a '_____' and a 'welfare society' in common debate about the definition of the term.
- The provision of welfare in society. In many '_____s', especially in continental Europe, welfare is not actually provided by the state, but by a combination of independent, voluntary, mutualist and government services. The functional provider of benefits and services may be a central or state government, a state-sponsored company or agency, a private corporation, a charity or another form of non-profit organization. However, this phenomenon has been more appropriately termed a 'welfare society,' and the term 'welfare system' has been used to describe the range of _____ and welfare society mixes that are found.

The English term '_____' is believed by Asa Briggs to have been coined by Archbishop William Temple during the Second World War, contrasting wartime Britain with the 'warfare state' of Nazi Germany. Friedrich Hayek contends that the term derived from the older German word Wohlfahrtsstaat, which itself was used by nineteenth century historians to describe a variant of the ideal of Polizeistaat . It was fully developed by the German academic Sozialpolitiker--'socialists of the chair'--from 1870 and first implemented through Bismarck's 'state socialism'. Bismarck's policies have also been seen as the creation of a _____.

a. 130-30 fund
b. 100-year flood
c. 1921 recession
d. Welfare state

8. In mathematics, an _____ is a statement about the relative size or order of two objects, or about whether they are the same or not

- The notation a < b means that a is less than b.
- The notation a > b means that a is greater than b.
- The notation a ≠ b means that a is not equal to b, but does not say that one is greater than the other or even that they can be compared in size.

In each statement above, a is not equal to b. These relations are known as strict inequalities. The notation a < b may also be read as 'a is strictly less than b'.

a. AD-IA Model
c. ACEA agreement
b. Inequality
d. ACCRA Cost of Living Index

ANSWER KEY

Chapter 1
| 1. b | 2. c | 3. d | 4. d | 5. c | 6. d | 7. a | 8. b | 9. d | 10. a |
| 11. d | 12. d | 13. d | 14. b | 15. b | 16. b | 17. a | 18. d | 19. d | |

Chapter 2
1. d	2. a	3. d	4. b	5. b	6. b	7. d	8. b	9. c	10. d
11. d	12. d	13. c	14. d	15. c	16. b	17. c	18. d	19. c	20. b
21. d	22. d	23. d	24. b	25. a					

Chapter 3
1. c	2. a	3. d	4. d	5. d	6. d	7. b	8. a	9. d	10. d
11. a	12. b	13. d	14. a	15. a	16. d	17. d	18. c	19. d	20. d
21. d	22. d	23. d	24. d						

Chapter 4
1. a	2. a	3. d	4. d	5. d	6. d	7. d	8. d	9. c	10. a
11. d	12. b	13. a	14. b	15. b	16. b	17. d	18. d	19. c	20. b
21. a	22. d								

Chapter 5
| 1. d | 2. d | 3. d | 4. b | 5. a | 6. a | 7. c | 8. d | 9. d | 10. b |
| 11. c | 12. c | 13. a | 14. d | 15. a | | | | | |

Chapter 6
1. c	2. a	3. d	4. c	5. b	6. d	7. d	8. d	9. d	10. b
11. b	12. d	13. d	14. c	15. d	16. d	17. d	18. b	19. b	20. b
21. a	22. d	23. d	24. d	25. a	26. d				

Chapter 7
1. b	2. c	3. a	4. d	5. c	6. a	7. c	8. a	9. d	10. a
11. b	12. b	13. d	14. d	15. b	16. d	17. d	18. d	19. c	20. c
21. d	22. d	23. b							

Chapter 8
| 1. a | 2. a | 3. d | 4. d | 5. c | 6. d | 7. d | 8. d | 9. b | 10. b |
| 11. d | | | | | | | | | |

Chapter 9
| 1. a | 2. d | 3. b | 4. d | 5. a | 6. c | 7. a | 8. d | 9. a | 10. b |
| 11. a | 12. d | 13. d | 14. b | 15. d | 16. d | 17. a | | | |

Chapter 10
| 1. c | 2. b | 3. c | 4. c | 5. d | 6. b | 7. d |

Chapter 11

1. d	2. b	3. d	4. a	5. d	6. b	7. a	8. a	9. c	10. c
11. a	12. d	13. d	14. a	15. b	16. d	17. b	18. b	19. d	20. d
21. d	22. b								

Chapter 12

1. d	2. a	3. d	4. a	5. a	6. d	7. d	8. c	9. d	10. d
11. b	12. d	13. d	14. d	15. d	16. b	17. d	18. a	19. a	20. d
21. a	22. a	23. d	24. d	25. d	26. b	27. c	28. b	29. d	30. c
31. b	32. c	33. d	34. b	35. a	36. d	37. d	38. d	39. c	40. a
41. c	42. d	43. b	44. d	45. d	46. d	47. c	48. c	49. d	50. d
51. b	52. c	53. b							

Chapter 13

1. b	2. d	3. d	4. d	5. b	6. d	7. b	8. c	9. d	10. d
11. d	12. d	13. d	14. c	15. d	16. d	17. d	18. d	19. b	20. c
21. b	22. c	23. d	24. a	25. c	26. c	27. a	28. d	29. b	

Chapter 14

1. d	2. c	3. d	4. a	5. b	6. d	7. d	8. d	9. d	10. d
11. d	12. a	13. d	14. d	15. a	16. b	17. d	18. a	19. b	20. d

Chapter 15

1. d	2. d	3. d	4. d	5. d	6. d	7. d	8. d	9. d	10. a
11. d	12. b	13. c	14. c						

Chapter 16

1. d	2. d	3. d	4. b	5. d	6. d	7. b	8. c	9. d	10. c
11. d	12. b	13. c	14. b	15. c					

Chapter 17

1. a	2. d	3. d	4. d	5. b	6. d	7. d	8. d	9. a	10. c
11. a	12. d	13. c	14. c	15. d	16. d	17. d	18. d	19. d	20. d
21. c	22. d	23. c	24. d	25. d	26. c	27. a	28. c	29. a	30. a
31. b	32. c	33. d	34. a	35. b					

Chapter 18

1. c	2. d	3. c	4. d	5. b	6. b	7. b	8. d	9. a	10. d
11. d	12. d	13. c	14. d	15. d	16. d	17. d	18. d	19. a	20. d
21. d									

ANSWER KEY

Chapter 19
1. d	2. a	3. a	4. d	5. b	6. a	7. c	8. a	9. a	10. c
11. d	12. a	13. d	14. a	15. b	16. a	17. a	18. d	19. a	20. d
21. b	22. b	23. d	24. d	25. d	26. c	27. d	28. c	29. a	30. c
31. d	32. a	33. a	34. d	35. d	36. d	37. d			

Chapter 20
1. c	2. d	3. a	4. c	5. a	6. d	7. a	8. c	9. d	10. d
11. d	12. a	13. a	14. d	15. c	16. a	17. b	18. d	19. b	20. a
21. d	22. d	23. a	24. b	25. b	26. c	27. c	28. c	29. b	30. d
31. a	32. d								

Chapter 21
1. d	2. d	3. b	4. d	5. b	6. d	7. d	8. d	9. b	10. b
11. d	12. d	13. c	14. d	15. b	16. d				

Chapter 22
1. b	2. c	3. b	4. d	5. a	6. d	7. d	8. c	9. d	10. b
11. b	12. a	13. c	14. b	15. d	16. b	17. a	18. c		

Chapter 23
1. d	2. c	3. b	4. c	5. d	6. d	7. d	8. d	9. a	10. d
11. c	12. d	13. b	14. d	15. b	16. d	17. a	18. a	19. d	20. d
21. d	22. a	23. d	24. c	25. b	26. b				

Chapter 24
1. d	2. d	3. a	4. d	5. c	6. c	7. d	8. d	9. b	10. d
11. b	12. a	13. d	14. c	15. b	16. d	17. d	18. a	19. d	20. d
21. d	22. b	23. a	24. d	25. d	26. d	27. b	28. c		

Chapter 25
1. b	2. d	3. a	4. d	5. a	6. a	7. a	8. c	9. d	10. d
11. b	12. b	13. a	14. c	15. d	16. d	17. d	18. d	19. d	20. a
21. d	22. d	23. d	24. a	25. b	26. b	27. d	28. d		

Chapter 26
1. b	2. b	3. a	4. d	5. d	6. d	7. d	8. d	9. a	10. d
11. c	12. a	13. a	14. b	15. c	16. a	17. d	18. d	19. c	

Chapter 27
1. c	2. a	3. a	4. c	5. d	6. c	7. d	8. d	9. b	10. b
11. a	12. c	13. b	14. d	15. d	16. d	17. b	18. c	19. d	20. b
21. d	22. d	23. c	24. c	25. b	26. d	27. d	28. d	29. b	30. d
31. b	32. d	33. d	34. d						

Chapter 28

1. d	2. c	3. d	4. d	5. c	6. b	7. a	8. d	9. c	10. d
11. d	12. a	13. d	14. c	15. d	16. d	17. b	18. d	19. c	20. b
21. a	22. b	23. b	24. c	25. a	26. b	27. d	28. a	29. d	30. c
31. d	32. d	33. b	34. d						

Chapter 29

1. c	2. a	3. d	4. c	5. c	6. d	7. c	8. b	9. d	10. d
11. a	12. d	13. a	14. b	15. a	16. c	17. b	18. c	19. d	20. d
21. d	22. b	23. d	24. d	25. d	26. d	27. d	28. b		

Chapter 30

1. d	2. b	3. b	4. d	5. d	6. c	7. c	8. a	9. c	10. c
11. d	12. a	13. d	14. d	15. c	16. d	17. d	18. d	19. c	20. a
21. d	22. d	23. d	24. d	25. d	26. d	27. d	28. d	29. d	30. b
31. d	32. d	33. d	34. d	35. b	36. d	37. d	38. b	39. d	40. a
41. d	42. d	43. a	44. a	45. d	46. d	47. b	48. d	49. d	50. d
51. a	52. b	53. c	54. a	55. d	56. c	57. c	58. d	59. d	60. d
61. d	62. b	63. d	64. d	65. d	66. d				

Chapter 31

1. a	2. d	3. c	4. c	5. c	6. a	7. d	8. b